MR BIG

MR BIG

Ozzy, Sharon and My Life as the Godfather of Rock

Don Arden with Mick Wall

ROBSON BOOKS

First published in Great Britain in 2004 by Robson Books,
The Chrysalis Building, Bramley Road, London, W10 6SP

An imprint of Chrysalis Books Group plc

Copyright © 2004 Don Arden

The right of Don Arden to be identified as the author of this work
has been asserted by him in accordance with the Copyright, Designs
and Patents Act 1988.

The author has made every reasonable effort to contact all copyright
holders. Any errors that may have occurred are inadvertent and anyone
who for any reason has not been contacted is invited to write to the
publishers so that a full acknowledgement may be made in
subsequent editions of this work.

British Library Cataloguing in Publication Data
A catalogue record for this title is available from the British Library.

ISBN 1 86105 607 9

All rights reserved. No part of this publication may be reproduced,
stored in a retrieval system, or transmitted in any form or by any means,
electronic, mechanical, photocopying, recording or otherwise,
without the prior permission in writing of the publishers.

Picture Credits
All photographs courtesy of author's private collection, except: Small Faces
(© David Magnus/Rex); Little Richard (© Dezo Hoffman/Rex); Black Sabbath
in concert (© Neal Preston/Corbis); Ozzy and Sharon's wedding (© Neal
Preston/Corbis).

Typeset by SX Composing DTP, Rayleigh, Essex
Printed and bound by Creative Print & Design (Wales), Ebbw Vale

Prologue

Looked at in a certain way, everybody's life must seem strange to outsiders. But you only have to tune into an episode of *The Osbournes* to understand why I say my life has been a lot stranger and more exciting than most. Sharon is my daughter, Jack and Kelly are my grandchildren and my son-in-law Ozzy is a rock 'n' roll icon. For millions of people around the world, they are the most outrageously dysfunctional family ever seen on TV, like a real-life version of *The Munsters*, with their Hollywood mansion, stumbling, mumbling father, weird kids, and supremely in-control but slightly crazy matriarch. For me, however, they are part of my life, a life over-burdened with millionaires and misfits, hit-makers and shit-stirrers, funny men and wise guys, talented failures and got-lucky schmucks.

For you it's a case of simply tuning in. For me, actually sitting here in Ozzy and Sharon's kitchen, watching it all unfurl around me – the chaos, the laughter, the dog shit – it's merely business as usual. You watch it in neat 25-minute bursts and laugh. To me it's more like a documentary than a reality/comedy show. It reminds me of how different things were 25 years ago, when Ozzy first came to live with me at my own mansion in Beverley Hills, after he'd been booted out of Black Sabbath for being too much for even them to handle. Sharon hardly knew him then and was terrified of him. Everybody was, unlike now. Then, Ozzy was at the height of his drugged-up, drunken madness and people used to get up and leave the room as soon as they saw him coming.

As Sabbath's manager back then, I was the only one who knew how to handle him. But then I'd had a lot of practice. Compared with my days working with people such as Gene Vincent, Little Richard and Chuck Berry, dealing with Ozzy, even at his worst, was a stroll in the park for me. People in the business said I was crazy to keep him on as a solo act; that Ozzy was all washed-up. As ever, I would make it my mission to prove them all wrong. Not just for the money; it had never been just about the money for me. It was about beating the other guy – by fair means or foul. Whatever it took.

I turned Ozzy into the biggest rock star in the world in the early eighties – then handed over his management contract to Sharon. She and Ozzy had fallen in love and decided to get married, so I gave it to them as a wedding present. That *should* have been the happy ending to the story. . .

But you can read all about that in this book. Right now, I just want you to know what it's like to be here for real, in the flesh, not just some image on your TV screen. The truth is, I find the whole experience quite strange but at the same time it fills me with pride. Once it was her father who ran the show, now Sharon is the one calling the shots. I certainly wouldn't be sitting here now as an honoured member of the family in her home if she didn't want me to be, and she wouldn't be sitting where she is, either, if I hadn't . . . Well, let's just say she reminds me of me, when I was younger. Maybe that's why we've had such difficulties over the years – not because of our differences but because we're so alike.

Is *The Osbournes* for real, though? Only in part. They cut out what they think are the boring bits. They don't think you would find it entertaining if they revealed how Ozzy is in fact extremely sharp-witted and blessed with an innate ability to know what's best. He is one the most complex and interesting men I have ever met – forget anything else I might have said. The kids come across as spoilt brats on the show, but in fact most of the time they are sweet and so considerate to others, especially those less fortunate than themselves. Lastly, Sharon. In *The Osbournes* you see her balls and all her talents but not her vulnerable side. It's just a shame the cameras weren't rolling 25 years ago. Then you really would have seen some shit about the place . . .

Am *I* for real, though? Ask anybody who ever received an unexpected visit from me how 'real' it felt. As you'll see, there have been enough of them over the years and I'm sure they'd be glad to tell you all about it – the ones that aren't dead. So, yes, I *am* for real and so is my story, and I've waited a long time to tell it. Almost until the end, in fact. I was going to say I hope you like it, but the truth is I don't give a damn. It was never about being liked or disliked for me, it was about fighting to get what you want, and I was one of those guys who came out of the womb fighting. Right from a kid in the street, I was always rougher, tougher, smarter, faster than the next guy. One way or another, I made sure I always won at everything.

Or almost everything . . .

1

As a true showbiz personality, it goes without saying of course that my real name isn't actually Don Arden. My real name is Harry Levy, and I was born in Manchester on 4 January 1926. My family were good Yiddisher folk – poor but terribly hard-working. You were expected to get up early every morning and, to quote my mother, 'get out and start making something of yourself'.

As a result, I belonged to a family where everything was happening. When we all sat round the table together for dinner at night – I and my parents and my sister, Eileen, who is three years older than I am – and told stories of what had happened to us that day, there was nothing that ever went by without comment or debate – nothing that didn't seem like the most important thing in the world at the time. My mother would tell us to write it all down in our journals, and we did. I used to sit there after dinner scribbling on a piece of paper, 'Got in a fight after school again today . . .'

My mother's name was Sarah, but she was known to her friends as Sal or Sally. She was born in a place called Riga, which later became part of the Soviet Union. That was the real Russia, in my grandparents' day, before communism had spread its nasty smell over everything. After the revolution, they were one of millions of Jewish families who were woken up at four o'clock in the morning and told to get out now – or die. Allowed to take only what they could carry, they were forced to leave behind everything else they had: their house, their possessions, all their family treasures – everything. Carrying just a single bag, my family walked to the nearest place there might possibly be a boat and finished up in England.

In those days, all the ships went to either Liverpool or New York. Understandably, my family were in a hurry and took the first available berth, which happened to be on the ship bound for Liverpool. I don't think they were very pleased by what they found there, though. Instead of being the Promised Land, Liverpool was just full of other people like them – jobless immigrants, mostly, barely able to speak the language. It must have seemed pretty hopeless. But they stayed there for a year and then set off for Manchester, where they were told there were jobs to be had. And, miraculously, there were.

My maternal grandparents – Sophia-Anna and Lazarus – were actually introduced to each other on the ship coming over from Russia. They were married on board by the travelling rabbi, who had told all the women that they wouldn't be allowed into the country if they weren't married. It was all bollocks, of course. The rabbi's real agenda was to try to ensure that all the Jewish women married Jewish men before they got a chance to meet any nice Englishmen, in order to keep Judaism alive in the 'new world'.

Being a good young Yiddisher girl, my grandmother dutifully married the first man the rabbi introduced her to – and never stopped regretting it until the day she died. She had six children by him, but she made it plain she absolutely hated him. Even as a small child, I could tell things were never quite right between them. He didn't hate her, but she definitely hated him. I always used to wonder why such a good woman wouldn't have any love for him, because he didn't seem like a bad guy. He certainly stuck by her. In the end, I think it just came down to the fact that she was *told* to marry him, this complete stranger. She never forgave him for that, even though it was hardly his fault. She just couldn't get it out of her system, even as she lay dying years later. Exactly the same sort of bloody-minded stubbornness, in fact, that would later surface in me as I began to grow up.

My father's name was also Lazarus – though he was always known to everyone, including my mother, as Larry – and he came from a big Jewish family in Poland, where it was the same story as in Russia. They've always hated the Jews in Poland and so my father's parents also ended up getting on a ship bound for Liverpool, before moving to Manchester for exactly the same reasons as my mother's family. More than that, I don't know. We never saw much of my father's family when I was growing up. We would see one or two of them occasionally, perhaps, when we were very young but I think his own parents died before he got married. It was my mother's people who kept us all together as a family. My mother always had this burning ambition and because of that she didn't really want anything to do with anybody else's opinions. She had her own ideas about how people should live their lives. For instance, even then, living in the ghetto, her dream was one day to own a house by Heaton Park – an area of Manchester only the richest Jews lived in. So much so that years later, when I started making big money, the first thing I did was buy her a house right opposite Heaton Park. She loved that house so much she said she wanted to die there! That is, until she started coming to America in the seventies and staying with us for months at a time. She loved being in America because she'd been dreaming of it all her life through going to the movies. She was like Alice in Wonderland.

For the first few years of my life, however, we lived at 13 Rugby Street, in Broughton, in what was then a Manchester ghetto: Catholics down one side of the street, Jews down the other, with the Protestants dotted about here and there. Everybody used to go to a different church in those days. That was how you found out who everyone in your neighbourhood was, by seeing which church they went to. Instead of religious divisions, however, there was a great deal of friendship back then among all the different religions that lived side by side in the ghetto. My grandmother used to suffer from chronic asthma, which is what eventually killed her. Her English name was Black and the Catholics used to come knocking on the door saying, 'How is Mrs Black today?' Most of them were Irish and they'd say, 'Don't worry because we've lit candles for her and we're praying to the Virgin Mary, so she'll be all right.'

My mother was the one who ensured that the family all stuck to Judaism. My father was more pragmatic. If they offered him an extra pound to work a Saturday, he would be running in there at six o'clock in the morning. My mother wasn't having any of that. Every Saturday, the Jewish Sabbath, all the family used to meet at my grandparents' home in Cheetham Hill. It was about a mile from where we lived and we used to walk there every Saturday morning all scrubbed up in our best clothes. My grandparents' six children had all married by then and had children of their own, so it was like a huge gathering of the tribe. It was never too strict, though. Some of my aunts and uncles would disappear down to the pub to get drunk; some would stay behind and entertain the kids; some would just clear off on their own to read the newspapers. We all became our own separate kinds of people for the Saturday visits.

My grandfather worked part-time in the local synagogue. He opened it every day and helped the rabbi prepare the services – the very religious Jews used to go there before going to work each day. My grandfather would give out the prayer books and make any announcements that needed to be made in English. That was how he got the job: because he could speak fluent English; not because he'd been to some big school in Russia like my grandmother but because as a young man he had been involved in the horse-trading business, buying and selling English and American studs, and he'd picked up the lingo through that.

By the time he came to England, my grandfather knew everything there was to know about horseracing. He used to come in on Saturdays and start showing off to all the kids. Always some story about the horses. 'This horse ran so fast he nearly died!' he'd cry. 'But he won and I won a thousand pounds!' We'd say, 'What do you mean, Grandpa? You won a *thousand* pounds? Show us.' Saying you'd won a thousand pounds then was like saying you'd won a million would sound today. We all thought he was mad. But he'd laugh and say, 'You don't understand. Here, in my heart, I won! I won!' Eventually, as we got older and horseracing became more respectable, he did begin to go to the racetrack again. He got to know all the jockeys and trainers and he became a friend of all the bookmakers. It also made him a very popular figure at the synagogue, where he was known for being able to place a bet or two, on the quiet, for the regulars.

My grandmother was a different story. Speaking English was about the only thing she had in common with my grandfather. She was highly educated because her people had come from money. One of my earliest memories is of seeing her on a Saturday afternoon, sitting reading a huge pile of newspapers in English, along with a similar number of papers in Russian and Hebrew. Eventually everybody in the ghetto knew how to speak English – or at least a version of it – but she and my grandfather were among the first to speak it as English people would.

Being Polish, my father was less flamboyant and just kept his head down and worked hard. He was what they called a 'waterproof-garment maker', which meant he made raincoats. He and the rest of the workers used to get paid according to how many raincoats they managed to turn out each week – what they used to call 'piecework'. He used to leave for work at seven in the morning and come back at eight at night, having churned out as many raincoats as he could, for which he usually managed to bring home about £3 a week.

The Rugby Street house was a typical two-up, two-down, as they called them, with one cold-water tap. We had to queue up at that tap to wash every morning, my father first because he had to go to work. You would stand there trying to wash yourself with ice-cold water while everybody stood behind you, watching and waiting. It was a hell of a way to start the day. You couldn't get away with just a quick wipe-round, either. We had to be absolutely spotless before my mother would let us out of the door.

It was the same with the house. Every day my mother cleaned it from top to bottom. Then, every Friday, while she cooked the Sabbath dinner for the next day, she would pay to have somebody else come in and clean the house 'properly'. Even though it was a slum in the middle of the ghetto, my mother always treated it as though it were a palace. She hated, for example, the fact that we had an outside toilet. The whole concept offended her. I didn't mind it so much: blokes don't need as much privacy for that sort of thing as women. But this particular toilet was pretty awful. You'd sit down for a shit and find yourself looking through the window at the bloke next door, who'd be sitting there having a shit on his toilet. Sometimes you would nod and say hello and the next thing you know you're stuck there chatting for an hour. You got used to it. If there was no one to talk to, I'd sit there for an hour anyway, singing my head off.

I understood only vaguely as a child that not everybody lived like this, that some people had more money than others and actually lived in houses with electric lights and hot water. My mother, however, knew better and she never stopped drip-feeding me with the idea that you could always do better for yourself. She taught me that appearances were important, that first impressions were usually the lasting ones. Therefore, you should always dress well, no matter how badly off you might be, and always make sure people remembered your name when they met you for the first time. It was good advice that I still follow today.

The first school I went to was Waterloo Road, which was just down the road from Strangeways, the local prison. I remember being fascinated by Strangeways and its big, imposing tower. My grandfather would sometimes put bets on for the prisoners there. They had these narrow slit windows high up in the walls, from which they would hang little bits of scribbled paper. Sometimes I would go with him to help him collect them, but, whenever I asked him what they were for, he used to say, 'Mind your own business, that's not for you.'

From the age of nine, I attended Heath Street School, which was considered a tough but basically good working-class school – the type of place where they made sure you learned. The regime could be harsh but there were very few kids who came away dummies from Heath Street. There was one teacher, a schmuck with a big mop of hair, whom we called Mr Moppy, and every morning as he came in he'd have something thrown at him: bits of bread if he was lucky, rocks if he wasn't. The headmaster came in and threatened us from time to time, but, as they never knew who was doing the throwing, there wasn't anything they could do to stop it. Mostly, though, we saw most of the teachers, the good ones, as pals – especially the young woman teacher who always seemed to have her skirts hitched up to her waist. We used to hide the ink pots in the fireplace just so we could feast our eyes on her gorgeous behind as she bent over to retrieve them.

The only snag about Heath Street was that there weren't any Jewish teachers there. Jewish teachers didn't really exist in schools like that in the thirties. So, after school each day, I and the rest of the Jewish kids used to go straight to what they called Hebrew School. We used to stop off in a Jewish bakery and get a penny cake and eat it on the way. Hebrew School was fine. There were certain lessons to do with religion and history, but it was also a good place to hang out after school. There were activities, sports, games, music. The only problem was that there was often a gang of English boys who liked to hang around outside, waiting for us to come out so they could start trouble. And that was when I first started getting involved in proper street fights. I don't mean the kind of drive-by gang warfare you see now on the streets of east LA: I mean the kind of fisticuffs we used to get involved in on the streets of Manchester in the thirties.

It wasn't just a one-way ticket, either. The Jewish boys could give as good as they got, and there used to be some frightening scraps between us. The streets we lived in were like a rabbit warren and, after dark, ambushes were common. We didn't have TV or anything like that to amuse us, so we used to end up just fighting each other. These fights would go back and forth for days, weeks. Sometimes you won, sometimes you lost. It was strange and sometimes scary but also in many ways quite exciting.

Where I grew up, you were either a fighter or you weren't. There was nothing in between. There was no such thing after school as, 'Oh, hello, Harry, do you think you'll be available for some cricket on Sunday?' If you said something like that round my way you'd have got your head smashed in. It was not a good environment for the physically weak or the feeble-minded and there were even suicides. I survived because I was a born fighter – and because I used my head.

For example, we were surrounded by rats in those days, especially in the small playgrounds we had. It was all rats and mice and other vermin. And we eventually decided between us – the Jews and the non-Jews – that the kid who could smash the most rats would be king. Some of the kids were dubious – they just wanted to fight – but I really built it up, really sold it to them as this huge test of manhood. Fighting each other was one thing, but what about fighting a pack of rats? You think you're tough? How about trying that?

And they went for it – we all did – and I was able to win quite often. We used to climb up onto the tops of trucks that would be parked in my street at night. There was a wall opposite and if you had enough patience you would see the heads of the rats as they crept out through cracks in the wall. That was the signal to try to smash them with rocks and broken bottles and anything else you could get your hands on. It wasn't easy: they were tough bastards, and, if there were enough of them and you got close enough to let them come at you, they would attack you. And you had to get close because you had to kill as many as you could.

Every time I won I made a point of carrying the dead rats down to show the other kids, who would act very strangely when they saw me coming, swinging them by their tails. A strange mixture of repulsion and admiration and . . . something else: fear. That was the first time I realised the power of fear. I was suddenly treated with the kind of respect I'd never known before. Seeing me nonchalantly swinging these dead rats by their tails put a question mark in their minds about who I was and what I was capable of. That made them more hesitant from then on in their dealings with me.

And that's the key to what I was and what I became: I didn't just smash the most rats, but I also got the others talking about it. That was when I first realised that a bit of swagger could be very effective, even intimidating, and that the threat of violence could be even more powerful than the act. And I noticed that, and decided it was a good trick I could use again whenever I needed to.

Soon I was the leader of the gang. Not because I was the biggest or the fastest, but because I was the one they most feared. I was Edward G Robinson. Or at least I acted like him. The only way bluff can really work, though, is if you've got something with which to back it up. Sooner or later you always get a challenge and you have to be seen to be dealing with it. Fortunately, even though I wasn't tall, I was always very strong. My physical strength came from my father. He was a dependable sort of guy who, if you interfered with his work, would give you two minutes of his precious time and, if you still didn't get lost after that, would simply knock you out. A simple, honest guy who knew what he wanted, which was to turn out as many raincoats as he could, sitting there with a cigarette in his mouth, proving he was the fastest in the factory by earning a few more shillings than the rest.

He was a hard nut to crack and I definitely inherited that bullish quality from him – that determination not to be put off the task at hand, no matter what. That was the sort of focus you needed back then in order to survive. Thankfully, my father was a man of action. Before the war, he was a member of the Young Jewish Brigade. He never made a big thing of it, never even spoke of it to me or my family until much later. It was just something he did on the quiet, something that he felt strongly about. The YJB made it their responsibility to deal with the British Nazis who thought the country should be a fully paid-up member of the German Reich. Their mistake was to hold their hateful little rallies on street corners in the ghettos, where the Jewish Brigade boys would have no trouble finding them and sorting them out. It was quite a gang, apparently. A lot of the early British boxers were Jews, some of them champions, and they would go out and lead the Brigade boys in the streets against the British Nazis. There were a few arrests here and there – the Nazis used to love fighting in the street – but it was the Jews in the streets who actively helped prevent the Nazis from becoming more powerful in Britain. The Brigade boys would be out there night after night, hoping to come across a meeting of those scumbags.

Despite my own running battles, I wasn't what you would call a bad kid. Certainly not compared with some of the kids I ran with on the streets. The only real scam I remember pulling was when I worked out a way to get chocolate for free out of this vending machine. We were always big chocolate eaters, my whole family. I used to crave the stuff all the time. And I would look at this particular machine they had in the school cafeteria, gazing at all the scrummy choccy bars crammed in there and think, God, I'd like to clean that whole machine out! So I gave it some serious thought and came up with the idea of cutting celluloid – small bits of plastic I'd taken from old camera film – into the shapes of the coins you needed to fit the machine. When I put the first one in and it worked, I couldn't stop laughing! In the end, though, I rammed so many pieces of celluloid in there that it jammed the whole machine, and that was that – no more freebies. Delicious while it lasted, though.

Any real brains I've got all came from my mother's side. She was also much more demonstrative and knew how to express herself, which is something I've always been good at too. She was interested in reading and music and the theatre – variety shows, as we called them, multi-act bills that would throw together comedians, singers, jugglers, impressionists, you name it. The sort of penny-a-ticket shows working-class families would often go to in the days before television. It was through my mother's love of the old variety shows that I first became interested in music.

As far back as I can remember, my mother was always nagging my father to buy us a radio. When he eventually relented and brought home a cheap second-hand set he'd managed to pick up somewhere, we had a party to celebrate! We were the first family in our street to have one, so my mother invited everyone in to have a listen. Before that, we'd go to the electrical shop in town, pretending to be interested in buying something just to stand there listening for a while to 'the wireless', as it was called then.

Once we actually had one of our own, she never turned it off. I used to love singing along to all the tunes. She used to sing with me. However, it wasn't until I joined the Bury New Road Synagogue choir when I was six years old that I realised I could actually sing properly. It was quite showbiz, actually. I did an audition, passed, and the next thing I knew I was doing a gig, so to speak. I even got paid – ten shillings a month (50 pence or a little under a dollar in today's money). I used to hand it all straight over to my mother. It was a big deal for me to be able to do that. It made me feel like a man.

Virtually from the first moment I arrived, however, I began to have arguments and fights with the cantor. The cantor is like the ringmaster at the synagogue, or the MC. He's the one who leads the singing and everybody looks up to him. I was six and should have been terrified of him, this big bear of a man with his long luxuriant beard and his impressive-looking robes. But for some reason I wasn't. Even then, I thought I knew better.

The problem was that I wanted to sing solos. Nobody sang solos at the synagogue until they had been there for years, sometimes decades. But I was six years old and I wanted to sing solos. I had this kid's thing in my head that if you were a famous singer you got to meet the king and the queen. So, right from the word go, I wanted to be that special person who sings – otherwise I'd never get to meet the king and queen. It seemed obvious to me. I certainly didn't want to be just another voice in the choir, one of the faces in the background. As usual, I wanted to stand out.

I don't think the cantor – who had been singing beautiful solos in synagogues all his life and had the most amazing voice – could actually believe what he was seeing and hearing. Nobody argued with the cantor. But I did, constantly. Eventually, he relented and allowed me to sing the occasional solo, and I grabbed my chance with both hands. I became so good at it that I became popular and, by the time I was ten, I was singing nearly all of the solos. It was just me and the cantor, backed by the choir.

In terms of my later career in showbiz, singing in the synagogue gave me some invaluable early experience of what it was like to stand before a crowd of very critical people and sing for them convincingly. It gave me a taste of what that might be like in an actual stage show, and I began to dream of bigger and better things.

My mother was absolutely crazy about the theatre, it became her whole life. She used to take me and my sister there: variety shows and the occasional music concert. We always used to sit in what they called the gallery, tuppence each for me and my sister and fourpence for my mother. This was the only real entertainment we had and we absolutely loved it. We got into the habit of going every week. I became aware that the people on the stage were seen as somehow different from the rest of us. They were stars and there would be headlines about them in the newspapers sometimes, as there are today, which just made the whole thing seem even more exciting.

By the time I was nine, my mother and I were already planning how I too was going to be a big star someday. Nothing happened by chance: it was all planned right from the beginning. From that time on, I was constantly rehearsing, honing my act. I didn't have anywhere to practise properly – we used to joke that the walls in our house were so thin that when you said your prayers at night the next-door neighbours said 'Amen'. So I used to practise out on the street or in the playground at school – especially if I'd been to the theatre the night before with my mother. For a while, I got a name among the other kids as a bit of a loony because of that. I'd be walking down the street to school in the morning doing my James Cagney. 'You dirty rat, you're the one that killed my brother!' I used to get carried away and the other kids poked fun at me. I didn't give a shit, though: I just wanted to get these things fixed in my mind. I knew my day was going to come sooner or later and, in the meantime, I was determined that, if I was going to do anything at all, it had to be better than the way the next guy did it.

Actually, it was marvellous for me because it gave me what I call a 'double-active' brain. I was thinking of so many different things at once all the time – school, work, the synagogue, singing, doing impressions – that juggling lots of different scenarios in my mind simultaneously became something I got good at doing. That's another reason why I think I succeeded so well in business later on, because I was always thinking several moves ahead.

I remember reading not long after I'd left my teens about when Al Jolson came back after the film of his life story had been such a big hit in the forties, and how overnight he was able to start charging $15,000 for a week's booking whereas before he'd have been lucky to get $3,000 a month. I used to read these things and try to imagine myself in the same situation, how I would handle it, what I would do. Right then, from a youngster, I was already working my way up to these situations in my own mind, preparing for them. And I never stopped doing that to this day, always working out how to get into that position of being one move ahead of the next guy. But I'm getting ahead of myself.

With what my father was now earning in the garment business and what I was able to bring him from singing in the synagogue, my mother decided in 1933 that we were now doing well enough to move to a slightly nicer part of town. We didn't actually go far – just a few streets away to Thomas Street, off

Bury New Road – but it was in what my parents had previously thought of as the 'posh' part of town. In other words, the sort of neighbourhood that never usually allowed Jews in it. But my mother had seen a house for rent up there that she liked and so she decided she would put on her poshest frock and go and see the estate agents. When she came home that day she told us all about it. She had charmed them with her sophisticated manners and eventually they had said, 'Well, love, we've not had you Jews up here before so you won't let us down, will yer?' And they gave her the house. The family never forgot that and, by the time we moved away from the area again a few years later, only Jews lived there.

Even though the new place was quite close to the old one, it meant quite a change for us all. At first we suffered from what these days we would call 'culture shock'. We didn't know what to call it back then, only that when we walked back down to Rugby Street to visit old friends they'd say things like, 'Oh, yer posh now, are yer?' It was depressing, and we didn't know where we belonged. It wasn't as though we'd gone to live in Buckingham Palace, but we *had* gone to a house that had things such as electric light, so we knew what they were saying. In fact, my sister and I stayed up for hours the first night we were there, going through the house and switching on the lights and looking at them and then switching them off again – then going back ten minutes later and putting them on again. In our old house we had had one room with one gaslight in it and the rest of the rooms had been filled with candles. In the new house, my sister and I even had separate bedrooms.

Once we'd moved out of the ghetto, our whole lives suddenly seemed different. We changed as people. I suppose it was the surroundings. I started at a new school, Cheetham Hill, known locally as the Cheetham Hill chip shop, and I suddenly became very studious in lessons. I even started doing my homework. For some childish reason, I believed you couldn't get a job as a singer unless you were a smart kid at school. Nobody ever told me that. I just got it into my head somehow. So for that reason alone I knew I had to learn. I still used to mess around and fight with the other kids but we used to do it *before* we went into class. Once we actually got in there, the teachers taught us well and we learned a lot.

Like every good Yiddisher boy, I had my bar mitzvah when I was thirteen years old. All the family were there of course, very proud, and there were all the men and boys from the synagogue choir and of course the cantor, plus my teachers. In fact, everybody who had ever had anything to do with anything was there – it was a real show we put on. How my mother and father managed to pay for it I don't know but somehow they did. I was able to help out a little because by then I was singing solos regularly in the synagogue, which meant I was now bringing in a bit more than before.

Not long after my bar mitzvah, Britain declared war with Germany. At first it seemed like the end of the world. But, as I was to discover, the outbreak of war also signalled the arrival of new opportunities for young men with ideas above their station. With so many of the young singers and comics being conscripted overnight into the forces, suddenly there were vacancies all over the country for new, young, male variety artists. All the travelling shows were suffering and every theatre in Manchester was suddenly advertising for new talent. Auditions and talent shows that would have been held once a year perhaps were now being held on almost a weekly basis.

I read all this in the newspapers and realised that this was my chance. I had been rehearsing my act for years – based partly on Jolson, of whom I did a fantastic impression, and partly on another American singer, Richard Tauber, whom I used to dress like, both on stage and off. But mostly my act was based around a singer and impressionist called Afrique, who I thought was just the greatest. Afrique was a Jewish guy from South Africa who sang and did impressions, and he was amazing. He was the first guy to become a major star through doing impressions. There had been others before him but none had ever succeeded on the scale Afrique did. He was a genius, a perfectionist. When he did his Churchill impression it was as if he'd been studying Churchill all his life. And then he would close the show by singing like Caruso! If Caruso was the greatest singer of his day, then Afrique must have been the second greatest, because he could do Caruso better than Caruso!

It was spellbinding. When somebody like that came around we would pester our mother and force her to take us two or three times that week. I used to watch everything intently, taking it all in, letting it burn itself into my memory. My mother used to take notes while we were in the theatre and my sister helped, too. Then I went to various music shops, got the sheet music for the songs they were singing, and put it all together from there. Afrique was my main inspiration, though. I used to look up at the signs above the entrance to the theatre where he was appearing and see his name in letters twenty feet high, and it used to give me a real kick. So I copied his act and, by the time I was thirteen, I could do everything he was doing – everything!

As ever, my mother did whatever she could to encourage me in these pursuits. My father was more English in his outlook. He was proud of my singing in the synagogue and he was all for my having an interest in music, but he also wanted to make sure I would know how to put some bread on the table. He insisted that I learn a trade, and so, not long after I left school at fourteen – which was customary back then, unless you were one of the rich kids who could afford to stay on and go to university – he announced proudly one day that he had pulled some strings at his factory and got me a job. I started the very next week.

I didn't know what to say. It wasn't as if he were being pushy, because he really did think he'd done me a favour. No way, though, did I see myself as a raincoat maker. But I thought, Well, there isn't anything else going on right now, so I might as well take it and at least keep the old man happy. I lasted three months. I did quite well learning how to cut the material and all that but, with the outbreak of World War Two, I thought, What the hell am I doing here? The whole world's going up in smoke and what am I doing – making raincoats! Then I read in one of the newspapers that Afrique was earning something like £400 a week – and that did it. I thought of my father, whose wages had improved over the years so that he was now earning £5 a week, instead of £3, and I decided I simply *had* to get out of there and do something else before I got stuck in the rut that he had.

It really started to get to me because by then I was going to the cinema, too, and I used to gaze in wonder at the screen, desperate to know how you got to do something like that – to actually be *in* a movie? I remember going down the side of a theatre once to the backstage door and knocking on it. I was never backwards at coming forwards, as my mother would say, and I was going to enquire whether they had any jobs going. I'd have done anything – made the tea, swept the floor – just to work backstage in a real theatre. I knocked but nobody came, so I tried the door but it was locked. I knocked again and this time some guy came out and said, 'What do you want, you little fucker?' I didn't do that again in a hurry.

I finally got my break when I won a competition for new talent that was taking place at the Manchester Hippodrome in Ardwick, the second biggest venue in town after the Palace. I had seen an ad for it in the paper the night before, but didn't say anything to my mother. I didn't want to make a big deal of it. I just left the house as normal the next day, but instead of going to work I went to the Hippodrome. I got there far too early, so I bought myself a sandwich and stood outside waiting for someone to let me in. Eventually they did, and the next thing I knew I was walking out on the stage.

Strangely, considering how much it meant to me, I wasn't nervous at all as I walked onto a stage for the first time in a professional theatre. I was always very confident I could do it. By then, I had been singing in the synagogue for eight years – for the latter part, soloing on some very difficult music. In order to sing in Hebrew in the synagogue, it's not just a good voice you need: it's a special kind of delivery. But, by the time I was thirteen, I was giving performances that men of forty weren't capable of. So I knew I could sing – and sing well – before an audience. Far from being nervous, I felt surprisingly at home.

The Hippodrome was a theatre I'd been going to for most of my life and I had fantasised about this moment often enough to have lived it many times over in my mind.

Nevertheless, I knew I would have only a very short time to show what I could do so I sang a song Afrique had made popular called 'None But the Lonely Hearts'. He was so huge at that time that I thought, If this doesn't get 'em nothing will. And blow me down if it didn't do just that and I actually won!

I knew I'd won as soon as I'd finished because all the judges immediately came up to me and started asking me all about myself. They knew I'd just copied Afrique's act but that only impressed them more. 'This is fucking marvellous son, how old are you?' asked this one guy. I thought quickly and said, 'Sixteen, sir.' I knew you had to be at least sixteen to work full-time in the theatre. 'Right,' he said, 'come back tomorrow and this time bring your mother or father or some other legal guardian with you. My name's Bernard Wooly and you can tell them I'm an agent and that I want to sign you up.'

I think I floated all the way home.

Bernard was a veteran of the local variety circuit and it was he who secured me my first professional engagements. He was never of the big time, but that wasn't the point. To be signed up by a professional theatrical agent – well, to say it was like a dream come true is such a cliché that it doesn't do justice to the incredible feeling it gave me. But that was what it was all right: a dream come true.

When I told my mother, she at first thought I was pulling her leg. Then, as the truth began to sink in, she started to become more and more excited. I think she was a little disappointed that I hadn't told her I was going for it; but, after I told her what had happened and what this guy Wooly had said, she couldn't have been more pleased for me. Even my father was pleased – though it would mean my leaving the job he'd secured for me.

The only part that worried me was when I had to admit I'd lied about my age. But that didn't faze my mother at all – in fact, she praised me for my ingenuity. When we went there the next day and they gave her the papers to sign – papers that would confirm my age as sixteen and give her consent for me to travel on the road with them – she signed without blinking. And that was it, I was in showbiz!

Almost overnight, Bernard got me spots on the bill of touring variety shows that would pass through Manchester. What a job! Getting the buzz from performing, plus enjoying all the fun and games that go with the backstage life, I couldn't believe I was actually getting paid to do it! But I was. In fact, the wages were miraculous. It nearly killed me with excitement when I got my first job on a show touring the country, but what made it even more miraculous were the wages of £8 a week! At a time when my father was working twelve-hour days just to bring home a fiver a week, I really did think that this was it, and I had made it! I'm fucking rich! I told myself.

What can I say? I was young. I didn't know the hardest part was yet to come. Fortunately, my mother was more astute and had already arranged for me to be enrolled for a two-year part-time course at the Manchester College of Music, which I diligently attended until I was fifteen. We had to pay for the privilege of course, but again my mother and father were somehow able to make the sums all add up until I was able to chip in with the money I started to earn on my own. It was a wonderful experience. There were all kinds of boys and girls there from different backgrounds, and so that was a new experience for me, too.

That was also the first time I tried singing opera. As luck would have it, we had one of the country's big operatic artists teaching us, a guy called Frank Mullins. Frank could be a cantankerous bastard but he was still active as an opera singer and so you had the benefit of learning from someone who was actually out there doing it, which was incredible. It was Frank who taught me all the difficult arias, for which I will always be grateful. I never fell in love with him personally as a singer, because he was a very cold deliverer of a song, and he took against me because of that. But he taught me a lot technically, such as how to breathe. Now that may sound strange to an outsider, but, if you're training to be a great singer, you'll know that having a good breathing technique is an absolutely crucial part of the kit. Frank used to say to me, 'Learn how to breathe properly now and you'll sing until you're ninety.'

There wasn't enough time to try to develop myself as a proper opera singer – I was in too much of a hurry to get back out there on the variety stage and start earning money. But I took that education into my budding new stage act. I wasn't doing opera but I was using the breathing techniques Frank taught me to improve not just my singing but my timing in general. By the time I was fifteen I had also started singing in a new synagogue called Higher Crumpsall. (My sister Eileen is still the secretary there.) And I took that learning into the theatre with me, too. The synagogue crowd was either hypercritical or half asleep. Either way, you had to learn to project yourself so that everybody paid attention. I learned that from the cantor. It was as much about his sheer presence as it was his beautiful voice. It was the whole package, something I understood the power of long before I got my chance in the theatre.

The bottom line is that I was always learning – and always very conscious of learning. Even when I started getting bookings, I never stopped watching all the other acts on the bill. Watching every little thing they did, trying to figure out how it was done, then how I would do it if it was me, how it could be done better. I would bury inside my head the way this man walked, the way that man talked. I was even following the way the women walked. I remember becoming obsessed with the sassy way Sophie Tucker had of making an entrance. I was just obsessed with the whole thing. And that was when I think it first dawned on me that you were either in the business totally one hundred per cent, or you weren't in it at all. There were no half-measures.

The other thing I quickly learned was that, once you did get there, actually walking out before an audience, your troubles really began. It wasn't like a normal job, where you moved steadily along. If you were a performer your career was always either on the way up or on the way down. You were either the greatest act in the world or the biggest piece of shit in the world, never anything between. And that was what I loved about it – that you were only ever as good as your last performance. You really were laying your life on the line every time you stepped out on that stage. That was how it seemed to me, anyway.

If it was a touring show, it would open in a new town every Monday and would play every night up to the following Saturday, before moving on to the next town on the Sunday. In the summer, I would sometimes perform at Butlin's holiday camp, which used to be one of my favourite gigs. All those girls on holiday looking for a good time – and a whole new coachload of them arriving every week! I thought I'd died and gone to heaven.

I was singing, doing impressions. My whole mini-Afrique bit. It went down a storm. We did two shows a day, including matinées, six days a week, in every northern town and city you'd ever heard of – plus some you never wanted to hear of again. We used to arrive in the town on a Sunday night and go straight to our digs. The longer you did these tours, the more you got to know every dosshouse in every town that could be used as 'digs': little bed-and-breakfast joints, if you were lucky, run by merry widows; a cot by the wall along with six other snoring, smelly blokes, if you were unlucky. You had to take what you could get.

As a result of my doing all the shows, my voice had started to develop. Most choirboys are finished as singers once their voices break. Often, they don't hear their singing voice again until they're about eighteen – if it ever comes back at all. Some of them don't. Some of the most beautiful angels at nine sound like dying frogs by the time they're fourteen. With me, though, it didn't happen: I was the odd one out again. I sang like a choirboy until I was sixteen, when my voice seemed to break overnight and I suddenly began singing like a man. I found the whole thing very strange, but other people virtually accused me of witchcraft. I remember these two old boys in the synagogue asking if I was a dwarf because of the mature voice that came out of this barrel-chested teenage boy.

Soon, through Bernard, I was getting regular bookings every week. We didn't have a telephone at home; hardly anybody did in those days. So I used to commandeer a public telephone box just down the road from us and use that as my office. The odd person did write a letter but most of the business was done by phone. By making sure I had access to a phone, I probably saved myself years of struggling. I was able to arrange bookings with Bernard and help build up some sort of momentum for my career. I didn't want to be down at the bottom of the bill for the rest of my life.

Every morning I would stand outside the phone box waiting for whoever was in there to finish their call, and then, once I got in, I never got out. I remember I felt very assured being on the phone like that, chatting up booking agents and theatre managers and the like. I even got my own business cards made up with the number of the phone box on them. I got away with it like that for over a year, using that old red box as my own personal office. I'd be on the phone, nattering away, eyeing the ever-lengthening queue of people waiting outside to use it, and I was pitiless. This one was taken. This one was *mine*. Hop it!

I brought the same single-minded determination to all my work. Doing auditions, for example, could either be very exciting or completely soul-destroying. But I always used to prepare thoroughly for everything. You had to have confidence to stand on stage at the Ardwick Empire at the age of fourteen, singing to two dozen sceptical non-Jews who were sitting there yawning and farting in the front row. But that was all that was important to me then, and I'd decided just to go for it come what may. Lying about my age, using the phone box as my office – the more ridiculous things got, the stronger I felt. If I had been confident before, now I was unstoppable. Nothing was going to get in my way.

It wasn't just the singing, though, or the lure of the spotlight. Whatever I had done I would have gone out of my way to make a big splash with it. That was because from Day One I always saw myself as different from Charlie next door. Charlie from next door had no chance with me. Even as a kid, you had to have something special to get one over on me. The older I got the more I noticed how certain men simply couldn't bear to be in the same room as I was in. I was so full-on, so confident and determined, they simply couldn't stand it; they didn't want to know. And that was when I knew beyond all doubt that I was going to become something big one day – when I saw the reactions of some of my male friends. That was when I knew I was striking oil.

My sister was similar, in her own way. Eileen was a star academically, winning a scholarship for the most expensive girls' school in the area – the only thing she had to pay for was the uniform. My mother was so proud. She had always had very strong aspirations for all of us, of course, but my father was equally proud of both of us. When I first started working professionally, he used to boast to all his pals at work, 'Oh, he's the greatest fucking singer in the world!' And he meant it. He wasn't jealous, the way some fathers get if their sons start to do well. He didn't have the head for that. He just enjoyed showing off.

Just like his little boy, in fact.

2

In 1944, my whole world changed again. What a year that was! Everything seemed to happen at once. I had turned eighteen at the start of the year and, with the war apparently no nearer reaching a dénouement, I was about to be conscripted into the army. It was also in 1944 that my parents broke up. As if all that weren't enough, it was also around this time, ironically, that I had decided to become engaged.

I don't know the intimate details of what went on between my parents – it was one of those things that they kept away from the children as much as they could – but my father more or less disappeared from our lives after that. He still loved my mother very much, I believe, and, for a while after they first broke up, he would call on her and want to take her out for treats. But she didn't want to know. Although she didn't stop him from seeing us, she never let him back into her own life again. Eventually, he took a new wife, whom he stayed with for the rest of his life. My mother wasn't interested in remarrying. She was too influenced by the movies. My mother loved the movies, but not just in the simple, adoring way of most movie fans back then. My mother learned things from the movies: that there were many other ways to live your life. And she stored that information away, I think, to help keep her strong after my father left.

I learned a lot from the movies, too. I was very like my mother in that respect. We both had ambitions way beyond anything my father ever envisaged, and we both lived our whole lives as though they were scenes from a movie: in her case a romantic adventure story, perhaps; in mine, a real action thriller with fights and explosions and steamy love scenes – the full nine yards. It's obvious to me now that everything I ever knew about life at that time came from the movies; everything I aspired to and wanted to become was right there on the silver screen. Even more than my mother, the movies shaped my whole life back then. They helped me become something entirely different – and much more interesting.

Meanwhile, I had met and fallen madly in love with an absolutely gorgeous girl who looked as if she'd just come straight out of a movie herself. Her name was Rita Marlowe, and Rita was an entertainer, too. She had beautiful reddish brown hair, dark glittering eyes and a wonderful figure. At the time, she was one of the most popular female singers in the country after Vera Lynn. I met her when we were both performing in a special show for overseas troops, which was broadcast on BBC radio sometime towards the end of 1943. Rita was always fretting about being called up for the war; the government was then actively involved in trying to persuade famous or well-known women to join up so as to encourage ordinary women to do the same. Rita had shrewdly decided that if she did shows for the troops she wouldn't be pestered into actually putting a uniform on. And while she was singing for the BBC, she was not only doing her bit for 'our boys' but also helping retain her star status. She was a real pro like that and in the beginning I admired her for it.

The only trouble was, she was 24 when we met and I was still just seventeen. We were having it off for about a month before I plucked up the courage to tell her how old I was. At first she refused to believe it. I literally had to get my wallet out and show her my credentials before she would take my word for it. After that, though, I think she was quite taken with the idea of having a young Romeo by her side. And the prospect of squiring this – as I saw her then – much older, incredibly sexy woman was certainly part of the charm for me, too. It was a very passionate, over-the-top relationship. We knew people whispered about us and we encouraged it. Her favourite thing was to have me service her right there in the wings just before she went on stage. She claimed it improved her performance. It didn't do any harm for mine, either, and we became engaged not long afterwards.

Engagements were common during World War Two. Men were being sent off to fight, women had to take strange jobs, whole families were being moved from one part of the country to another at a moment's notice – you never really knew from one week to the next what your long-term prospects were. Becoming engaged was partly a way of flying in the face of all that and trying to establish a bond at a time when such things were almost impossible to sustain. They didn't really mean much in a practical sense, unless you went ahead and actually got married. It was more a case of having something to hold onto, something warm to nurture in your heart while the rest of the world was falling apart or around you.

When I told my mother, though, she hit the roof. The timing of my announcement, admittedly, was not exactly auspicious, what with her just then going through the breakdown of her own marriage. But, in my foolishness, I at least thought she'd be pleased for me.

Instead, she went nuts. 'What have you done?' she cried. 'Have you gone mad?' I tried to tell her what a wonderful woman Rita was but she said she knew exactly what kind of woman Rita was – an older one. One much too hard-faced and experienced for me. And, although I didn't want to hear that, in retrospect I feel she was probably right. There was more to Rita than that, though, things about her my mother either couldn't or wouldn't see – her talent, her beauty, her spirit. But my mother had seen the unpalatable things about her that I had either ignored or chosen to see rather as charming affectations. The only thing my mother approved of about Rita was that she was Jewish. The seven-year age gap between us, however, she just couldn't get her head around at all. She couldn't understand what a woman like Rita would see in a young boy like me, her bubba.

Not that that deterred me – any more than a mother's disapproval will ever deter any son from doing what he will when it comes to affairs of the heart. If anything, it spurred me on to want to get married – just to prove her wrong. Fate, however, took a hand in things and early in 1944, not long after we had become engaged, I received my call-up papers for the army. I was in a show at Wolverhampton at the time and I remember the terrible sinking feeling I got as I opened the official government-stamped envelope. I had been expecting them but it was still a shock to have them in my hands. I think they said I was to report to the army induction centre within 24 hours, or something ludicrous like that. Knowing I would soon be called up, Rita had begged me to marry her before I was sent off to fight. But, while I was still trying to bring my mother round to the idea, the induction papers had arrived and, the next thing I knew, that was it: I had disappeared inside a uniform.

I started off at a boot camp for infantrymen in Weymouth. Needless to say, Rita was not exactly thrilled by this latest development. She wrote me a letter in which she didn't pull her punches. 'I want you to get permission to marry me before you get sent off to fight,' she wrote, 'or I'm not waiting for you.' You might have thought my mother's dire warnings would have come back to haunt me at that point – but no. I was so lovesick, and I went straight to the commanding officer of the camp I was in and begged him for a brief leave of absence so that I could get married. I explained how my fiancée was nearly 25 and so couldn't afford to wait around for me. But the CO, who had obviously had a bit more experience of this sort of thing than the moon-faced recruit standing before him, refused to let me go. 'No,' he said abruptly. 'I'm not going to OK this. This marriage sounds like it will be too much of a burden for you.' I just stood there, speechless for once. 'You'll be shipping out to Germany to fight in a few weeks,' he added. 'If she's not prepared to wait for you while you do that, she's not worth marrying anyway.'

I was devastated at the time but the old CO had done me a favour. If he had said yes and let me go I would have gone and married Rita and my whole life would have turned out to be very different. I would still have been in showbiz, I have no doubt of that. But my whole focus would probably have changed – I think Rita would have insisted on it – so that all our energies were channelled towards her career. But it obviously wasn't meant to be. When I wrote and told her I had been refused permission to leave she wrote back straightaway saying how terribly sorry she was to hear that but, not to worry, she'd definitely stay in touch. Good as her word, she dropped me another line about a month later to say she'd married someone else.

I just stared at the letter in my hands in disbelief. It turned out she had married this taxi driver we both knew – an ignoramus who claimed to have ambitions to become an impresario in America. Rita always was America-mad, and so off she went. We still stayed in touch, though, writing to each other off and on, for a couple of years, until finally she wrote to me one day saying she was living in New York but that the schmuck she'd married had gone rotten on her, and that she was coming back to England. By now, though, I'd learned to read between the lines and this time I didn't bother to reply.

There is, however, a small, melancholy footnote to the story of my affair with Rita. Over thirty years later, when I was living in Beverly Hills, I discovered by chance that someone called Rita Marlowe was performing in the cocktail lounge of this hotel in LA, singing and playing piano. I couldn't resist going down there for a peek, just to see if it was really her. I went on my own. It was a classy place and when I walked in she was at the piano singing. As soon as I heard the voice, I knew it was her. It was exactly as I remembered it from the forties and I was momentarily transported back to the war. It was very odd indeed.

When she took a breather I took the opportunity to go up and say hi to her. I didn't say who I was. I just said, 'Hello, I just wanted to say how much I like your singing.' 'Thanks,' she said.

As soon as she spoke, I knew something wasn't right. She turned to face me and that was when I realised. She was blind, poor thing. 'Well, sweetheart,' I said, 'I don't want to keep you. I just wanted to say I think you've got a lovely voice.'

I wondered if she had recognised mine, but she hadn't. I decided not to make a big thing of it, in case it embarrassed or upset her. She had a silver tips tray on top of the piano and I pulled out a hundred-dollar bill and left it there. I looked at her one last time as she turned back to the piano, and said, 'So long, sweetheart, lots of luck.' And then I got out of there. It was just too much, all too much. It still makes me sad to think of it.

The timing of my army call-up didn't snooker only my love life, though: it completely ended my career. By then I was a regular performer on the touring circuit, working my way up the bill. My agent was now Joe Collins, who was big time (and whose daughters, Joan and Jackie, would also become famous later on as Hollywood actress and blockbuster novelist, respectively) and things were going well. It was always the same sort of show: there would be me and maybe five other guys, most of them gay, and about thirty girls. 'This is the life,' I used to say to myself as I stared into the mirror in my dressing room, psyching myself up to go on. I was still sixteen, earning a good living and having a hell of a lot of fun. There was a war on, of course, but in a strange way you got used to that. I remember when I first went with a show to London. It was at the height of the blitz and every night German bombers and British artillery fire lit up the sky. You could either stay in your house, hiding under the table, or you could go to one of the bomb shelters. Or you could do what I and the rest of the show people used to do and just totally ignore it. Or, rather, not ignore it, but just accept it as part of the landscape, part of the fun.

Not that everything was a laughing matter. My future brother-in-law, whose family lived in London, was caught out one night when the bombs started dropping and so he went to a shelter and stayed there until morning. When he finally got home the next day, however, he found his house gone, completely flattened into rubble – and his entire family with it. So do not think I am being flippant if I say that most of the war years were great fun for me. I am just describing the way we dealt with it at the time as young people, not really knowing what else to do. It was the old cliché: you could either laugh or cry. These days they would probably label it as some form of 'denial', but that wasn't it at all. We were young; we were on the stage, on the road, earning good money and having a great time fucking ourselves stupid. The fact that the sky was exploding every night just seemed to be part of the general live-for-today excitement.

I wasn't a star yet but I was certainly raking in the money. Just before I was called up I was doing shows that would sometimes pay as much as £25 a week. That still wasn't much compared with the hundreds that someone like Afrique would make, but it was certainly a lot better than what my father had been bringing home before he left us. The nearest I came to being a star before the war was when I actually became the understudy to the great Afrique himself. He had got to hear about this kid who had more or less ripped off his act, but he took it all in great humour. He saw it as a compliment, and by the time I was seventeen we had met and become quite friendly. When on one occasion he became ill, he asked me to stand in for him. That was by far the biggest job I'd landed, up to that point, and I took it very seriously. I did his regular headline spot for a couple of weeks and absolutely revelled in it! The only trouble was he got well too quickly and before I knew it I was back down the bill again. But, hey, that's showbiz – a world I was getting to know better each passing day.

That all ended abruptly, though, with the arrival of my call-up papers.

Joining the army was an eye-opener, to say the least. The training camp was a dismal, depressing place which filled me with foreboding. After I had lived the life of Riley for nearly four years as a professional entertainer, the idea of roughing it with a bunch of unwashed, unworldly, largely uneducated lads my own age was a frankly appalling one. If the thought of being sent off to fight in Germany wasn't enough to keep you awake at night, the smell of fifty other men's smelly feet and arseholes definitely was. I'd got used to being on stage and in digs. I'd got used to being the centre of attention. I thought, How did I end up having to share my bedroom with these second-class cunts?

The one thing we had in common was that nobody wanted to be there. We were all conscripts and, apart from one or two idiots who thought they were off to become heroes, the rest of us all thought we were going to die. I admit that even I was worried. It's one thing to face someone in a fight, man to man, but to put yourself in a place where you're expected to face up to a landmine or a bomb, or some bloody sniper you don't even see – well, I didn't fancy that at all. Sod being a hero: I was eighteen and all I wanted to do was be out there on stage, making money and having a good time.

Fortunately, my theatrical background would come to my rescue. I didn't know it yet but I was about to give the performance of my career – one that was, possibly quite literally, lifesaving.

It started when it became known that I had been on the stage and I was asked by one of the high-ranking officers if I would be interested in trying to prepare some regular entertainment for the troops. There was no one else in my barracks who had been anywhere near show business – or, rather, no one else who had owned up to it. Once I started geeing people up, however, it turned out there were more than a few singers and performers – mostly amateur but some semi-professional – who had been hiding the fact in case any of the other boys got the 'wrong' idea: they didn't want them to think they were sissy. But I brought them out of their closets, so to speak.

After that, I was invited to apply for a posting with ENSA – the official entertainments division of the army – and I started arranging shows for army bases in places such as Catterick,

Chester and Southport. The officers wanted regular shows as morale boosters, they said. In truth, it was more to do with the fact that they enjoyed being able to bring their families and friends down for the weekend. They all came from rich families who, when we were in Southport, would book suites at the best hotels. This northwestern town was considered a high-class English beach resort in those days. Once I grasped this, I started aiming a little higher than just low-key variety shows featuring the actual boys in the barracks and started to bring in some proper professional talent.

There was an agent I was in contact with called Harry Roysten, who was great at finding acts for those weekend soldier shows. I thought that, if I could entertain the officers as they'd never been entertained before, maybe they would find a way to keep me there indefinitely and I wouldn't have to go and have my balls blown off.

For a while it looked as if my plan was working as my 'shipping-out' date kept getting postponed. The only thorn in my side was this one guy, who didn't like any of this airy-fairy theatrical stuff at all. In fact, he hated it and did everything he could to try to get it stopped. Or, if he couldn't do that, just get me removed personally. He used to say to me, 'You're as strong as an ox, you're eighteen, why aren't you going off to fight?' He thought he was a tough guy because he had two stripes on his arms, but I used to look at those stripes and think, He's nothing, fuck him!

'I'm not going to fight,' I'd say, 'because I've been told to do something else by the officers – to sing and produce a show.' And as I said it I'd sort of flutter my eyelashes at him, which would send him into an even greater rage. He really had issues with the whole showbiz thing. He couldn't bear to see men dressed as women; he couldn't bear to see men dressed as anything other than soldiers. The more I realised this, the more I used to wind him up about it. Once you know what enrages a man, you've found his Achilles' heel. I used to speak to him in showbiz patter with a heavy lisp and put my hand on my hip and say, 'Oooooh!' It would drive him mental. 'You fucking poof!' he'd scream at me. 'Go back to fucking London!'

What got me was that he was a Jewish corporal. A Jew from Hackney who thought the war was the best thing that had ever happened and that I just wasn't taking it seriously enough. He was wrong. I took the war very seriously, which was why I was doing what I was doing. I just wasn't taking *him* seriously enough. In the end, though, no matter how many times I made him look stupid, he just wouldn't quit. I discovered that you get that quite often if you're in the business. It can go two ways: you either get people who are fascinated by the whole process, or who hate everything about it – and you most of all. The not-so-kind corporal fell into the latter category. For a while, I thought he was their leader. Eventually, it got so much I made it known in a discreet way to the officer who had put me in charge of the shows that I was being harassed by this old cunt, and he stepped in and sorted him out. I don't know what he said exactly but it must have been good because he never came near me again.

Just as one problem was disappearing, however, another even more worrying development had reared its head. Although I carried on putting on top-quality shows, the officers couldn't keep me there for ever, they said, and eventually I was given a firm leaving date. The weekend before I was due to ship out, I was given a 48-hour pass to go home and say goodbye to my mother. As soon as I walked through the door she knew something was wrong. When I told her the news, she became distraught.

'When do you go?' she asked me, the tears rolling down her cheek.

'The day after tomorrow.'

She nearly fainted. And that was when I made up my mind.

'Don't worry,' I told her. 'I ain't going anywhere.' She looked at me doubtfully, but I put my arms around her and reassured her. 'If you do what I ask you to do, then there won't be a problem.'

'What do you mean?' she said.

'I mean,' I said, 'that tomorrow afternoon I want you to phone my barracks and tell them that your son, who is on leave, has fallen ill, very, very ill, and that they are to send someone to get him.'

And that's how it started – my mystery illness. I hadn't really thought it through before I got to my mother's. But, having seen her like that, I just knew she was right. I wasn't going anywhere! I was too young to die, I really did think that. Good as gold, the next day my mother phoned and spoke to the CO's office, and the next thing I knew I was in the army hospital being looked after by the prettiest nurses I'd ever seen.

All sorts of tests were run on me over the first few weeks but nothing 'conclusive' had emerged, said the army doctor who tended me. Nevertheless, I had some disquieting symptoms, the main one being an inability to do anything other than lie flat on my back, giving out no signs of life at all: a vegetable. The other one was not being able to talk properly, conversing with the doctors and nurses in a manner that gave them the impression I could manage to utter only two words out of five. In other words, I was a little crazy – a very hard thing to test for back then. Not that it stopped them from trying. But, while they did that, I was going nowhere – exactly as I had promised my mother.

I confess, I wondered at first how long I would be able to keep it up. It didn't take long, however, to realise that I was hardly the only soldier there suffering from some unspecified illness. As I looked round the ward, it seemed the prospect of being sent overseas to fight had induced similar distresses in a number of young men. The guy in the bed next to mine, for instance, was definitely at it. He came from some rich old Jewish family and there was absolutely nothing wrong with him, but he used to pretend he was suffering from shell shock. He'd walk around like a cripple and slur his words. He had them all going. Only his wife and I knew the truth.

The only trouble was that he was too convincing and whenever his wife came to visit him – this pretty 23-year-old who obviously loathed the whole idea of hospitals – it was clear she couldn't stand it. We were in the army hospital in Southport and she used to come all the way up from London to see him, stay about five minutes, wrinkle her nose in disgust and leave again. He would ask her to go for a walk with him along the beachfront and she'd pull a face and say, 'If you think I'm going out with you looking like that you're very much mistaken!' Or she'd give in and take him and he'd be leaning on her and slobbering over her all the way down the corridor. He knew she hated it but he didn't see what else he could do. 'Just a little longer,' he kept telling her. It never crossed his mind that she might grow so tired of the whole charade that she would eventually just turn him in, but that was what happened. Down on the beach one day in front of several officers and doctors, she just pushed him off and walked away. He started to run after her and that was when they nabbed him. They sent in the redcoats – the army police – and put him in a wagon and that was it. I woke up one morning and his bed was empty. One of the nurses later told me they had sent him straight to the second front.

Fortunately, I didn't have to worry about a wife letting me down. The only immediate cloud on my horizon was that most of the army doctors were Jewish and they were very wary of being seen to go out of their way to help any of the Jewish patients – particularly one like me, about whom they already had their doubts. They had to be careful because, if it turned out that I wasn't really ill, it might look as though the doctors had been covering up for one of their own. And that would have been seen as treason, for which there was only one punishment in wartime: execution.

But, if that all sounds quite serious, I should say that most of the time at the hospital the atmosphere was more one of faint hilarity. The war, which had been going for over five years by then, had induced a very different state of mind in everybody, far more accepting of things that would have been considered strange or even outrageous in peacetime. All the nurses, for example, were young women from well-off families who had volunteered to help the sick. They all had cut-glass accents and were all immaculately turned out, but, instead of being stiff and unworldly, they were a very switched-on and amusing bunch.

One of them winked at me one day as she was tucking me into bed. 'I must say, I think you're doing a marvellous job of fooling them all,' she smiled. 'I can see why you're on the stage.' I had to be careful in case it was a trick and so I just played dumb. But inside I took it as a compliment.

The stage was in my blood. As a result, I had one of those bizarre illnesses that seemed to go into remission whenever we had another army show coming up. In fact, I spent the latter part of my so-called army career either appearing on the stage or lying in my bed in the hospital. I wasn't sure which was the greater acting job, but I certainly gave some Oscar-winning performances along the way. The officer behind the shows never even used to ask where I'd been hiding. I think he just knew. They all did, I'm sure of it. It was the last year of the war and I think most people were at it in one way or another. The golden rule, as ever, was not to get caught.

And then something strange and unexpected occurred: I became ill for real. I'm sure it was through always being at the hospital, surrounded by sick people, that I suddenly came down with pneumonia. I was completely out on my feet for months. My mother came to visit me and was shocked by what she saw. I'd lost weight and had sunken eyes. I think she thought I was a goner. But she would make me get dressed and take me out for a walk down to the beach while I held onto her arm for support. It did seem to do me some good and after that she would visit often, bringing extra food and always making sure we had a walk down by the sea no matter what state I was in.

In those days, pneumonia was even more serious than it is now. There was no known cure and people died of it all the time. Bizarrely, this worked in my favour when the army doctors sat down to decide my fate. By then, it was 1945 and the talk was all of how the war would soon be ending. With the hospital already so overcrowded, the army administrators balked at the idea of treating a long-term patient who had very little chance of recovering in time to send overseas. So out of the blue they just decided to send me home. Just like that. Ironically, now that I really was ill, they just couldn't be bothered with me and I was honourably discharged early in 1945. It was a real bolt from the blue. By then I felt as though I was probably three-quarters better anyway. But the head of the hospital made his own law – they were left to run these hospitals the best they could during wartime – and I was given some official papers to carry with me, explaining my condition and the reason why I wasn't in uniform, and told to clean out my locker and go.

I didn't need to be told twice. I packed up my troubles – and everything else – in my old kit bag and, as the song goes, smiled, smiled, smiled.

There was never any doubt in my mind about what I was going to do once I got home to Manchester. My mother wanted me to give it a few more weeks, until I had got all my strength back, but I was in a hurry. I had wasted enough time already being stuck in the army and the first night I was home I bought the *Manchester Evening News* and studied the theatrical ads. I got a pencil and circled a few and the very next morning I was on the phone. Within weeks I had got back with a new agent – a little Yiddisher fellow by the name of Hymie Zahl – and I was booked into a touring show.

I had expected to be a little rusty but because of all the army shows I'd done I wasn't finding it tough being back at all, and quite quickly I started working my way up the bill again. Now that I was older, I was also really able to put myself forward. When I had been first starting out, what I did was almost a novelty act – people used to get a kick out of seeing this kid doing Afrique or Al Jolson. But now I was nearly twenty and I wanted to be seen as a grown man with a talent and personality of his own – a potential star in his own right. Then something happened that blew the whole thing out of the water again.

I was appearing in a show at the Hippodrome in Huddersfield, and I'd picked up a girl I'd met in the greenroom – the rest and hospitality room backstage. I was a bastard for going to the greenroom after the show each night and picking up girls. All the artists met and drank there, along with a few of the patrons and theatre management and various guests, and so there were always a lot of girls hanging around. This particular week I had met this sweet young thing in there who was about my age. I met her on the Wednesday, and on the Friday, as I was in my dressing room getting ready to go on, she asked me to sign her autograph book. I was puzzled as to why she hadn't asked me before. She said she had intended to but that, the first night she had turned up at the theatre asking for me, the backstage manager had stopped her, saying, 'What do you want that fucking Jew boy's signature for?'

I knew who the prick was because all the artists knew him. He was the guy running the whole thing and so it paid to stay in his good books, which until then I thought I had managed to do quite successfully. When I heard that, though, I knew different. The fact that he had said such a snide thing, not to me but to this innocent young girl, made me angry. But it also embarrassed me in front of her – which made me even angrier. I decided there and then that something would have to be done. I went off to find him.

In those days, I thought I could take anybody. I'd spent my whole life doing deep-breathing exercises, which is why I ended up with such a barrel chest – every three months I'd have to buy a new suit because my chest kept expanding. It paid off, though. I had tremendous lung power. If the audience didn't like me all I had to do was sing a high note and hold it there until they started clapping and cheering – a trick I'd learned from my days singing with the cantor.

I also had tremendous strength. It was just a part of me, anyway – the Russian part – but this power surprised even me. To keep it up, every day, wherever I was, I would be out running or walking. I would keep going until I was collapsing. I equated physical fitness with mental fitness, and mental fitness with success. There were no gyms to go to because I was travelling all the time, so I would devise other ways of keeping fit. Every Sunday, for example, the acts would share taxis from the digs to the train station. All the acts, that is, except me. At first, they thought it was because I was a mean little bastard who wouldn't spring for the fare. But that wasn't it. I just wanted to keep fit, so, instead of going in the cars with everybody else, I would trot down the street after them with a big, heavy suitcase in each hand.

As a result, I was all muscle, no fat. The girls in the show used to call me Tarzan. I'd go to the wings with my shirt off and just a towel round my neck and I'd see guys staring at my physique – big barrel chest and big muscled arms and legs – and I knew what they were thinking, God, look at that guy, you'd have to hit him with a hammer to knock him out. They would take one look and not want any part of it. I loved it. I took it as a gift in return for all my hard work. The trouble was, I also had a quick temper and I built up a reputation after I had left the army of being the kid who would take you on, no matter who you were, if you tried to mess with him. As the stage manager was about to find out . . .

The show had already started but my anger wouldn't keep. I found him by the side of the stage, working the curtain. I tapped him on the shoulder and said, 'Here, did you call me a fucking Jew boy?' I thought he would at least try denying it before he stammered out an apology, but he didn't deny anything. He just stood up and faced me and said, 'Yeah, so what?' That was when I knew I had to hit him. He had left me no option. If I had backed down, he'd have had me pegged in his mind for ever as the guy who bottled out – and I wasn't having that.

We were standing in the wings, the curtain was up and there was an act out there doing his stuff. I applied a few good blows to the body and head and he went flying – literally flying – through the air! He ended up lying half on and half off the stage, his head in the orchestra pit. The audience laughed – there was a comedian on stage at the time and they thought it was all part of the act.

However, the theatre owner, Louis Benjamin, had seen it all and knew different. Louis was the one responsible for booking the acts from the agents. I had been back in my dressing room only a few minutes when he knocked on the door. I still had the girl with me but he said, 'Excuse me, I want to speak to your boyfriend.' And he shoved her out the room. Then he looked at me and said, 'How much are you on this week?' I told him: 'Twenty-seven pounds.' He said, 'I can't give you that this week. Instead, I'll give you a figure that's minus two days – tonight and tomorrow.' I asked what he meant and he looked at me sternly and said, 'I'm not paying you for tonight or tomorrow night because you will not be appearing on stage at this theatre tonight or tomorrow night – or indeed any other night. You might not have noticed but this is a theatre, not a boxing ring.'

He was very smartarse about it and I was tempted to give him a dig, too. But that really would have had me finished, so instead I tried to soften him. I tried to explain what the cause of the ruckus was, but he just didn't want to know. He told me simply to get my things and leave. I went back to my digs that night and locked myself in my room. I couldn't sleep at all, but I just lay there on my bed all night thinking about it. Surely, once people knew the full story, they would understand – wouldn't they? Then why had I just been sacked? I finally went to sleep that night just as daylight was beginning to peep through the curtains. All I knew was that I had better get myself down to my agent's office first thing Monday morning – and start doing some explaining.

Hymie was part of the Foster agency, one of the biggest in London. I travelled down on the train from Huddersfield on the Sunday, checked myself into the usual showbiz digs and at 9.30 Monday morning I was waiting outside his office in Lower Regent Street. Which just shows how rattled I was: I knew full well that Hymie never usually turned up until after eleven. This particular Monday morning, however, Hymie was there waiting for me. He had already heard the news, of course, and was not happy.

I said, 'Hymie, you gotta understand, this fella called me a fucking Jew boy. I had no choice.'

He said, 'So what? You never heard that before?'

He was right. I had heard it all before. But this had been different. If he had spoken like that to my face, I still wouldn't have liked it but at least it would have given me the chance to say something back. The fact that the little shitbag had said it behind my back – and not just to anyone but to this girl I was trying to impress – had been what set me off. I tried to explain some of this to Hymie but he just held up his hands, signalling for silence.

'Look,' he said, 'whatever this schmuck called you, the fact is you've beaten him up pretty bad. I've had reports that he's in hospital and the rest of the staff at the Hippodrome are having a whip-round for him.'

I said, 'What the fuck are you talking about? I hit him, I didn't kill him.'

'Whatever you did,' said Hymie, 'this man is now lying very ill.'

'Where? Where is he ill?'

Hymie just looked at me. 'How the fuck do I know where he's ill?' he shouted. 'But I'm telling you they're making collections for this man and you are the one getting the blame for it!'

I turned away. I couldn't understand what Hymie was telling me. When I had walked out of the theatre on the Friday night the guy had been on his feet, still operating the curtain. I said, 'Look, Hymie, I'm telling you, something's going on here. Something's wrong.'

He said, 'Oh, something's wrong all right. They've banned you from the circuit for two years, that's what's wrong!'

I couldn't believe it. Word had already gone out and it wasn't just the Huddersfield Hippodrome I was in trouble with now: it was every Hippodrome in the country.

'And not just them,' Hymie frowned. 'Nobody wants you! Not for two years!'

It took a few moments for the implications to sink in. As far as I could see, not being able to appear in any of the country's theatres meant not being able to work at all. For two years.

After the time I had already lost in the army, this was an almost unbearable prospect. 'I might as well retire,' I joked feebly.

'Kid,' said Hymie, 'you already have.'

I looked at him. 'What am I going to do?'

He just shrugged. 'I love you, my boy, but I just can't help you with this.'

There was nothing left to do, it seemed, except say goodbye.

'Don't worry,' he said as he saw me to the door. 'We Jews can fight for ourselves, always remember that.'

Maybe so, but those words offered very little comfort on the long journey home to Manchester that day. Blackballed from the profession for two whole years – that's me finished, I thought. I might as well go home and slit my wrists. And for what – some girl I hardly knew? My mother would be devastated. And how would we pay the bills? My sister Eileen had only just got her first job as a trainee secretary and wasn't bringing in much money yet. That meant I'd have to get a job, go back to earning a fiver a week – if I was lucky. I thought of nothing else as the train slowly wended its way home. Until then, I had considered myself a pretty smart cookie. Now I was beginning to feel like a schmuck.

Help, however, was just over the horizon, and Hymie's words came back to me more than once over the next couple of years. Just as he had predicted, it was the Jewish community that eventually came to my rescue. At first, I had gone home to Manchester and just sat around for a couple of weeks not knowing what to do. In the army, I had acted shell-shocked. Now I really was. The prospect of getting a so-called proper job again definitely was not on the menu, but what else was there without the stage?

I had been kicking around like that in a daze, not knowing what the hell to do, when I bumped into an old chum from my army show days. At that point, I was ready to consider anything and so, when he started going on about this Yiddisher agent down in London who worked mainly with Jewish artists, my eyes lit up. Her name was Julia Golden and her thing was to put on these shows to raise money for various organisations connected with the Jewish community – the sort of specialist entertainment that ran outside conventional show-business lines.

I got her details and bought myself a ticket on the next train back to London, going home first just long enough to pick up some sheet music for a few Jewish songs. I didn't even bother ringing ahead for an appointment, didn't even think about digs, just got to London, jumped on a bus and went straight to her office. Fortunately, Julia was a class act and nothing fazed her. She saw me straightaway and I began telling her what I thought I could do for her, which was basically the same act I'd always done but with a slightly more Jewish slant to it in the songs and impressions and so forth.

She shook her head and said, 'Never mind singing Jewish songs. Can you actually sing in Yiddish and Hebrew?'

'Of course,' I said.

'Great,' she said. 'I've got a show on this Sunday night at the London Palladium – can you be there?'

Could I be there for the London Palladium? Was she kidding? The London Palladium was the king of variety-show venues, the sort of place you dreamed of playing one day. I was incredulous. She said she had a spot there for a Jewish artist who could sing in Hebrew. I think I was still in shock when I walked out on stage at the Palladium three days later. I hadn't expected to be thrown in at the deep end like that and it wasn't until I got there and started setting up that I realised the only sheet music I had with me was written just for piano. Thankfully, the old boys in the orchestra swung it for me. They knew all the songs already of course and, even though I'd never sung them with an orchestra before, they were bloody marvellous. They really helped me out and made me look good.

Julia was there, watching from the wings, and, even though I did my best to ignore her, it made me unusually nervous, as though I were a little kid again, auditioning at the synagogue. We hadn't even discussed money yet: she'd said she wanted to hear me sing first. When I came off stage, though, she was standing there waiting for me with a folded paper bag in her hand. 'Here, this is for you,' she said. I opened the bag and looked inside. There was a bundle of notes – it looked like about thirty quid. The only time anybody had ever given me that much was for a whole week's work. I was still pondering that when she opened her engagements diary and started reading aloud. 'These are the dates when I need somebody,' she said. 'Is it possible you might be available?' I resisted the urge to bite her arm off and said yes, it was possible that I might be available.

That was the start of a wonderful working relationship that lasted for the entire two years I was 'banned' from the mainstream theatre. I started out filling in here and there on these Jewish-only bills Julia specialised in and ended up headlining my own shows at the Palladium and other places. I really knew how to work the orchestra by then, knew how to put on a top-of-the-bill show, and was getting paid accordingly. By 1948, I was getting £350 per show, which was berserk money in those days. Star money.

Late at night, after the show, as I sat with a large glass of whisky in my hand and a pretty girl on my knee, it was hard not to see it all as the result of my having punched out that racist little schlemiel in Huddersfield two years before. And that was when I learned never to regret anything. By the time my so-called 'ban' from regular theatre work had been lifted, instead of a career in ruins, I was suddenly slammed with theatre work. I was fielding calls from every big agent in the country. In two years I had gone from being a popular turn halfway down the bill in a travelling provincial show to the star of the London Palladium. Now I intended to stay there, and so, even after my ban was lifted, I continued working for Julia, too. I fell into a routine of doing the regular provincial theatres during the week and then travelling down to London or wherever for the special Jewish concerts at the weekend. I was so excited to get back on the road again that I felt as if I had enough energy for ten shows!

*

It was at this point that I decided to change my name. After coming back into mainstream showbiz, I never thought about going back to Hymie, who I felt had washed his hands of me too quickly. Instead, I got a new, more high-powered agent named Johnny Riscoe. It was Johnny who first brought up the subject of my name. He kept complaining that 'Harry Levy' simply didn't sound glamorous enough. 'I think you can go all the way, kid, and I want to represent you but your fucking name has gotta go!' He was one of those guys – old school.

Eventually, I decided he was right. 'Harry Levy' was awful, not because it was Jewish, but because it just didn't sound like the name of a big singing star. If I had been a comedian, it would have done fine. But I wanted to be known now primarily as a singer – I was convinced that that would be my passport to the big time – and so I needed a new name.

Johnny said, 'Leave it to me. I'm going away on holiday for a couple of weeks. I'll have your new name for you when I come back.' Sure enough, when he came back two weeks later Johnny called me into his office and said, 'OK, forget Harry Levy. From now on you will be known as Don Arden.' And that was that, thank you very much and goodnight. I found out later that he got the 'Arden' from Robert Arden, the Hollywood actor, and the 'Don' from another Hollywood star named Brian Donlevy. I was quite chuffed when I found out. I used to love Brian Donlevy because he always used to play these semi-gangster types who walked a fine line between right and wrong in order to do what they had to do. I used to love all that as a kid. I understood.

As soon as I changed my name to 'Don Arden' I discovered another strange fact about showbiz: the importance of having the right name. I was still doing the same act but almost overnight my fortunes were transformed. The act had evolved a great deal by then, too. It was still a mixture of singing and impressions, but best of all was when I could combine the two – like when I did the black pianist and singer, Hutch, who was rumoured to be having it off with Earl Mountbatten's wife. That always went down well. I used to sing in my own voice, too, but I used to mix it up with laughs by doing my impressions of people like Churchill, Mario Lanza, Edward G Robinson, Bing Crosby . . . I found that, despite the age difference, I could do all those people. Often, it was just a question of getting the right hat. Take Churchill, for instance: I got a hat like his, which had become his trademark as much as the cigar, and I would put it on, start doing the voice, which I was good at, and the next thing you knew I was Churchill!

I would keep the act fresh by adding new voices all the time. I no longer did Afrique, for example, who was now out of fashion. Instead, it was Johnnie Ray. When he became the hottest thing on two legs, my impression of him was one of the most popular bits of my show. I still did Al Jolson, but by now it had developed into a much longer piece, which I would perform occasionally in one-man shows. I didn't do the black face though: it wasn't necessary after the war. People had seen the movie *The Al Jolson Story* in which Larry Parks played Jolson, and it was that characterisation that I focused on – that and his marvellous singing voice. Mario Lanza was another one who always used to go down a storm. I'd use my impression of him to do the holding-one-note-until-they-applauded bit. The audience loved it more than ever and it became my gimmick – I would undo my tux and really let go. One or two other performers tried it but they couldn't live with me. I'd been doing that little number since I was a kid.

By the early fifties, however, the showpiece of my act was my Marlon Brando impression. People liked it not because it was good in the conventional copycat way, but because it was clever and sophisticated. I couldn't actually do the voice – I tried and tried but I just couldn't make it. But I had studied him as a human being – the way he walked into a room, the way he used his body – and I contrived the whole performance around that. I would black out the stage for thirty seconds, which is a long time in the middle of a performance – no sound, nothing. But, when the lights came back on, I was Brando! I'd studied everything, even the colour of his skin. I changed the colour of my face to match Brando's by having the lighting guy put this certain amber gel over the spotlight. And I had a jacket especially made that was exactly like the one he wore in *On the Waterfront* (1954). The magic was in the way I just stood there under this certain light, in this hat and jacket. There was something, too, about the movements and the mannerisms. The whole thing was so heavily stylised that it just immediately worked and, although the whole thing was essentially done as a mime, the applause for Brando was bigger than for almost anybody else in my show back then! Even though I couldn't do the voice, I used to think I was the best in the world at Brando. And of course, all the women wanted to be laid by him. I can't say I minded that, either!

There were girls everywhere, of course, just as there are now at pop concerts. Variety was the most popular form of entertainment there was until TV came along in the fifties and changed everything, and, like everyone else, I took full advantage of that fact. As a young man in his early twenties, earning a fortune and starring at the top of the bill, I wasn't attracting only the women, either: I remember these two gay male singers we had on one tour who would actually fight each other for the honour of washing my underpants!

Apart from the girls, the other main forms of recreation on those tours would be gambling – gambling and boozing. There were no recreational drugs back then – that sort of thing didn't come in until later, when the rock-'n'-roll thing took off. Drink was our drug: Scotch, and plenty of it.

Despite all that, I never used to forget to phone home to my mother each night. I used this routine, in fact, to help keep my feet on the ground. I'd give her all the news and gossip and keep her clued in with what was going on. I was earning big money now – really big money – and I wanted to splash it around a bit, but I'd always go home first and give some of it to my mother. It was amazing the effect that money had, though. It opened doors to a whole new world for both of us.

There was occasional jealousy of course, just as there is in any walk of life – it's just that in showbiz that jealousy gets amplified a hundred times. Usually, it was over money. I soon discovered that every artist, no matter how big or small, always thinks they are better than all the other acts on the bill – and therefore should be paid more money. If it wasn't money, it would be stupid little things. With me it was money and everything else. My confidence, mainly – they couldn't stand that. Or the fact that I very rarely got nervous before I went on. Most of the acts I worked with, no matter how many years they had been on the stage, never lost their pre-show nerves. You'd see them standing at the side of the stage waiting to go on, rubbing their hands and stamping their feet, unable to stop twitching. I used to stroll up to them, a big smile on my face, slap them on the back and say, 'What's the matter? You cold or something?'

When we appeared in places like the Glasgow Empire, where the audiences were notoriously tough, they would be shitting themselves before they went on. They'd lost it before they'd even set foot on the stage. I used to enjoy it, though. To me it was like a boxing match, with me in the red corner and the audience in the blue. You had to be ready for anything, and I made sure I always had plenty of sharp one-liners prepared for whatever they might throw at me. Otherwise, as soon as they heard your English accent, you were done for. What I discovered was that it wasn't witticism that impressed that crowd: it was sheer muscle. One night in Glasgow it got so bad that I just lost it. They were all yelling from the gallery and in the end I just put up my fists and went: 'Grrrr, you come down here and say that! I'll knock your block off!' And the audience started to applaud, they loved it! After that, I was off the hook. They loved me up there. The other acts on the bill hated that, of course.

I didn't care. I was a perfectionist – determined to be the best at what I did, no matter what it entailed or who it rubbed up the wrong way. It was an attitude that would often win the day for me, but it was also one that would get me into trouble on more than one memorable occasion throughout my career. You might have thought I'd have learned my lesson after my bust-up in Huddersfield. But no: in the end, I'd seen that as a victory. Not because I'd given that prick a pasting but because it had made me work my balls off to get where I was now. Yes, I'd had luck, we all need that, but luck alone won't do it: you have to have the talent to make the most of the luck when it comes your way. And that's where I came in. I had talent but, more than that, I was a worker. I had physical strength and sheer force of will. I never gave up.

Most people, however, weren't like that. Worse still, they resented anyone who was. It meant I was continually clashing with people. Usually, I would just laugh it off. But sometimes it did spill over into more serious situations. For example, as I was doing my Brando impression one night, instead of putting the usual amber gel on the light, so I got the correct flesh tone for the illusion, this idiot used a red that tore the whole act to pieces. It ruined everything for me and the audience. So, of course, as I came off stage that night the first thing I did was hunt down the moron who'd wrecked my act.

I went upstairs to the lighting gantry and confronted him. Instead of apologising for his error, he just shrugged and said he couldn't find the amber gel and so thought the red 'would do'. I couldn't believe what I was hearing. It was this shiny scarlet colour that had made my face look as if it were on fire. I tried to explain what the difference was and why it was so crucial to the act that he use the right gel but he just stood there looking at me, as if I were making a big fuss about nothing. When I finished he just looked at me and said, 'Fuck off, sonny. You're not the star here.'

Maybe I wasn't that night. But that didn't make what I was doing any less important to me. This schmuck obviously needed to be shown just how important. I grabbed him and put him up against the wall. I was only going to rough him up a bit, but he made the mistake of trying to fight back – and that was when I really lost it. With the adrenaline from the show still pumping through me, all my frustration came out and, although he had a go, he just couldn't live with me. I knocked that prat every which way, then rolled him down the stairs like a bundle of old rags. When he reached the bottom, I jumped on him again. In the end they had to pull me off him.

Needless to say, I was the one they fired. 'You'll never work again,' the theatre manager told me as I exited that night. Now where had I heard that before?

3

In the mid-fifties, I was at the height of my success as a performer. On the variety circuit, I was second only to the comedian Max Miller, with whom I toured. It was great to watch an old master like that up close, just to study his timing. He was one of the most relaxed performers I'd ever seen – a quality I greatly admired. He worked an audience beautifully. The only bit of advice he ever gave me personally, though, was always to make sure that you shaved. 'How many stars can you name with beards?' he once asked me. I wasn't sure how serious he was being but if you thought about it you could see his point.

Beard or no beard, though, Max's day was drawing to an end and there was already a new generation of comics coming along – Tommy Cooper, for example, who later became a huge star on British TV and influenced generations of comics from Benny Hill to Lee Evans. Tommy and I had the same agent – Johnny Riscoe – so we worked together quite often in those days and became pals. We were a good double bill: I at the top with my very professional all-round act, and Tommy with an act that was basically just Tommy being Tommy – but exaggerated to the nth degree. When we were travelling on the train to shows he would take his shoes and socks off, knowing his feet always stank – so that we would have the compartment to ourselves. It worked, too – God, his feet hummed! And of course he was famously tight with money. I was in a clothes shop in Glasgow with him once and he wanted to buy a tie. He kept trying it on and taking it off again, before trying it on again and admiring himself in the mirror. Finally, he asked the girl behind the counter how much it cost. When she told him he pulled a shocked face and clutched his chest as though he were having a heart attack. Then he took off the old tie he was wearing and asked her how much she'd give him for that in part-exchange. It was hard to tell with Tommy sometimes when he was joking and when he wasn't.

By then I had moved from Manchester and was living full time in London. It was important for my career to be where the action was, and in England that would always mean London. I also had another reason for wanting to move. In 1950, I had fallen in love and married the woman who was to become the bedrock of my life for the next forty years and the mother of our two beautiful children: David, born in 1952, and Sharon, born in 1954.

Her maiden name was Hope Shaw – though everybody always called her Paddles – and before the war she had been an acrobatic dancer under the stage name of Paddy O'Shea. She came from a show-business family: her father was a famous Irish tenor and her mother, Dolly, had once led a well-known troupe of dancers called the O'Shea Girls.

After she retired, Dolly opened up what soon became known as the best showbiz digs in London. Her biggest clients were the comedians Morecambe and Wise, a double act who would become even more popular in Britain than Tommy Cooper over the next twenty years. Artists used to like staying there because Dolly had been in the business – or the 'biz' – herself and so she treated them all like one big, happy family. She prepared all the kids for the Christmas shows at the Palladium each year and everybody who stayed there became friends.

I met her daughter when she turned up backstage at one of the shows I was appearing in at the time. She had come with a group of friends common to both of us, and, from the moment I was introduced to her, I was smitten. I had served my two-year ban by then and was now back with a new name and a new career – bigger and more popular than ever. Meeting silly starstruck girls backstage was no longer as appealing as it had been. Paddles wasn't like that. She was almost ten years older than me and already had two children from a previous marriage: Richard and Dixie. But she had a fair complexion and wise, smiling eyes, a warm, inviting personality and a wonderful sense of humour. She was also very comfortable in her own skin – confident, relaxed and intelligent. All of which I found enormously attractive. The fact that she also came from a showbiz background – which meant I didn't have to explain anything to her about the life I lived – made her even more attractive to me. I began courting Paddles – my own pet name for her – immediately, and we were married in a small registry office just a few months later.

The only fly in the ointment was my mother. Not only was Paddles considerably older than I was – and with children of her own, already! – but she wasn't even Jewish. I knew my mother would never have approved, so I just went ahead and did it without telling her. In fact, I didn't tell my mother or my sister until my son, David, was born – at which point I couldn't keep the news from them any longer. My mother was furious, as expected, and at first refused even to meet Paddles or the children. It wasn't until after Sharon was born that my mother finally accepted the fact that I now had a wife. Then they became firm friends.

By this time, I had moved the family down to Brixton, in south London. I had leased a huge old Victorian mansion from Winifred Atwell, the black pianist, who had shrewdly bought up a lot of property in that area, specifically to rent out to other artists. This particular place was on Angell Road, near the White Horse pub, and I had never lived in such a house before – it had four floors and seven bedrooms! We used the top flights as the family home and the ground-floor front room as my office. I had two telephone lines put in – which was very unusual in those days, when most homes didn't even have one phone – and Paddles occasionally rented out the rest of the rooms to showbiz people.

Brixton, at that time, had become a gathering place for all sorts of theatrical types. The father of the future British prime minister John Major lived around the corner. He was an acrobat, like Paddles. But there were also dog acts, jugglers, singers, dancers . . . It wasn't advertised: it was all word-of-mouth. Paddles would always let you have a room if you were playing in town and you were a friend of a friend. Variety stars such as Conrad Vince, Sunny Dorks and the Crazy Gang – whom the queen supposedly loved – all stayed with us throughout the early fifties. It was quite a scene – some of the happiest, most carefree days of my life, in fact. I was far too young and full of spunk to appreciate that at the time, though. There was still a big wide world out there waiting for me to conquer it.

Meanwhile, partly because I was newly married and starting a family and so didn't want to be away from home so much – I'd been a pro on the road for over ten years when I married Paddles – and partly because I was always looking to develop my act anyway, I was starting to work more in London, where I could at least go home every night.

For a while I starred in my own one-man show – *Don Arden as Al Jolson* – which had a long run at the London Casino. I also sang once a week at the Astor Club, which was famously owned by the twins, Ronnie and Reggie Kray, then overlords of London's organised-crime world. The Astor was a classy place, an American-style nightclub that really got going only after midnight. I got to know it through the singer Don Black, who was a pal of mine and also worked there from time to time. I had a regular spot there for years. I got to know the Krays, of course, because that was their headquarters. But the twins loved show business, so they were always very helpful and friendly. If anyone in the audience dared make a sound while the act was on, they would have them thrown out immediately. So everybody was always very respectful and the acts all loved it there.

By contrast, after the kids came along I started doing things like Christmas pantomimes. The most memorable occasion was when I appeared in *Aladdin and His Magic Lamp*, which also starred the comedian Vic Oliver, a big star at the time, whom I took under my wing (and who was later rumoured to have married one of Churchill's daughters). Frankie Vaughan, who later topped the charts as a singer, was also in the show, as was Bernard Spear, a Jewish entertainer who would later be transformed into a fine stage actor in the West End. I played Abanazer – Aladdin's evil uncle – which I loved, getting booed at by all the kids. I also sang – which was about the closest I ever got to opera!

With TV now coming into more people's homes, I also started to make my first appearances on the box. I had done radio before of course, but this was a completely different story. Whether there was an audience in the studio or not, it didn't matter. You had to learn to ignore them and perform direct to the various cameras. It was very different from performing in a theatre, and there was a whole new set of tricks to learn. TV was mainly broadcast live in those days, too, which meant you really had to be spot on – there were no second chances. But I revelled in the excitement of that. It made of it more like a real show.

Much as it galls me to say so, I suppose the highlight of my short-lived TV career was in 1955, when I was booked as special guest for a twenty-week run of *The Black & White Minstrel Show*. I say 'galls me' because it was this old vaudeville-style show on BBC TV that all the male singers had to black up for. It was part of the show's shtick, but I hated having to do that. It was something I never did for my Jolson impression on stage. But the show was hugely popular – it was the BBC's main Saturday night attraction – and so the deal was very good. I used to come on and do Eddie Cantor; it was the solo highlight of the show. And because it was weekly it meant I could still do other things as well – including other TV spots in which I could go on with my real face.

Fine though all that was, however, I was beginning to feel increasingly restless no matter what I did. I was nearing thirty. I didn't fancy still being on a stage somewhere when I was fifty. But what else could I do? Before I could even contemplate any alternative, though, I felt that I first had to fall out of love with the idea of being on stage – and that wouldn't be easy. Nevertheless, I had begun to think seriously about what I would do when I did step down as a performer as early as 1954, the year Sharon was born. By then, I'd made enough money to go into other things – but what exactly those 'other things' might be I hadn't yet decided.

Then two things happened that showed me exactly the way I needed to go: the first was entirely self-motivated; the second was more like a shove in the back. It began with my increasing disenchantment with my various agents. I wasn't a kid any more and it became obvious to me that, while some were fine when it came to making a deal for the big stars, most of them were truly average – guys who just answered the phone, wrote things up in a book and counted the money. There was also a new generation of agents in the mid-fifties who had somehow got it into their heads that they could actually instruct an artist on how to perform their act. None of these schmucks had ever been on a stage themselves, of course, but because they were the paymasters they felt they had the right to express an opinion. I simply refused to tolerate them – they might try that crap with me once, but they never tried it again. You were never able to make it go away completely, however, and in the end I thought, To hell with them! Why do I even need an agent? I can be my own agent! And that was when the idea of becoming an agent myself first began to flower in my mind.

The second thing that happened – and what put the final nail in my coffin as a performer – was the advent of the very music that would later, ironically, help make my real fortune: rock 'n' roll. Because I was always on the lookout for new people to impersonate in my own act, I had developed very good antennae for public taste – like when I dropped Afrique from my act and started doing Johnnie Ray instead. I felt I could always see what was coming around the corner and by the mid-fifties there was no doubt in my mind that rock 'n' roll was what was coming next.

Initially, this caused me some concern. In the past, whenever new trends appeared, or new showbiz personalities, I was able to incorporate them into my act. But rock 'n' roll was so different from anything I had ever done that this time I honestly didn't know how. I was starting to look over my shoulder at these mere kids, half my age, just coming into the business and having a big hit with their first record, and I'd think, Do I really want to try to compete with that? No, I did not. I'd been on stage for over fifteen years. I'd topped the bill at the London Palladium and starred on TV. Now I was a variety artist at a time when variety artists were about to bite the dust. I saw it coming and decided to get out at the top. There was no point hanging around trying to prove I could sing louder than these kids.

There's a saying: if you can't beat 'em, join 'em! Well that's how I felt about the new rock-'n'-roll stars who were coming out of America. Just because I couldn't compete, it didn't mean I couldn't get in on the action in some other way. That was when the idea of becoming involved full-time in the business side of things really took hold. It seemed the most sensible move. Back in my army days, I had organised some of those soldier shows practically single-handed. How difficult could organising these rock-'n'-roll shows be compared with that? All I needed were some acts of my own to represent.

I didn't announce my retirement or just suddenly stop performing or anything foolish like that – I still had a family to support and I was careful not to jump out of the frying pan and into the fire. I just started pushing things that way slowly, letting it build under its own steam. By 1956, however, with the onset of TV and rock 'n' roll, the variety scene in Britain was starting to close down. I was ready to try my hand at anything: producing shows, representing artists, still doing gigs myself, whatever. But for the first time in my career I was struggling. We all were. Many is the night I recall from that period when I would be sitting at the kitchen table with some of the other artists, bemoaning our fate and wondering how we were going to pay the bills.

Determined to make the most of whatever was still left out there, though, I began putting little shows on. There was plenty of unemployed talent to pick from and we did all right for beginners. I would MC at those shows – to help draw a crowd and because I saw it as my safety net. If the agency business didn't work out, I could always go back to just being a performer. That worked well enough for a while. But I didn't really start to make money as an agent until I had the bright idea for a package I could sell on the Continent, specifically to the US military bases that were now all over Germany.

Through performing at some of those places myself, I had learned that they always had tremendous problems getting decent acts to play them. Until then, army officials had relied on local German agents to provide the talent. But the war was still fresh in everybody's mind and, because all the big American stars were handled by Jews, these German agents had no chance. The old American Jews who ran the business – all of whom came from families that had been persecuted somewhere down the line by Jew-hating fascists all over Europe – wouldn't even take their calls. The US soldiers would ask for Elvis or Little Richard and end up with Fritz the local yodeller and his dancing bear.

I clocked all this and it got me thinking. Here was a demand for talent – big demand, for those US bases paid top dollar – that was going unfulfilled because of a totally unrelated set of circumstances that nobody knew how to resolve. Spotting my chance, I stepped in and offered to put together some top British talent for them. It wasn't exactly Elvis, but it was better than anything else they had, and suddenly I was in. I would package three or four variety acts and send them off to these American and British military bases in Germany and France for six or seven months of the year. I had them doing four shows a night, five nights a week. It was a tough schedule but they got paid per show and so everybody did well out of it. As 'producer' of the shows, I was often there personally to collect the dough – paid in cash, the best-tasting bread there is.

Always, though, I would be pestered about bringing American stars to the bases and soon I was cooking up a new plan. The answer seemed obvious to me. All the Germans needed was someone who could talk on their behalf to the American agents, someone those guys would take seriously and listen to. At the same time, all the Americans needed, it seemed to me, was someone they could deal with who didn't have a German accent! Someone, in fact, just like them: a show-business Jew. Then everyone would be a winner: I, the Germans, the Americans, the artists and most of all the soldiers stuck out there on those dreary bases.

I decided that I should be that someone. Positioning myself successfully in the middle of all that, though, would need some plotting – and some luck. I was old enough by now to realise you should never underestimate the importance of luck in any given situation. In this case, however, it came from a most unexpected quarter: my old agent Hymie Zahl.

Hymie and I had recently become friends again. I had been in touch with all the agents in London in my new guise as a promoter and Hymie just happened to be one of the first to get back to me with some big names. What I didn't know until later was that Hymie was then responsible for all the overseas tours for the William Morris Agency, then the biggest talent agency in America – and, though Hymie didn't know it, home of most of the biggest new names in rock 'n' roll.

Hymie became another regular guest at the house in Brixton, where of course he fell in love with Paddles, as everyone seemed to do. The only thing was, Hymie was quite old and frail by then and he seemed not to know me at all. I had changed my name since we'd last met nearly ten years before, of course, but it wasn't just that. His eyesight and his memory seemed to be getting worse by the day. Every time you saw him he had a different pair of glasses on. In the end, he actually died not knowing it was me – his former trouble-making artist. It didn't matter. Names and places all eventually get consigned to history in showbiz; it's just the way of it. I'm pleased at least to say that, when Hymie died, we parted as friends.

Before he died, however, Hymie inadvertently helped me kick-start a whole new chapter in my career when he asked if I would be interested in promoting some shows for an American singer he'd just taken on called Gene Vincent. 'I got this wonderful girl singer for you from America,' he said. 'Oh, you'll love her! She's marvellous!'

I'd heard the name Gene Vincent maybe once before in my life but I never for one moment thought he was female. Hymie, though, in his increasingly bumbling way, kept going on about this 'lovely girl' for whom he wanted me to produce some shows. In the end, I got someone in America to send me over some photographs. I looked at them and thought, Thank God, he is a fella! Then I stopped kids in the street and showed them the picture and asked if they knew who it was. I was amazed to find that most of them knew instantly. Not all of them knew, but the ones who did were saying things like, 'That's Gene Vincent, man! He's the greatest, daddio!'

That's when I made up my mind to go for it. Not just as the promoter, but agent as well. It was obvious that Hymie, bless him, just wasn't up to the task any more. He didn't know Gene Vincent from Jean Harlow – and he didn't want to know. Rock 'n' roll had come far too late for an old timer like Hymie. I thought, He's going to lose this one completely if I don't step in and help him. Either that or someone else is going to take it off his hands.

I went to him and talked it through, and, being a shrewd old bird, he knew that what I was saying made sense, and he gave me his blessing. In the end, I did that very first British tour with Gene as a co-promotion with the professional wrestler Paul Lincoln, who put in some dosh upfront to get the ball rolling. He and his business partner, 'Rebel' Ray Hunter, owned the 2i's coffee bar in Soho, which was the in place at the time. We were so successful that Gene came back again not long afterwards. But that was on a package organised by another agent called Tito Burns. I wasn't best pleased when I discovered that – I felt Tito was reaping the rewards of my original gamble.

Nevertheless, I felt vindicated. The success of those first tours by Gene just proved what I'd been saying and that the time was now right for acts like that. After that, I went for every major American rock-'n'-roll star I could get. I was pissed off with Larry Parnes, who was then the main promoter for home-grown British rockers such as Cliff Richard, whom I always thought of as a pathetic imitation of the real thing. But all Parnes's acts were like that. He used to say Billy Fury could hold his own with Eddie Cochran, and that was exactly what he did – stood there on stage holding his own cock. Billy Fury wasn't fit to wipe Eddie Cochran's arse for him. I decided after the success of Gene that I was going to show everybody in Britain what rock 'n' roll really was.

That was when I persuaded Hymie to fix me up a face-to-face meeting with the William Morris guys in New York. At the time, I saw it as my big opportunity, my once-in-a-lifetime shot. Not just because I knew it could unlock the key to a fortune for me personally, but because by then my options were narrowing by the day. The acts I was sending out were now past their sell-by date even in Germany and I knew it was only a matter of time before I was back where I started. I needed this William Morris contract.

If I wasn't hyped up enough already, just being in New York brought its own special charge. I recognised so many of the buildings and places from the movies that the whole thing was dizzying and only served to make me even more determined not to blow it. I felt instinctively that I was going to get only one go at doing something big in this town and that I had better do it fast if I was to have any chance at all of making my mark here.

I went into my first meeting all guns blazing. That said, I don't think I actually went in person even once to the William Morris offices the whole time I was there. None of the top guys in America ever seemed to do any business at their actual offices. Everything was done in hotels and restaurants. It was that kind of enclosed scene where you not only had to know where the right places were to eat or be seen eating at, but they had to know you, too, otherwise you'd never even get through the door.

At first, the guys at William Morris thought I simply wanted to talk to them about taking over Hymie's business. Hymie may not have known who the hell Gene Vincent was, but he knew all about guys like Tony Martin and Bing Crosby. Which would have been great, except that wasn't what I was interested in any more. You can't make your mark with old-established stars like that, anyway. It's all been done by then and I wanted to be the greatest, not just the latest. Having seen people go crazy for Gene all over Britain, I could see clearly that rock 'n' roll was here to stay, and I was determined to make sure I got in on it now, before everybody else had the same idea. Until then, none of the original fifties generation of rockers like Elvis Presley, Jerry Lee Lewis and Little Richard had ever played outside America, and I made it clear that these were the sorts of acts that I felt I could do something special with. All I needed was the go-ahead and we would all start making money.

This was music to their ears. They had sent acts overseas before – big American stars such as Bob Hope and Danny Kaye, who would come and do a run of shows at the London Palladium, perhaps. What I was suggesting was a whole new concept, though. I wanted these guys like Gene and Richard out touring the provinces, playing in places like Leeds and Doncaster, real working-class English cities with real people absolutely starved of top-class entertainment – just as I used to do, in fact, in the old touring show days.

Once they started to go for that, I threw in the idea of maybe doing some of these equally lucrative US military bases in Europe too. 'It'll make money and be good for their image,' I said, 'doing their bit for the boys in uniform.' 'Great,' they said. 'When can you start?' I tried to act nonchalant. 'I'll get back to you,' I said. But when I left New York I made sure I did so with a signed agreement in my hand, witnessed by lawyers.

I had one big ally at William Morris, Sol Shapiro, who later became head of the music department there and remains one of my closest friends. But I soon grasped that most of these guys didn't know the difference between Sheffield and Strasbourg – and didn't care. With the acts overseas anyway, as long as they were earning them money, they could be playing in Timbuktu for all they cared. 'Just make sure they come back in one piece,' was all they said. I assured them that as long as they were with me they would be looked after properly, that nobody would have to worry about a thing, that they should just leave everything to me. In other words, William Morris didn't have to lift a finger. All they had to do was say yes and then wait for the money to roll in. More music to their ears . . .

And mine. When I returned home to London from that trip, I did so with two signed contracts in my briefcase that would literally change my life. The first, the one I had gone out there determined to get, was for the next Gene Vincent tour. The second, which I had only hoped for, made me the sole UK and European representative of the William Morris agency. I was so high when I got on that plane that I could have flown it home myself!

Those bits of paper meant that, as of now, pretty much every major rock-'n'-roll star in America who wanted to play outside the country would have to come through me. That was how I suddenly became known in the newspapers as 'Britain's Mr Rock 'n' Roll'. Practically overnight, I became the biggest, most talked-about agent in London – literally the talk of the town.

Most of the older, more established agents at the time, such as Harold Davidson, thought I was nuts. 'He'll lose his trousers,' he said. Even Larry Parnes told me that rock 'n' roll was 'just a passing thing'. Meanwhile, younger, hipper agents such as Arthur Howe and Tito Burns looked at what I did and decided they wanted a piece of the action, too. Well, they were all too late. I had got there first. Mr Rock 'n' Roll.

With the William Morris contract under my belt, business back in London took off in a way even I had not previously imagined possible. I was now the biggest agent and promoter for rock-'n'-roll music outside America. Normally, you would be one or the other – the agent or the promoter. The agent got his cut direct from the artist's fee, a standard 10 per cent paid by the promoter, who took his cut from ticket sales. I looked at that and sensibly decided that, if I did both jobs, I could cut out the middleman, as it were, and keep the money from both the top and bottom ends for myself. It was sweet: all above board and very lucrative.

With all the American artists, however, you were required to put down a sizable deposit upfront of their arrival in the country. For Gene's first tour it was something like £20,000. Because of that, when the American acts came over, I always made sure they did so for lengthy tours that would sometimes last three or four months. As long as you felt sure you would sell plenty of tickets, it always worked out well. For that first tour with Gene, I think the deal would have been something like £4,000 a week, for six shows a week. That meant we had paid the deposit back within the first few weeks. After that, whatever happened, you knew you were making money.

After Gene's 1958 tour the acts began arriving thick and fast: Brenda Lee, Freddy Cannon, Johnny Preston, Conway Twitty . . . To cope with the sudden change in our lives, Paddles and I closed down the guest part of the Brixton house and turned it back into a proper family home. My office also now expanded beyond the front room to take over the entire ground floor, and I started a new company, which I called Anglo-American, specifically to deal with the artists William Morris were now sending over. After the first year or so, once I had shown what I could do, it wasn't just William Morris I had on the phone now, either. Other big American talent agencies like Universal Attractions started putting some of their business my way, too. I was building up a reputation as the guy who handled things for the big boys outside America. Word went out: you just put the act on a plane and left the rest to Don.

As the business rapidly expanded I would be forced to take on more and more staff. For the first few months, though, during that initial period that all new businesses go through when all the money is going out of the door and none is yet coming in, I did virtually everything myself, from making arrangements for forthcoming tours to doing all the secretarial work – as well as keeping up all my other usual activities in

London. It was crazy. I don't think I slept for about six weeks. I didn't care. I knew this was my big opportunity and I was determined to do whatever it took to ensure the thing was a success from the word go.

It did lead to some funny situations sometimes, though. For instance, one of the first acts I booked for William Morris was Brenda Lee. For that I would actually be on the phone to her mother – who acted as Brenda's manager – pretending to be my own secretary! Brenda was half Native American and her mother's name was Doris Rainwater. She was a very nice lady but quite straight and proper, so I'd put on this nice polite female voice whenever I spoke to her on the phone as my secretary. I'd be ever so lovely and accommodating. I sounded like an elderly English matron. But I felt it was important to give the right impression. I didn't want Doris thinking she was bringing her precious daughter all the way to England to be looked after by one man and his dog – which, effectively, was what I was at the time. It reminded me of being a kid and using the red phone box at the end of my street as my office. I discovered that, as long as you kept up appearances, people were ready to believe anything. I nearly got caught out, though, when I went to meet Brenda at the airport. As soon as Doris stepped off the plane she asked where my secretary was – she said she'd been so nice and helpful that they'd brought her a gift. I had to think fast and explain that unfortunately my secretary had now moved on – but that I would forward the present to her.

Soon, however, I did have a secretary – and an assistant, and a driver, and several other agents doing the donkey work for me. People like Colin Berlin, who later managed the singers Adam Faith (who died in March 2003) and Tom Jones.

Brixton was still a bubbling house, though, and we stayed there until 1963. People like Tony Secunda (who later managed the Move and T Rex, among others) and the songwriter Lionel Bart (who would win a Tony award in 1963 for *Oliver!*) used to come by all the time in the early sixties. Sometimes people would come to visit and end up staying for days and weeks at a time. Billy Preston was like that. He would later have a successful solo career, as well as working with the Beatles and the Rolling Stones. Back then, though, he was the keyboard player in Little Richard's band, which I first brought to London in 1962. He stayed at our house so much I thought Paddles had adopted him. She was always adopting waifs and strays. Wee Willie Harris was another. We used to have regular canasta evenings with his managers, the husband-and-wife team Les and Nora Bristow. Willie would come too but because the old boy couldn't read he never sat down with us. Instead, he would sit and play Monopoly with David and Sharon. The kids understood and whenever his dice landed him on a 'Chance' or 'Community Chest' card, they would make a big fuss, pleading for him to let them read the card first – just so he wouldn't be embarrassed.

The kids were like their mother in that respect: tremendously giving. Not because these strays their mother took in were famous – it could be anybody. I remember one nutcase Paddles's lawyer asked her to look after for a few days when his parents died. His name was Nigel Heathorn and he had inherited just enough wealth at nineteen to buy himself out of the army and still have some left over to move into a nice little place of his own in London. But after he got out of the army he didn't know what to do. So he came to dinner at our house one night – and never left again!

Nigel would hire chauffeur-driven cars to take him out every day – then come back to Brixton at night and kip in one of the backrooms. An odd character, but very generous. He was always bringing us presents. Once, he came back with a film projector and some huge speakers he'd bought on a whim. For weeks he would rent the latest movies and project them up on the back wall of the house. You would have all the neighbours, passers-by, everybody hanging over the wall, watching the movie. In the end, the fool spent every last penny of his inheritance – and at the end of it he was still living with us! So I did the only thing I could think of and bought him a guitar and put him out there on the boards as a singer, to help him earn his keep. It turned out he had a penchant for country-and-western and for a while he actually became quite popular in those circles.

Then there was Henry Henroid, who became the tea boy on some of the early tours I promoted. We literally found him hiding under a pile of coats in the dressing room after a Gene Vincent concert. Paddles said, 'He can't stay here!' And that was that. Henry came home with us to Brixton – and didn't leave again for four years! He was another one I made pay his way, though, and eventually he moved from being tea boy and general all-round gofer to being Gene's driver, then his tour manager. He, too, later became a manager in his own right, most famously in the seventies for the legendary British DJ, Emperor Rosko.

By the end of the fifties, I had taken the plunge and gone into artist management myself – though that happened more by chance than design. At the end of his next tour with me, Gene decided out of the blue that he didn't want to go back to America. I was actually standing there with his plane ticket in my hand when he said, 'You know what, Don? I like it better here. So I'm gonna set a spell. Hey, you can manage me!'

I was flattered but at the same time I knew his career in America had hit the skids. Despite his having had million-selling hits back home with 'Be-Bop-A-Lula' and 'Lotta Lovin'', Gene's dark, sinister image had begun to work against him as the new, much cleaner-cut era of young American singers like Fabian and Ricky Nelson came along. In short, he wasn't the big star in America that he had been, while in Britain and Europe they still couldn't get enough of him.

I thought quickly and told him that I'd look after him and turn him into the biggest rock-'n'-roll star in the UK – which I did – but only if he agreed to do things my way. First off, that meant he couldn't expect American money. I would make sure no one else in Britain earned more than he did, though. And he was happy with that. We shook on it and for the next five years I ensured that Gene remained the biggest-selling live rock-'n'-roll act in Britain.

It was me, for example, who put him into the black leathers for the first time. He'd arrived back in London for that tour without any luggage whatsoever. He'd just turned up at the airport and jumped on the plane, drink still in hand. I was furious with him for being so unprofessional. But it turned out to be a stroke of luck because I was forced to take him out and buy him some new stage clobber. The first thing that caught my eye was this display in the front window of Cecil Gee's in Shaftesbury Avenue. They had dummies dressed in these skin-tight black leathers and I thought, Yes, this'll do nicely. And so I took him in and got him fitted up with some tailor-made leather suits.

Gene was reluctant at first – I think he thought he looked queer in them – but I told him to shut up and get on with it and that he looked amazing. Sure enough, the first time he walked on stage in them I knew we had a winner. The black-leather look really fitted the dark, creepy image Gene had already created for himself. He'd walk on stage in his shiny new leather gear, limping because of his gammy leg, looking like Dracula, and the crowd would go absolutely crazy. He was magnificent, truly scary! (The gammy leg was the product of a motorbike accident, which I'll tell you about later.)

The guys loved it, of course, but a lot of the girls just didn't want to know. Gene was simply too much for them. If it hadn't been for the bad leg, though, I think he would have been right up there in the popularity stakes with Elvis. He sang in an exaggerated, stretched-out way I'd never heard done before. It fitted in so well with the music that it was almost like another instrument, another texture to the overall sound. And his diction was fantastic, each word thrown at you like a knife. My only regret was that I never got to record him at that time. He was still tied up in a long-term contract in America with Capitol Records. So it never really came up, which is a pity.

Instead, I had him on the road more or less round the clock, playing all over Britain and Europe. Some weeks we had him doing double-headers, two shows a night, six nights a week. It was a killer pace, but Gene just ate it up. If he wasn't on the road he only got into trouble anyway. It was better just to keep him working, moving from place to place before he could cause too much damage.

When he wasn't on the road, he at first lived in a hotel just off Tottenham Court Road in which I used to put up a lot of my American artists – nothing flash but comfortable. It was run by a lovely old Italian couple who treated Gene like a son and he generally kept his nose clean while he was staying there. But then he got married to an English girl named Margie and I found them an apartment to rent down in Streatham, not far from my own place in south London – and that was when all hell started breaking loose.

By then, I was more than just Gene's manager: I seemed to have taken over the day-to-day running of his entire life. And what an introduction to man-management that was! Years later, I would manage Ozzy Osbourne during his most drug-induced, self-destructive years in Black Sabbath – but that was nothing compared with the lunacy of Gene Vincent in his prime. Left to his own devices, Gene was one of the most self-destructive people I have ever known – and I have known a few in this business. He was just out of control. I had to have a permanent 24-hour, seven-days-a-week guard on him. Not to stop him getting into trouble – no one was ever quite able to do that – but just to have someone there to help get him out of it again once it started.

To that end, I gave him the use of my own personal driver – a chancer I knew from the fringes of showbiz named Peter Grant. Grant would later find his own kind of infamy, in the seventies, as the grossly overweight manager of Led Zeppelin. In fairness, he always admitted he learned everything about rock management from working for me. But I had to laugh whenever I read that. He was so desperate to be seen as a tough guy that he was probably hoping a little of my own reputation would rub off on him. But, whereas I was the real thing, Grant would lie and tell people he had once been a professional wrestler. What crap! Peter Grant could barely wrestle his own dick out of his trousers!

I first met him at one of the US army-base shows I did in my days as a performer. He was just a kid in his twenties with a Volkswagen bus that he hired out to take the artists to and from the airport. I used him again when I started sending my own packages out there, and then I hired him as my chauffeur, and he worked for me in London. His most important job each day was taking the kids to school. In truth, he was a big, three-hundred-pound bag of shit – so fat you couldn't tell if he was twenty years old or thirty. But he was a good driver and reliable, and so I sent him to work for Gene. I told him, 'Make sure that fucker gets to the shows in one piece – and make sure he stays off the whisky!' Which Peter did manage to do quite successfully – most of the time.

Sometimes, Gene's antics could be funny. Because of his gammy leg, he couldn't drive himself, but, whenever I sent Peter in the car to pick him up, instead of sitting in the back and taking it easy, Gene would insist on sitting in the front, riding shotgun next to Peter. No matter how fast he drove, Gene would always be yelling at him to go faster. Gene would grow so impatient he would throw his walking stick down on the accelerator – he had a lethal aim with that thing – until the car was finally moving fast enough for him. People used to get out of a car ride with Gene and Peter with white hair.

Sometimes, though, Gene's outlandish behaviour wasn't so funny. His first Christmas in London married to Margie was one I'll never forget. He was stinking drunk by midday and started a big fight with Margie, accusing her of sleeping with other guys while he was on the road. It wasn't true, but when Gene got drunk the world disappeared and he was in charge. Then he got it into his head somehow that Margie was having an affair with the guy who lived in the apartment next door. I think the worst the poor schmuck had done was smile and say hello when they passed on the stairs. But Gene knew better. 'You're fucking him, you whore!' he screamed at her.

Peter Grant was there and he tried to calm things down but Gene turned on him, too. 'I'll kill you, you son of a bitch!' he cried and stormed out of the room. When he returned seconds later he was holding a loaded revolver in his hand. (I didn't know it until then, but Gene always carried at least one gun with him wherever he went, a habit I would also acquire for a period some years later.)

Next thing, Gene has run out the flat and stuck the barrel of the gun through the letterbox of the neighbour's front door. 'I know you're in there, motherfucker!' he's screaming. 'And I know you've been fucking my wife! Well, now I'm going to kill you!' And then he starts firing, managing to get three or four rounds off before Peter can wrestle him away from the door.

And this was Christmas Day! Never mind peace and goodwill to all men, Gene wanted someone dead. Peter phoned me in a total panic and I went straight over. I had the most awful time trying to get the gun off him. I had to tell him the cops were outside before he eventually relented – and then it was all sobbing and remorse. My main concern at that point, though, was whether the guy next door had been shot. We broke down the door and looked inside but, thank God, he wasn't in. Like everybody else in the building, he had either gone away for the Christmas holidays or was out getting drunk. It cost me a bundle in cash to keep him quiet when he did eventually return but it didn't end there and the guy moved out not long after. I couldn't blame him.

Every day with Gene was like that – every day for all the years I managed him, right up to one of the last things we ever did together: a tour of South Africa. He nearly got us all killed when it was discovered he had bedded a fifteen-year-old girl.

The hotel manager where we were staying actually warned me that the police were planning a raid – that was, if the lynch mob didn't get us first. 'If you don't get out now,' he said, 'this fucking maniac's gonna get you killed.' So we came up with some excuse to delay the start of the first show while we got Gene out of there in a hurry. We were that close, apparently.

Another time, Gene and Peter were staying at a high-class hotel in Italy, right next to a mountain. Gene got drunk and decided he was going to climb the mountain. Peter tried to follow him but Gene was suddenly making serious tracks up the side of the mountain and the big fat lump couldn't keep up. He was huffing and puffing so hard he thought he was going to have a heart attack. But Gene kept going and going, gammy leg trailing behind him, and, by the time Peter finally reached him, his hands were all bloody, his clothes were ripped to shreds and he was crying his eyes out.

As he got to where Gene was, he realised they were on a ledge overlooking the horizon. The drop to the next ledge was only a few feet but Peter didn't know that yet, and Gene just looked at him, smiled and said, 'That's it, baby. I've had enough. I'll see you around.' Then he jumped off the ledge and disappeared. Grant was apoplectic! For a moment he thought Gene had actually thrown himself off the side of the cliff! And what the hell was he going to tell me! I think his whole life must have passed before his eyes.

Then he gathered himself and actually took a peek over the edge, expecting to see Gene's crumpled body lying several hundred feet below. Instead, he saw Gene squatting on the ground about four feet down, silently laughing his arse off! At which point Peter totally lost it. He jumped off the ledge and landed straight on Gene's bad leg – all three hundred pounds of him! It would have broken an able-bodied man's leg, but in Gene's case it nearly finished him off for good. He had to be put into plaster up to his waist and flown back to London.

If it had been anybody else, I would have killed them for doing that to one of my artists. But I was only too well aware of the bullshit Gene put people through and so I accepted it as a one-off. Gene and Peter would have escapades like that practically every day and they actually ended up becoming friends. What a time of it Gene gave him, though. Even working with Led Zeppelin, who enjoyed a pretty wild reputation themselves, must have seemed like a picnic by comparison to his days dicing with death with Gene.

Ironically, Gene's most famous misadventure had occurred before the incident on the mountain, and it had been while he was actually asleep, when he nearly died in the car crash that killed Eddie Cochran, in April 1960. The two had been sharing a ride back to London from a gig they had just done together in Bristol. Eddie was just 21. Like Gene, despite million-selling American hits like 'Summertime Blues' and 'C'mon Everybody', Eddie was now actually bigger in Britain than at home in America. Poignantly, his final single, which had just been released, was called 'Three Steps To Heaven'. But, while Eddie was killed outright, Gene escaped with just a broken collarbone – and, it has to be said, his aura of vampire-like invincibility was even more enhanced. But that was Gene. It was all true, based on fact, not fantasy.

People used to ask about the leg, whether it was really busted up or just part of the act. It was real all right. Gene had smashed his left leg badly in a motorbike accident when he was a kid in the US Navy. They had operated on it but the leg was never the same again. Not only did he limp but it caused him constant pain, which is one of the reasons he used to drink so much, to try to deaden it. Then the leg actually started to rot and so I took him to see Dr Bobby, my own family doctor, a private consultant in Harley Street who knew the score.

When Dr Bobby looked at Gene's leg he was aghast. In effect, he said, the navy doctors had put the broken leg back together the wrong way round – which was why it had never healed properly. They had also put a chain inside his leg to hold it together and now it had begun slowly eating away at the inside of the leg. It was a horrible thing to see. If Dr Bobby hadn't taken him straight into hospital and operated on him, Gene would have lost first the leg, then possibly his life, as the poison started to spread.

We patched him up and put him back out on the road, which is the only place he ever really felt comfortable, anyway; but it was all downhill from there. Not because of the leg, but because Gene was an alcoholic, pure and simple. I asked Dr Bobby what he thought – if there was any chance we could cure him. 'What do I think?' he said. 'I'm thinking, Why is this man even alive?' He was serious. He said Gene was so far gone that, if we didn't give him a drink every day, he would probably die even sooner.

I was so upset that I sat Gene down for a heart-to-heart. I was like a father figure to him by then and I could do that. I said, 'Look, baby, the top and bottom of it is like this. If you don't mend your ways and at least cut down on the drinking you're going to die.' He just nodded his head sorrowfully and said, 'I understand.' But of course he didn't. He was just lying as usual, to me and to himself. He was always surrounded by these ponces, coming in through the back door of the theatres to give him his bottle of this, his bottle of that. It was suicide, it was just suicide. But that was Gene Vincent. Nobody told him anything.

We eventually parted in 1964, when his wife persuaded him to go back to America. She thought that if he went out to Hollywood he'd become a movie star. She was wrong. He came back for another tour of Britain a few years later but by then it was all over for Gene, and he died not long afterwards, still drinking. I was sad but hardly surprised.

Meanwhile, I had other fish to fry. Which is one of the secrets of success: the ability to keep as many plates spinning in the air as possible – all that stuff they teach you today in college that nobody even thought about in the fifties. Nobody, that is, except a few guys like me, who were always planning two or three moves ahead. And that's the other secret of success: never rest on your laurels. The minute you think you've made it is the minute the whole thing starts to crumble again. I'd already seen it happen a thousand times in this business and I wasn't going to let it happen to me. Oh, no!

4

It was also through my association with William Morris that I first got involved with the Star Club, in Hamburg, in 1959. Now best remembered as the place where the Beatles honed their skills in the early sixties, the club itself was small by comparison with the army-base halls, but it was open every night and the acts did several sets. As long as you worked hard you could always make money. The problem, as with the army bases, was that they couldn't get any of the big American stars near the place. That was where I came in. Shrewdly, however, instead of using me as their booking agent, the owners of the club actually invited me to become a full-time partner – giving me a vested interest not just in providing top-class talent but actually helping turn the Star Club into the greatest rock-'n'-roll club in the world.

Situated in the red-light district of Hamburg, then probably the sleaziest docking point in Europe, the Star Club was already the roughest, toughest club in the world when I first started there. You had to know how to handle yourself. There was just one fight after another. The audience was this strange mix of mad drunken sailors on shore leave, druggy art students pretending to be bohemian, and a sprinkling of tourists wondering what the hell they'd got themselves into. There had even been a killing there, so when I got involved I imposed a rule: the first sign of aggro and you were out – literally. As soon as anybody started getting out of hand, the boys were under instruction to go wading in and knock them out cold, then throw their bodies into the street. That proved to be a great deterrent and the club became a much friendlier place to be after that.

Of course, once I'd helped make it famous, there would be a few of the amateur bad-guy types calling in whom joints like that always attract – small-time hoods who thought they could throw their weight around. But I was ready for them too and I always made sure we had plenty of muscle visible on the door and behind the bar. Once they saw that, if they had any sense at all, anyone with the wrong idea would probably shit their pants and leave very quickly. Sometimes they weren't so sensible, though, and needed to be taught a lesson. It wasn't pretty. Those German boys were tasty: they would literally try to murder people for me while I stood there at the bar watching. There was one guy we had working there who became a good friend of mine, a local boy named Horst Fasher. Horst was the most feared of all the guys working at the Star Club. He wound up doing three years in prison for breaking a sailor's neck. He was that sort of guy. I made him the manager.

The Star Club may have been rough, but it wasn't dirty. We didn't go looking for trouble. We just did what we had to do to survive, according to the environment we found ourselves in – in this case, an extremely dangerous one – and by the early sixties the Star Club had become the most famous rock-'n'-roll club in the world.

My partner and co-owner was Manfred Weisleder. I liked him right away. He was in his forties, a real character who loved his rock 'n' roll and didn't take shit from anyone. I bought a white Chevy Impala from him not long after we had first started working together. I had never seen anything like it before: it even had a record player in the back! A man like that deserved the best, I thought, and so I did everything I could to give it to him. Jerry Lee Lewis, Little Richard, Bill Haley, Ray Charles, Fats Domino, the Beatles – I put them all on at the Star Club in the late fifties and early sixties, and we shared the profit. It was the only club in the world that regularly had those stars. Other clubs had an occasional big star if the owner knew a particular artist well, perhaps. They all did the Star Club, though. I made sure of it.

It was Manfred who first brought the Beatles to Hamburg in the summer of 1960. I saw them and decided they were just another group of typical British rock-'n'-roll copycats. Manfred saw something more in them, perhaps, but neither of us really thought them anything special. At least, nowhere near as special as their manager Brian Epstein was always telling us they were.

Manfred never understood Epstein at all, whereas I had him figured out from the word go – a lower-middle-class poof who longed for respectability and to be accepted by the British establishment. Well, he had no chance of that. Not because he was gay, but because he was a Jew. He hadn't figured that out yet, though: he still thought money and success would do it for him. He was wrong. Like me, they saw him for what he really was: just another Yiddisher boy from the north who got lucky.

Not that he was a bad guy. I always liked Brian. He didn't really know what he was doing; he just went out there and did it. In that respect, you had to take your hat off to him. He worked hard and there wasn't anything he wouldn't do for his boys. Like the time when he shafted me over Little Richard. I had brought Richard over to the UK for some shows in 1962 and he phoned me up in the middle of the night and said, 'Hey, man, why you put me second to this group in Liverpool?' It was the Beatles. Epstein had promoted a show for them at the Liverpool Empire. This was before they had broken through nationally, but he wanted to prove they were already the biggest group in Liverpool – and he wanted another big name on the bill as insurance: to make sure it was a sell-out. But, when he rang to enquire about booking Richard for the show, he sold it to me as a headline slot. Epstein used to put on shows only occasionally – we had done a similar deal for the Beatles to support Gene Vincent at the Cavern just a couple of months before – and because he didn't know any better he always used to pay more than anybody else. So I agreed to let him have Little Richard – at double the usual price. But then he pulled a stroke of his own and put the Beatles on *after* Richard!

Oh, he could be slick. When it came to the serious stuff, though – the big-money contracts with the record companies and so forth – he was out of his depth. He more or less admitted as much to me when he told me the story of how he signed the Beatles' song-publishing rights to Dick James Music (DJM).

Epstein had been happy for EMI's in-house publishers, Ardmore & Beechwood, to handle the first Beatles single, 'Love Me Do', which came out towards the end of 1962. With so few artists actually writing their own material, song publishers had a much bigger role in an artist's career then than they do now, when they are chiefly used to collect and distribute songwriting royalties. Back then, they would be involved in the actual promotion of the records, arranging TV and radio spots, not to mention encouraging as many covers of the songs from other artists as possible. Epstein – probably rightly – felt that the EMI team had covered the basics on 'Love Me Do' but hadn't actually gone out on a limb for the group. Most of all, he disliked their superior attitude. He didn't know how to counter it. He felt intimidated by the big boys – which was why he went to an unknown publisher like Dick James. He probably felt James would be easier to dictate terms to.

If so, he was wrong. Dick – whose real name was Isaac Vapnick – had started out as a singer around the same time as I had, and he knew the score. Back in 1948 he'd actually had a hit in America with a drippy ballad called 'You Can't Be True, Dear'. He used to bill himself as 'Britain's Romantic Singer of Songs' and he used to wear this terrible wig that he must have got from Woolworth's. It looked as if someone had glued a dead rat to his head! His only hit in Britain had been in 1956, when he sang the theme tune to *Robin Hood*, a new kids' TV series.

Now he was a small-fry publisher with a one-room office in Charing Cross Road. I think it was George Martin – who'd actually signed Dick as a singer to Parlophone back in the early fifties – who had suggested him to Epstein. Brian later told me the place was so dead when he walked in there that Dick was sitting with his feet on the desk eating a sandwich. Hardly surprising: DJM was barely a year old at the time. But James immediately did a number on him and Epstein fell for it. Knowing through a contact that the producer of the TV show *Thank Your Lucky Stars* wanted to book the Beatles for an appearance, James pretended to cold-call him while Epstein watched, going as far as arranging a date for the group to go on the show. Epstein just sat there with his mouth hanging open. After that, he couldn't sign the contracts fast enough.

Dick James pulled his real masterstroke, however, after the first Beatles single he published – 'Please Please Me' – went to Number 1. The Beatles were so hot by then that this record would have been a hit whoever published it. Epstein was feeling validated, however, for having ditched the EMI team in favour of an unproven newcomer. So when Dick suggested an even more lucrative arrangement – for him and Epstein to form the group's own publishing company, for which Dick had even come up with a name: Northern Songs – Epstein jumped at the chance.

Essentially, the deal meant the group – and Epstein – would get 49 per cent to share between them and Dick and his accountant, Charles Silver, would get 51 per cent, as well as final veto on any business decisions. It was a relationship that would endure until 1973, and, while it undoubtedly made more money for the group than they would have done under the normal publishing deal, it also made vastly bigger sums for both Epstein and James. Dick was so reliant on the success of the Beatles' songs he took out insurance policies on Lennon and McCartney worth £500,000 each. He knew he was doomed without them. The only other major artist he ever signed as a publisher was poor old Elton John, who later sued DJM in the eighties for all the millions Dick had conveniently overlooked to pay him.

But after Epstein died the group started to turn on him and so he cashed in his chips to the TV overlord Sir Lew Grade. Unfortunately, the group didn't bother to check the small print when the new contracts were put before them and they effectively signed away their rights to all their early songs. He may have been a mediocre publisher, old Dick, but he was a terrific con artist. As a result, Lennon and McCartney have earned very little dough in songwriting royalties from any of the first fifty or so songs they released as the Beatles, including all their biggest hits, up to the end of 1964. You can't blame Dick, though. He was only doing what good publishers do: make as much money as possible out of their artists. It wasn't Dick's job to protect the group's interests: it was Brian's.

It was the same ill-advised set-up with the record deal he signed with Parlophone. Initially, the contract Epstein had negotiated for them gave them exactly one penny for every double-sided record sold, split five ways equally between the group and Epstein. This was in the days before decimalisation and there were still 240 pennies to the pound. So for the first million sales of 'She Loves You', for instance, the guys actually *in* the group would have made about £800 each. Even though that was fairly standard in the early sixties, the deal had improved only slightly even by 1967, going up another penny, so that the income for a million-seller then would have been just over £1,600.

That just shows you how easy Epstein was to manipulate. I used to laugh when I read all the stories in the papers about their being millionaires. He may have come across as suave and sophisticated in Liverpool but Epstein had no background in the biz whatsoever and when he got to London he was eaten by the sharks. I could have taken the Beatles from him, of that I have no doubt. You could see, even then, that John and Paul sensed that he wasn't all he cracked himself up to be. If I had made my move at that moment I believe they would have followed me in a second. But I didn't want to do that to the boy. I already owned a Rolls-Royce, and I didn't need to take anything from the likes of him.

Manfred couldn't figure Epstein out at all, though. It didn't help that he was always haggling for more money for his 'boys'. He had the unfortunate habit of speaking to Manfred about it openly in front of his staff, which Manfred regarded as strictly *verboten*. Epstein would be standing there striking a pose, mouthing off. 'You know, Manfred, your own people believe my boys have made the Star Club what it is. We really should be paid more money.' This was two years before they'd struck any oil. I remember walking in one time as he was telling Manfred, 'What you have to understand, you see, is that my boys are going to be bigger than Elvis.' That killed Manfred because he absolutely worshipped Elvis. He called me over after Epstein left and said, 'Don, this guy, he has shit in the head! His boys bigger than Elvis? Tell him he *never* says this to me again or I kill him!'

The truth is, the real stars of the Star Club were always people like Jerry Lee Lewis (who was still setting his piano on fire each night), Ray Charles, Little Richard and the rest of the American stars I was able to bring over – the ones Manfred called '*Schaumacher*' (roughly translated: the 'show makers'). We originally booked the Beatles only because they were cheap and could fill in on those nights when we didn't have anyone well known booked, or when they were used as a backing group for Tony Sheridan. To begin with we paid them only a few hundred quid a week – good dough for them back then but a pittance to us. And for that we would have them working every night, eight hours a night.

Nevertheless, it was invaluable experience for them: they learned to work an audience to the extent that they were now attracting fans of their own. By the time 'Love Me Do' took off, we were paying them more like two grand a week. They were under contract to us for a two-week residency with Little Richard at that point but of course Epstein was straight on the phone demanding more money. We held out but he wouldn't leave it alone, and when they arrived at the club he said something to Manfred again to the effect that his boys were bigger than Elvis, and this time Manfred lost it.

He grabbed me and said, 'Don, I told you, the next time he gives me this shit about Elvis, I kill him!' I asked what he was going to do and he said, 'You wait and see.' At first I thought he meant it and that he was actually going to do the guy some damage. But Manfred was far too professional for that. It wasn't that he merely didn't like Epstein: he just couldn't stand him!

The Beatles' final shows at the Star Club involved a fourteen-night stint over the Christmas and New Year period, 1962–3. You could see they were only going through the motions to begin with. They knew they were past doing places like that by now. But, as Christmas drew nearer, they suddenly started getting into the spirit of things and really did some great shows. The final night, New Year's Eve, was very emotional. We all knew they'd never play there again, that they'd probably never play anywhere remotely like that again, and that this was goodbye – not just to the Star Club, but to earlier, simpler times.

After the club closed that night, however, Manfred had the staff tie some tablecloths together into a sheet, and, when Epstein emerged from the dressing room, the guys all grabbed him and threw him onto it and proceeded to give him the sailor's toss-up. Manfred wouldn't hurt him because he knew Epstein couldn't fight a cold. He just wanted to get his own back on him for being such a pompous, middle-class wanker. I remember standing there roaring with laughter as Epstein was bounced up and down about ten feet in the air. He was screaming, 'Stop! I'm warning you! I'll sue!' It was hysterical.

You messed with Manfred at your peril, I discovered. Once we had got to know each other well enough, he introduced me to the *real* people who are known to the world at large and who owned and controlled the Star Club – the Israelis. It was this semi-secret cabal of extraordinarily wealthy and highly dangerous Jews who had interests behind the scenes in every major moneymaking business, legitimate or otherwise, along the Hamburg shoreline. As a result, they were raking in over a million dollars a month – big, big money in those days.

Manfred took me over for dinner one night at this old Jewish boy's place in the harbour and introduced me to some of them. I was impressed, not just by the hospitality but the unexpected warmth. I was welcomed like a kindred soul and I left that night feeling like one. After that, I was invited to come by any time I liked. It was all very civilised. They would never let you buy a drink and you could talk to them about anything. The only thing Manfred warned me not to do was ask them directly who they were or what it was they actually did for a living. 'You don't want to know,' he advised me sternly.

This was one gift horse whose teeth I didn't feel like counting. All I knew for sure was that they loved what I was doing for them at the Star Club. Because of the quality of acts I brought with me, I was able to help Manfred turn it into a big international attraction – and that, in turn, brought more people not just to the club but to all the bars and strip joints around the area. Everybody benefited, and we had some great times.

One of the funniest was when I took Bill Haley there in 1960. Haley was much older than most of the other rock-'n'-roll acts – he was actually born the year before I was and had released his first record, a hillbilly tune called 'Candy Kisses', back in 1943. He had been on the road, more or less, ever since, but it wasn't until the mid-fifties that he finally cracked it, having an American Number 1 with 'Rock Around the Clock' and notching up a further dozen or so copycat hits in Britain alone. By the time I took him to the Star Club, however, his career was on the wane. Unfortunately, as is often the case with these things, everybody knew it except him.

But, if he was a prick, what did I care as long as he did the business? If I worked only with people I *didn't* think were pricks I'd hardly work at all. Bill had never been out of America before when I booked him into his first British tour. That had been in 1958. A huge success ticket-wise, it was the tour, ironically, that more or less finished him off for good once the kids actually saw how fat and old he was in real life. But then the following year I took him to the Star Club, where the audience were older and not so interested in what the acts looked like, so long as they could play. And if there was one thing about Haley, it was that he knew how to put on a show. Just one hit after another, everybody up dancing, exactly what you want in a club.

Then, during rehearsals the first day, Bill took me to one side and said, 'Don, I heard the broads here in Hamburg are the best. Could you arrange something for me?' That was a first. Usually the last thing the singer has to ask the promoter for is *more* girls. I thought, If this guy's so ugly he can't get any, that's his problem. 'Look, Bill,' I said, 'I'm a rock-'n'-roll promoter, not a pimp.' But he was desperate, pleading. He wouldn't let it go until finally I had to say yes just to shut him up. But I wasn't happy.

I talked to Horst about it and we came up with a plan to fix the bastard. Horst arranged for me to meet one of the 'girls' from this restaurant he knew that was staffed by transsexuals. My eyes nearly popped out of my head when he took me there – some of these guys were more beautiful than any woman I'd ever seen! How they worked that I don't know, but with the help of Horst I arranged for this one absolutely gorgeous 'girl' with huge tits to come to the club that night. When she arrived I sent word to Bill and he came out of his dressing room dressed in his best suit. I had a job trying to keep a straight face. When he saw those tits he just went mad. I thought he was going to attack her there and then.

'Well, goodbye everyone,' he said, grinning like a fool. Then he took her by the arm and led her back into his dressing room and locked the door.

Horst and the boys and I leaned against the door, listening. You could hear her squealing, *'Nein, nein, nein!'* as he chased her round the room. Finally, he must have got his hands up her skirt because there was this almighty explosion. He just went insane! You could hear him screaming in there! Then the dressing room door flew open and he went for me! In all my life, I never saw a man lose it quite like that. He started screaming. 'I can't believe you would do that to another man!

It's monstrous! It's against nature!' But I couldn't stop laughing. The angrier he got, the harder it was to stop laughing – which only made him even angrier of course. He was trembling with rage. 'I'll never sing for you again!' he cried. 'Never!'

His manager, this old time Yiddisher fella, called me on the phone from the States the next day and said, 'I don't know what the fuck you've done to Bill but he says he'd rather kill himself than do another show for you.' Maybe I had gone just a little bit far with poor old Bill. Oh, well, I thought, he wanted a fuck, and by God I gave him one – right in the head! It still makes me laugh to think of it.

Another lunatic I brought to the Star Club regularly back then was Jerry Lee Lewis. He didn't make life crazy for you the way Gene Vincent did, but there was nothing vulnerable or lovable about him, either, as there was with, say, Little Richard. Jerry Lee was just plain nasty. The first time I put him on tour in England I had arrived late at the airport to meet him, but instead of waiting for me they had all pissed off to the hotel. When I finally got there the door to his room was open and I could hear them all talking, him and the clowns he'd brought with him from the American record company. I stood at the door listening and I realised they were talking about me. 'I heard about this English Jew boy,' said one of them. 'He thinks he's tough. Well, he better not try to fuck with us, 'cos we'll show him.' They were mad red neck idiots and I took an instant dislike to them.

Still, I made money out of him and I got my own back for the slurs the next time I brought him over by booking him onto the Israeli airline, El Al – with which I'd recently done a deal to handle all my business. Jerry went crazy because the Jews on board all got up from their seats halfway through the flight and began to pray. He was such an ignorant red-neck that he thought they were praying because the plane was about to crash! Sometimes I wished it had.

When his baby drowned in the swimming pool – a story that made headlines all over the world at the time – I was devastated for him. We had a tour coming up and my first thought obviously was that we should cancel it. But he called me up after the news broke and said he wanted to go ahead despite the tragedy.

The one guy I never managed to get my hands on – which was a great pity, since I would have been absolutely the perfect guy for the job – was the king of rock 'n' roll himself, Elvis Presley. He never did come to Britain in the end, of course, but I came closer than anybody back then to making it happen.

It was in 1961. Like every other agent and promoter in London, I'd been told for years that his manager, Colonel Tom Parker, would never let Elvis leave America. Nobody really knew why. The thing about the Colonel's wish not to travel overseas because he was really an illegal alien and worried about not getting back into the US was being whispered about in showbiz circles even then. But that was a crock. Nor, I think, was it anything more sinister than that – though I did wonder for a while. At the end of the day, I think the Colonel's reticence came down to simple indolence. I think the man just didn't see the need to send Elvis anywhere further than he really had to. He would never have left Memphis at all, I believe, if making films for Hollywood didn't mean having to live in Los Angeles for periods. The only reason he ended up playing those dreadful hotels in Las Vegas was because the Colonel practically lived there by then! They'd give him a free suite and he'd just sit there for years at a time, gambling.

So of course everybody just laughed when I said I wanted to bring Elvis to London. It was just a total nonstarter, they said. But then they had said that about virtually everything I'd ever done and that hadn't stopped me. I thought about it and decided that maybe the Colonel just hadn't been offered the right bait. I knew that money alone wouldn't do it. The Colonel didn't need to go all the way to London to make money for Elvis. It had to be something else then – something even better than money. Some form of acclaim they still craved, perhaps, or something else that might spark their imagination.

Then it hit me: what was even better for your image than making money? Giving money away! That was it! Some sort of charity concert in London, which Elvis could headline. It would have to be something major, though, something the folk back home in America could relate to as well. This was decades before concerts like Live Aid and at first I struggled to think of a cause that would catch Elvis's or the Colonel's eye. I went to the library and found a book that contained lists of official charities and found myself going automatically to the ones with royal patronage – it just instantly legitimised them in your mind. Then I noticed how many boys' charities and general youth programmes the Duke of Edinburgh lent his name to and I thought, That's it, perfect! I'll write to the duke and ask him if he fancies having Elvis Presley perform a special fundraising concert in London for all his charities.

And so that was what I did, and a couple of weeks later I spoke on the phone to one of the Duke of Edinburgh's official aides, who invited me over for a meeting. It turned out the old boy was a bit of an Elvis fan on the quiet and thought it was a 'splendid idea' to have him come and do a special show. All the duke's office needed to know was when exactly Elvis would be available so that they could start to make the appropriate arrangements. Inside I was jigging with delight but I kept my poker face on while I made it clear that, although the concert was ostensibly in aid of the duke's various charities, a 'consideration' would obviously have to be made to Elvis and his organisation for giving us his time. They readily agreed – and at last I had my bait.

I wrote to the Colonel at his office in Los Angeles, spelling the whole thing out. I thought, I bet he gets a hundred of these a month and I never hear anything back. To my amazement, however, he wrote back almost immediately to say both he and Elvis thought it was a wonderful idea and that they would be honoured to accept. He suggested I phone him and, after I had read the letter through a couple more times, I spent the rest of the day in a state of nervous excitement. The Colonel was in LA, eight hours behind me in London, and, as I waited impatiently for the hours to pass before I could call, I thought about how bringing Elvis to London on behalf of the husband of the Queen of England would be the peak of my career as a promoter. I felt sure of it, as though it were my destiny – and now I had this piece of paper in my hand telling me so.

I waited until nearly eight o'clock that evening before I phoned – noon in LA. I didn't want to be the first guy in the Colonel's face when he got out of bed that morning. I wanted to be cool. I gave his secretary my name and she put me right through. I don't know what I expected but to my surprise he came across on the phone as a thoroughly charming man as he reiterated what he'd said in the letter: that Elvis would love to do the show. He did, however, have one stipulation: a 'special request' from Elvis, he said. 'We want the duke to invite him personally.' He wanted a letter written to Elvis from the Duke of Edinburgh, inviting him to come to London and play for him.

At first, I didn't take it too seriously; I just put it down to general ignorance on his part. I explained how the duke wasn't allowed to invite anybody directly to give money to any cause he represented; that he was virtually the King of England and that just wasn't how they did things here. But the Colonel was insistent that I at least go back and ask. I told him I would do that and get back to him. Of course I never did. Instead, I rang the Colonel back a few days later and explained again how the duke just wasn't allowed by law to do anything like that, but that he would personally be at the concert, where he and Elvis could meet and chat and have their picture taken together – pictures that would have made the front pages of newspapers all over the world.

Not good enough. Nothing I said would sway him. He just wanted Elvis to go on American TV with that letter in his hand. You can picture the scene he had in mind: Elvis, looking solemnly into the camera and explaining how 'I got this letter today from little old England, from the husband of the queen. They want to know if I can go over there and help them . . .'

I was heartbroken when that potential coup died, because I had come so close.

Apart from Elvis, the other guy I always wanted to bring over to England was Little Richard. Even more than Elvis, for me, Richard was the one who started it all. Those early records like 'Good Golly Miss Molly' and the million-selling 'Tutti Frutti' were unbeatable. I never heard so much energy coming off a record before. But I had never seen him play, except on TV and in the film *The Girl Can't Help It*. Nobody outside America had. I thought that, if I could go to him and say, 'Hey, I'm the guy who took Gene Vincent and Jerry Lee Lewis to England and made them money,' it might persuade him to let me do the same for him.

So, early in 1962, I made some initial enquiries, but to my surprise everybody I spoke to told me that Richard had virtually retired as a rock-'n'-roll singer – and that he was now preaching in a church! At first I thought they were putting me on but then I thought of my own upbringing and how I still liked to go into the synagogue sometimes, just to hear the singing, and I started to get a better picture of the man – or so I thought. I was told I had next to no chance, however, of getting him to change his mind – and especially not to go all the way to somewhere like England.

But that information, of course, only acted on me like an aphrodisiac. I now saw it as a challenge: my personal crusade to get Little Richard out of retirement and over to Britain. Why not? Stranger things have happened at sea. The trouble was that William Morris had virtually given up on him by then and so I'd have to pull this one off on my own. I couldn't do that just by talking to people on the phone. For this sort of business, where I knew I would have to be at my most persuasive, I needed to *be* there, in his face, to let him see who – and what – he was dealing with. I decided to take a punt and get myself over to Los Angeles, where I planned to track Richard down.

I had never been to LA before, and at first I felt like a stranger in a strange land. But on another level – one that related all the way back to my childhood and so many nights spent sitting in the darkness of the local cinema with my mother and sister – I recognised it immediately. Going to LA meant going to Hollywood, and that was a place I felt I already knew well. It certainly knew me – or at least my kind. Showbiz wise guys out to build empires. For once, however, the reality was even more vivid than my imagination. I flew out on my own but any trepidation I might have felt on the long journey over was swiftly dispelled on the drive from the airport. Just looking at the palm trees or, best of all, that wonky white Hollywood sign in the hills overlooking the city, I felt immediately at home. I had been living my own movie in my mind for so long, even then, that it all just somehow made sense.

I checked into the Beverly Hills hotel and once I'd got over the jetlag I started phoning around the various churches and mission halls I was told Richard had been preaching in. No dice. For a man who was now supposedly devoting himself to spreading the good word he was awfully hard to track down. I decided to aim my sights a little lower and start checking out the local bars and clubs, on the off-chance he might be preaching the gospel direct to the sinners. The William Morris guys had given me some names and addresses and I just went from one shithouse to another asking if anybody knew where I could find Little Richard, until I finally found somebody who said, 'Oh, I see him every night, but it's a terrible place. Are you sure you wanna go?'

It was a place in downtown LA – the poor, sleazy part of town – which Richard apparently still liked to frequent. I arranged to be there the following evening. It was one of those strange bars that back then existed only in places like LA – not exactly gay, not exactly straight, just a mixture of both with heavy sexual overtones. I can't remember the name of it now but I recall the look on the taxi driver's face when I gave him the address. Clearly, he knew what I was letting myself in for. But he just shrugged and told me to get in. Perhaps he looked at my short hair and dark suit and tie and thought I was in some kind of drag.

When I got there, I admit, I was taken aback. After Hamburg, I thought I had seen pretty much everything – but I had never seen a place like this before. I know it's a cliché but you really couldn't tell which were the girls and which were the boys – most of the people there looked like a bit of both. Not least the man I had actually come to see. I discovered him occupying a back booth. It was almost midnight when I arrived (I had been told he never usually turned up until about then), and he was already there, sitting with a battered-looking old bible in one hand and a glass of champagne in the other.

So this was the so-called religious freak I had been told would never sully himself again by playing that nasty rock-'n'-roll music! Despite my uneasiness at the surroundings, I have to say I felt greatly encouraged by the discovery that Richard was no ordinary 'preacher'. It meant there was hope yet.

I went over and introduced myself and he said he'd heard of me and invited me to sit down. He was very amiable but it was clear that his mind was on other things. The table was surrounded by freaks of all persuasions who couldn't keep their hands off each other, so I decided to leave him to it and arranged to come by and see him again the following night. Which I did, but this time a little later, to give him a chance to have his fun first before I tried to concentrate his mind on more serious matters.

We danced around the subject for a while. I told him about myself, that I had been a performer too, and that I also had a religious background, but that I loved rock 'n' roll – and his records especially. He'd be right with me up to when I started speaking about rock 'n' roll – and then he'd frown and go, 'Oh, but, you know, man, I don't *do* that now. I sing gospel now.'

'Of course you sing gospel,' I would say, treading carefully. 'But you haven't stopped singing rock 'n' roll for ever, surely?' He'd shake his head. 'No, sir, I've stopped! The devil is in rock 'n' roll, the devil!' He told me the story of how he was on a plane that was struck by lightning. 'It was the devil that nearly killed me in that goddamn plane!' he cried, and I could see he meant it.

I started to back-pedal a little and asked him if he would be interested in bringing the gospel to England, maybe, and he began to relax and get back into it. I told him how many fans he had there and how excited the whole country would be if he came at last, and he really started to get into it – as long as he could sing gospel. 'OK,' I said, 'and what sort of money would you want for that?' It was average money, two or three grand a week. But then his eyes started to wander again as new faces started to congregate around us at the table and I decided to leave it there again for another night.

Now that we were starting to talk business, I decided I had to get him out of that place or we'd never get anything done. As I rose to leave I asked if he would like to have a meal with me the following day and to my relief he said, 'Yeah, let's have lunch.' We spent the whole of the following afternoon having lunch at a swish place he favoured in Beverly Hills. And that was when we started to get to know each other properly. We talked about everything under the sun and I found him to be an extremely beguiling character full of strange contradictions. He loved sex and he loved God, he said – and he really did seem to think rock 'n' roll was the devil's work.

I tried to get him to see a tour of England as another way to spread the gospel. Why not mix the two – the gospel stuff with a little of the old rock 'n' roll? Just so the folk got something they were familiar with too. They had never seen him before, so surely he owed them the chance to see the gifts God had bestowed on him, I said.

He liked the idea of that, you could tell. It appealed to his vanity, which, as I was to discover, was bottomless. He softened and said, 'Well, man, you tell me exactly what you want me to do and I'll do it – and you can buy me another lunch tomorrow when I'll tell you how much money I want!' He was very witty with lines like that, but that was how we did the deal. He came back for lunch at the same place again the next day and I agreed to pay him something like £5,000 a week for six shows a week. We got the lawyers in and when he signed the contract I was euphoric. I'd gone out there on a mission, and

I'd accomplished it, and, in so doing, proved the doubters wrong – again.

Once I'd gone back to London and started putting the dates together, though, I admit I was nervous. Despite having it written into the contract that he would do some rock 'n' roll, I didn't really know for sure until Richard arrived what songs he was actually going to sing. My intuition told me it could go either way. Richard was the type of guy who doesn't give a shit. If he was in the mood, he was a genius. If he wasn't, you were in big trouble. Sure enough, at the first of two shows we started the tour with in Doncaster, he forgot all about the rock 'n' roll and just did gospel – and he died! He was so dead I thought we were going to have to carry him out. Meanwhile, the crowd – who had come expecting to see the king of rock 'n' roll, as I'd billed him – were on the verge of rioting. It was only the matinée show but I had to get the heavies in to come and clear everybody out. I thought, Shit, now what?

I had put him on a co-headline bill with Sam Cooke and in the end it was actually Sam who saved the day by offering to talk to Richard personally. I'd already been in there and read him the riot act, but it just fell on deaf ears. 'But I have seen the light, honey!' he pouted. I came that close to putting his lights out for good but Sam stepped in. Sam was a class act – not just immensely talented, but probably the handsomest man I have ever seen. His physique was perfect and he had the face of a film star; and his voice and his style were just unbelievable, both on stage and off – a genuinely special individual.

Sam came up to me and said, 'Don, do you mind if I talk to Richard alone? Because I feel I'm as big a part of this as you are.' It was Sam's first tour of Britain too and he desperately wanted it to be a success. So I said go ahead and Sam ripped into him! He tore him to pieces! 'You are so full of shit!' he shouted at him, which – coming from Sam, who never swore – sounded really heavy. 'You say you're spreading the good word – well, out there tonight you killed every bit of good feeling we had in that room! You killed me, you killed Don, and if you're not careful you're going to kill this whole fucking tour!'

Richard looked like a man who has just been kicked in the balls. In a sense, he was. After that, he was contrite. 'Well, man, what you want me to do?' he whimpered. Sam calmed down and said, 'I want you to go out there for the second show tonight like a gentleman and sing what Don is paying you to sing. Because if you don't this tour is coming off tonight.'

I couldn't believe Sam had put his neck on the line like that for me. No artist had ever spoken up for me like that before. Later, when we were alone, I told him, 'Sam, any time you ever want something – *anything*, doesn't matter what it is – you just give me a call.' He was such a gentleman, another perfectionist. After he'd done his own set at the second show, he stood on the side of the stage to watch Richard's and as a joke he shook his fist at him as he walked by. I don't know whether or not Richard took it seriously, but he went on and did the rock-'n'-roll stuff and absolutely slaughtered them. From there on in, we were in business, big time.

In order to create some excitement for the tour, I'd hired a young whiz-kid publicist I'd come across in London called Andrew Loog Oldham. Andrew was only about seventeen then but he was already on his way to becoming the full-blown character who would manage the Rolling Stones through their earliest, most exciting years. He really knew how to sell a story to the papers and things were going great until he arranged for an article in one of the London papers that said something about how this was the most sensational show ever and that the kids were going to go crazy and rip the seats up in every theatre Richard played in. It was great publicity, because immediately everybody was talking about it and wanting to see it. But then I got a letter from the lawyers of Cecil Bernstein, then the head of Granada and owner of most of the venues on the tour, saying that unless we dropped our PR he would cancel the tour. It was a real kick in the guts but there wasn't anything I could do, as the tour had already started. I showed the letter to Andrew and he understood, but I hated having to let him go like that, without even being able to put up a fight.

The ones everybody still wants to hear about from those days, though, are the Beatles. My memory is that they were good boys, mostly, always up for a laugh – though it was hardly sophisticated humour, more like Scouse hooliganism. They behaved as any young lads would who had never been away from home before. When they weren't playing they were often pulling pranks. Like the time John Lennon dressed himself up in bed sheets to look like the pope and began pissing out of the window of their hotel. It was a Sunday morning and, although the club was in a street full of strip joints and brothels, in the middle of everything was this beautiful, three-hundred-year-old church, which a lot of the local residents, particularly the older ones, still attended. This particular Sunday morning, however, John had decided to do some 'anointing' of his own. As soon as he saw these old dears tottering up the street on their way to church, he would pull up his sheet, dangle his dick out of the window and start pissing all over them! Someone eventually called the cops.

When the group became famous, so many people claimed to have seen them at the Star Club first that you could have filled Madison Square Garden with them every night for a year. It was the same with the Cavern, the shoebox in Liverpool they also used to play regularly. Even now, I meet people who probably weren't even born then who swear blind they saw the Beatles either at the Star Club or the Cavern long before anybody else had ever heard of them.

The Beatles loved playing the Star Club not just because they could run riot but because they got to rub shoulders for the first time with genuine American rock-'n'-roll stars like Little Richard, Ray Charles and Gene Vincent. They'd always be pestering them with questions about America, the places, the stars, Elvis, you name it. To describe what they did on those early records as the 'Liverpool sound' was such bullshit, I always thought. That youthful exuberance, that cheerful defiance, that sense that a bomb had just gone off and no one knew what might happen next – all of these things that characterised the early Beatles hits, to me, had nothing to do with Liverpool. That was the sound of Hamburg and the Star Club at its giddy height.

What no one had anticipated, however, was the profound effect the astonishing success of the Beatles would have on everything else, both positive and negative. Ironically, for example, it killed the Star Club stone dead. At first, it had benefited, as suddenly everyone wanted to visit the place just to say they'd been to the famous venue in Germany where the Beatles started out. What screwed it up for us, though, was that people actually thought the Beatles were still going to be there! When they weren't they went away disappointed and never came back again. It wasn't just the club that suffered, either: their success had the knock-on effect of killing off an entire generation of fifties rock stars. Overnight, Gene Vincent, Jerry Lee Lewis, Little Richard and the rest became old hat.

As a result, my whole professional life was about to change again. I was supposed to be Mr Rock 'n' Roll. If that music was now dead, where did that leave me? While I pondered that, the Star Club went downhill rapidly and by the end of 1963 we were actually forced to close it down. It was tragic. The whole thing ended just like that. I remember standing on the corner of the street as we locked the doors for the last time and put the CLOSED sign up. Manfred, who was six foot four of prime German beef, stood there crying his eyes out like a baby. He said, 'You see, Don, what happens? We make them stars and they do this to us!' He was upset and not making much sense but I knew what he meant. The Star Club had breathed life into the Beatles. Now they had somehow taken it away from us.

Even as we walked away down the street together, though, I had to admit there was something intoxicating about the success of the Beatles, something that suggested we were about to enter yet another new era – both in music and in the world generally. And we were hardly the only ones in the business to be adversely affected by it – at least in the short term. I hadn't really seen it coming this time, but I was no less determined not to be left out. I said goodbye to Manfred, flew back to London – and immediately began plotting my next move.

5

Earlier that year, I had moved the family out of Brixton and up into the West End of London, to a beautiful old mansion I'd found in Mayfair called Barclay House. I had already moved my business out of Brixton the year before to Royalty House, in nearby Curzon Street (Ken Pitt, who managed Manfred Mann and David Bowie, was in the office below). Right in the heart of London's most expensive neighbourhood, the new family home was the most ostentatious place I could find. For five years I had been the biggest agent and promoter in the world outside America. Now I was also the richest. I could afford the best of everything and I made sure I got it. I didn't have a Rolls-Royce any more – I had three Rolls-Royces! As soon as I got a scratch on one, I dumped it and got another.

Of course, that kind of attitude doesn't always sit well with those less fortunate, shall we say, and there was a great deal of jealousy towards me, as there had been in one shape or another for most of my working life. In sixty years, I have never seen one agent or promoter go up to another and say, 'Congratulations, man, you're the fucking greatest!' I might have heard something like that, but when you looked in their eyes you knew they were lying. It always happens wherever there is one man in charge – nobody wishes him well and everybody plots against him. Make no mistake, they would all kill you if they could. My attitude was, Let them try – I'll be waiting.

Meanwhile, I was looking after so many artists in the late fifties and early sixties, even though I was no longer a performer myself, that I suddenly found myself out on the road again almost constantly. One night it would be the guitar legend Bert Weedon in Margate; the next night it would be the Kay Sisters (a fifties Spice Girls) in Birmingham. Sometimes it was one-offs like Little Eva, who had one big hit with 'Locomotion', then disappeared. She never managed to follow it up but while it lasted she was hot. Same with the Shirelles and Brian Hyland: nice people to work with – and lucrative while they lasted – but you could tell they wouldn't be back. Chubby Checker was another, a charming man who went from top of the pile one minute with 'Let's Twist Again (Like We Did Last Summer)' to absolutely nowhere once the fad had worn off. For a fat guy, he had unbelievable success with the ladies. But it all faded very quickly once people got bored with doing the twist.

The artists who interested me most were always the Americans – guys like Carl Perkins, who had a hit with the original 'Blue Suede Shoes'. Carl wasn't as big a deal as someone like Gene Vincent or Little Richard, but he was very talented and a genuinely nice fellow and so I was always willing to do something for him. (A decade later I even signed him to my record label, Jet.) Bo Diddley was the same. He wasn't a star: he was just a well-known name. So there was no ego, just a happy-go-lucky guy. All he ever asked me was, 'What time am I on and when do I get paid?' I liked that.

Of course, not all of them were so easily pleased. Duane Eddy, for example, was another one of those guys who now relied more on their names than their record sales to sell tickets. He was a one-trick pony who'd had a few similar-sounding hits and had then run out of ideas. Now everybody had to pay. He couldn't help you with anything. He was the type of prick that if a light bulb burnt out during his set he'd blame you personally. 'How dare you allow the lights to burn out while I'm on stage!'

Then there were the ones you just couldn't fathom at all, like Sophie Tucker. Sophie didn't listen to anybody. She just did her own thing. William Morris asked me to fix a UK tour for her when she was invited to appear before the queen at the annual Royal Command Performance at the Palladium. It was a big televised event and so I fell for it and arranged some dates for her – and lost a small fortune!

Until then, I had idolised her. On film, I thought she was sexy, funny, and had a surprisingly good voice. But, by the time I got to know her, her voice and most of her looks had gone. When the tickets first went on sale, they did OK, but, after people saw how ragged she was on TV, sales dropped off completely. The whole thing was a disaster.

Towards the end of the tour, when it became clear we weren't going to make any money, she phoned and asked if she could come to my office. Ordinarily, if Sophie wanted a meeting she would insist on my going to see her, usually for lunch at the Savoy. But we made the appointment and the next day she walked in with the Kray twins, one on each arm. I had to laugh. She was desperate for cash and she thought that, if she turned up with Ronnie and Reggie by her side, I'd be so intimidated I would cave in immediately and give it to her. What she didn't know was that the brothers and I already knew each other from my days at the Astor, and the first thing they did was come up and slap my back and kiss my cheeks. She couldn't get over it that they hadn't told her.

Speaking of jokes, I definitely thought the William Morris guys had lost the plot when they sent me Johnny Preston for a tour. Johnny had just had a huge Number 1 hit with 'Running Bear', which was supposedly a modern version of an old American Indian song, but nobody in Britain really cared. They knew the song but they didn't really know him. They didn't even know what he looked like. The William Morris boys pushed him to me hard, though. 'He's this big, handsome, Red Indian chief,' they told me, 'and he's got all these gorgeous Red Indian dancing girls around him going whooo-whoooh! Don, how can you refuse?'

A few weeks later I'm standing at the arrivals gate at London airport waiting for a Red Indian giant to step off the plane, but there are no giants, no Indians, no dancing girls – nothing. I'm just about to turn back when this guy, no more than five feet tall, taps me on the arm and says, 'Hey, Don.' I look at him and say, 'Hello, are you with Johnny?' He says, 'No, I'm not *with* Johnny – I *am* Johnny!'

I told him to piss off but he was insistent. I looked him up and down. He was the shortest, whitest, most clean-cut Red Indian giant I had ever seen, wearing a suit that looked like something he'd stolen from a thrift store. I suppressed my rage and took him to the hotel. Then I returned to my office and got straight on the phone to New York and asked them what the hell was going on – was this some form of sick joke?

Apparently, it was. I could barely believe my ears. Some of the younger guys had done it to me as a gag! I was furious but the dickhead I spoke to just kept laughing. 'What harm can it do?' he said. 'Besides, Johnny's a great singer.' I could see the funny side, from their point of view, but what made me mad was what it symbolised in my mind. The sixties were about to explode and the rock-'n'-roll department at William Morris was now being run by a much newer, younger crowd. I didn't have anything against that. I recognised the value of having people on the ground who were the same age and related to the same things as the younger, newer artists who were coming along – which is how both my own children came to work for me when they were still teenagers. What I objected to was the fact that they would go to such lengths just to give themselves a cheap laugh one slow afternoon in the office.

But I decided to play it cool with Johnny himself – at least until I'd seen for myself what he could do. We opened at the Empire in Leeds but when I walked in on rehearsal he was standing there singing 'Danny Boy'. I thought, This joke isn't funny any more. I went back to my hotel and got on the phone again to the smart boy who'd done all the laughing. I said, 'I've got bad news for you: I'm sending him home tonight.'

'But why?' he asked. 'Johnny's just been Number One!'

I said, 'Yes, but not with fucking "Danny Boy", you prick! I've sold tickets for people to see a giant Red Indian singing "Running Bear" and all I've got is a fucking midget singing "Danny Boy"! If I let him go on stage like that I'll be done for murder! They'll tear him apart!'

But he pleaded with me and it was too late to do anything about it now anyway: the tickets had all been sold and the show was about to start. So I sent the poor schmuck on and prayed that nobody would get killed when the riot started. But to my amazement he got away with it! How, I'll never know. He looked like a bank clerk, singing 'Danny Boy' – and they loved it!

Then there was Little Richard. Once I'd got him over here that first time I was able to keep bringing him back for more, and by 1963 he was a bigger star in Britain than he was in America. He'd walk on stage in the same suit he wore in *The Girl Can't Help It*, hammer straight into 'Tutti Frutti', and the crowd would go absolutely wild! It never failed.

Of course, Richard had his wayward side too. I made the mistake once of walking into his hotel room unannounced. He had left the door wide open and so I just went in to tell him the bus was ready and that we were all waiting for him downstairs – and then wished I hadn't! He was lying naked and unconscious on top of the bed with half a dozen other people – men and women, all naked on the bed with him. There were empty champagne bottles lying everywhere. I picked one up and began banging it with my car keys. 'Wakey, wakey!' Richard eventually roused himself. Far from being embarrassed, he just smiled and said, 'Mornin', Don. What time's breakfast?' You couldn't embarrass Richard. He just got up and put his trousers on.

He was another one who fell in love with my wife. They both loved fine jewellery and used to chat for hours about clothes and stuff like that. And he always liked my son, David, who started coming to some of the shows when he was twelve. I had to keep my eye on things though: I didn't want David walking in the dressing room when Richard was in the middle of one of his scenes. That didn't stop David getting more than he bargained for, though, the time he decided to take a peek inside that damn bible Richard always carried with him. He took it everywhere, he said, so he could preach to people 'on the street'. But when David picked it up and looked inside it one night his face turned bright red. It was this huge old bible with big Roman lettering, and down all the margins Richard had written the names of all his lovers over the years, along with detailed descriptions of what they did when he shagged them. That was his message to God.

I took him to one side and said, 'Look, sweetheart, you don't have to carry that thing around with you any more. You're the biggest name in rock.' Which was a lie but I had learned to appeal to his vanity first whenever I tried to get him to listen to me. 'Carrying something like that around makes you look cheap.'

The next day Paddles and I went out and bought him a beautiful new bible – an old-fashioned, ornate-looking thing that came with a gold key. When we presented him with it that night, the tears were rolling down his cheeks. 'I'm throwing the old one away,' he said. 'I'll never abuse my bible like that again!' He was an absolute liar, of course. I knew he'd never throw that old bible away. It did stop him leaving the damn thing lying around all the time, though.

The only artist at that time I took more pleasure in working with than Richard or Gene was Sam Cooke. Sadly, we were destined to work together only briefly. After the tour he did for me with Richard in 1962, I had planned to bring him back for his own headline tour. Sam was managed by Allen Klein, the New York lawyer who would later become involved in the affairs of both the Beatles and the Rolling Stones. It was Klein, in fact, who sent me the contract for the next tour. But the day I actually flew to New York to sign it was the day Sam was murdered.

I had been at my hotel for only about an hour when I received the phone call telling me the terrible news. I couldn't believe it. I was devastated. As for the story we got – that Sam had been shot after some altercation with a hooker in a downtown motel – I never believed that for a second. That just wasn't his style. What the truth is I don't suppose we'll ever know now, but, had he lived, I think Sam would have become my biggest attraction. I really do believe he was destined to become the world's greatest. It took me a long time to come to terms with his death.

And then the Beatles came along and it all went out of the window again. At the start of 1963, the year the Beatles became big in Britain, I had a whole bunch of tours running concurrently – Sophie Tucker; Johnnie and the Hurricanes; Joey Dee and the Starliners; Brenda Lee; the Everly Brothers – and all of them died a death. I lost every dime I put into them. The Beatles had killed everything. People who had been stars all their lives suddenly became milkmen.

The only tour I was able to salvage was the one by the Everly Brothers. I think we sold something like eleven tickets for the first night, so I put the rest of the dates on hold – I think we said one of them had the flu – while I hurriedly came up with a Plan B. I phoned Richard and said, 'You've got to help me, I'm in the shit.' He still wanted the same dough he would have got for topping the bill but that was all right, and within two days, bless his heart, he was here. Then I managed to get Bo Diddley at a reasonable price and then, at the last minute, the Rolling Stones, whom I secured for £40 a night. At this point, we opened the box office again and we sold out. Of course, there was no profit – I finished up losing two or three grand – but at least it gave the tour the appearance of success, which is almost as important as the real thing.

Remarkably, by 1964, the Beatles' success had even spread to America, where they became the first British group to become massively successful. Despite the occasional hit record, there had never been a consistently successful British rock-'n'-roll artist in the US charts before. Now the path to American success had never seemed more straightforward. You just needed a group like the Beatles to do it – a new, fresh-faced, young British group who did mainly original material.

Hardly my forte at that time, it has to be said. I had always regarded the domestic British scene as frankly pathetic compared with the American acts I dealt with. A few of the more theatrical, comedy things were all right, such as Screaming Lord Sutch, or Wee Willie Harris. But I could never understand how someone like Cliff Richard was allowed near a stage. It was the same with all the domestic talent. I remember on a Jerry Lee Lewis tour once I took a chance and booked Heinz as the opening act. He'd just had his first hit but the Jerry Lee crowd didn't care about that – they just thought he had a funny name. (Of course, the British fans simply associated his name with Heinz Baked Beans.) Sure enough, as soon as he came on he was pelted with baked beans. I called his manager, Joe Meek, and told him to forget it, but Joe insisted and so Heinz spent the rest of the tour being pelted with beans.

Now things had changed – the Beatles had seen to that – and it wasn't about the Americans any more. The charts were now dominated by new copycat Beatles groups like the Rolling Stones, the Hollies and the Dave Clark Five, many of whom wrote their own material. For the first time in my career, it was about being British and making records – and not just any records but *hit* records, which was a side of the business I had very little hands-on experience of at that time. It was going to be a steep learning curve for me, a lot of new business I would have to become involved in, but, as ever, I was determined to win through. I was 37 at the start of 1963 and I had no plans to retire just yet. Whatever the Beatles had done, they would never change the colour of money, and there was still plenty of that to be made out there – of that I was sure.

My first brush with the record business – and my first real success – had been with Brenda Lee in the early days of my association with William Morris. Known as Little Miss Dynamite, Brenda stood just four foot eleven, and she totally lived up to her name – I thought she was sensational. As part of my plans to promote her first UK tour, I went to see her record company in London, Decca, to see if they wanted to release a single to coincide with the shows. But I found them surprisingly reticent.

The guy running the show at Decca at that time was Dick Rowe, a wonderful person who would later become famous as 'the man who turned down the Beatles', which he did, before Epstein got EMI interested. It was the sort of thing that happens all the time to record companies. Most big stars have been turned down by dozens of people before they strike any oil. The Beatles were no different: everybody in London turned them down at one time or another. The problem was that the Beatles then became the biggest act in the world. Even though Dick then went on to sign the Rolling Stones, who became the second-biggest act in the world, he paid for that one slip a thousand times over. But Dick was a shrewd fellow who knew the record business inside out and we became great friends over the years. He was one of the few people I actually trusted. A gentleman in a ruffians' game.

When Dick explained that Decca had never actually had a hit with Brenda Lee outside America before, I was amazed because to me she was a star and I just assumed she was a big seller everywhere. Dick assured me that was not the case. But the dates had already been booked and it was too late to back out now, so I threw my hat into the ring and offered to help promote the record if he would at least agree to put something out. Even if it was played only a couple of times on the radio, it would be like a poster for the shows. I might even get her a TV appearance.

Dick listened patiently and eventually agreed. The clincher was the offer to get on the phones and help promote the record myself; that showed how serious I was and so he let me go for it. Dick chose a song from one of her old albums called 'Speak To Me Pretty' and I came in and frantically worked the phones, badgering people up and down the country to stock the record in their shops and put it on their jukeboxes. Then I pestered my contacts at the BBC to try to get someone to play it. It was my first attempt at promoting a record and I have to say, I didn't really know what the hell I was doing. Dick gave me a few pointers where I needed them but basically I just rang everyone I knew and tried to get them to do whatever they could for the record.

Three weeks later 'Speak To Me Pretty' was Number 1 in the UK charts and Brenda Lee had her first hit outside America! Not bad for your first throw of the dice. And of course the tour sold out every night. To say I was feeling lucky at that point would be something of an understatement. I was shitting gold!

But, while I might have felt like the king of the castle, in reality my bank balance had not been improved one iota by the success of 'Speak To Me Pretty'. Yes, the success of the record had helped drive ticket sales for the shows I promoted and the record had sold hundreds of thousands, yet I never saw a penny of that. I had no part in the writing or recording of the song. I was just the schmuck who turned it into a hit. Not that I begrudged Brenda her success. She was a lovely girl, a real trouper who would do anything for you. But I noticed how everybody at Decca used to stand to attention whenever I walked in now and how intently they listened to what I had to say. None of it escaped my attention and so, when a few years later I decided to make some records of my own, it was inevitably to Dick Rowe that I turned for encouragement and support.

The success of the Beatles didn't just change the face of the music business: it changed the way people lived their lives. Everybody's hair grew longer and their clothes changed, too. But it wasn't just that. The success of the Beatles changed the way people were thinking. To a certain degree, that meant I had to change the way I thought about things too. No problem: adapt and survive – I had done it before and I would do it again.

Some changes, though, I found harder to accept than others. The heavy-drugs scene, for example, which began to emerge in London in the mid-sixties, was something it took me a long time to come to terms with. Partly, it was my age. Although I had been around entertainers most of my life, I had never knowingly mixed socially with anybody who was into drugs, even the so-called soft stuff. Mostly, though, it was because I was – and remain – firmly against drugs. I couldn't tolerate them or the people who used them, and anybody who came near me or my artists with that shit in the early days was in for big trouble.

It wasn't until I got involved with groups like the Small Faces that I realised the full extent of what I was up against, though. There was no way I could ever have stopped the Small Faces popping pills or smoking pot, the way I had tried to in the past with Jerry Lee and others. I didn't approve but I realised they were half my age and from another world. Drugs were so prevalent on the streets of London by then that I couldn't have stopped them anyway. It wasn't like the days when you saw that shit only at the shows themselves. Now it was everywhere.

Drug dealers would actually come to the backstage door expecting to be let in. Unlike most promoters, however, I always made a point of telling them to get lost. I hated the idea that I was putting on these shows, making good money for the artist just so they could give it away to some shithouse drug monkey who didn't care if they lived or died. So I made another simple rule: no drugs allowed anywhere backstage at my shows – the old one-strike-and-you're-out rule from the Star Club. Those foolish enough not to heed the warnings got the worst that I could give them – broken arms, legs, jaws, whatever. They had to learn.

Not that that stopped them for long. I found out that drug dealers were like rats: they never stopped multiplying. You killed one and another two jumped up to take their place. It didn't help that in the case of someone like Jerry Lee he allowed these scumbags to crawl all over him. Knowing what a jerk he was, I shouldn't have been surprised to discover he was on dope – but I was. I had no idea until one night I actually took a girl, who turned out to be a major dealer, backstage to meet him. She was young and, when she knocked on the door and told me she was an old friend of Jerry's, I saw no reason to disbelieve her. The worst I thought she might be was an old girlfriend. It never occurred to me that she might be selling something.

So like a dummy I called up the stairs, 'Jerry! Somebody here to see you, kid!' And off she trotted to his dressing room. 'Have a nice time,' I said as she waved goodbye. The rest of the crew, some of whom knew what she was, saw this and took it all the wrong way of course, and word went round that Don Arden didn't mind dealers coming by any more. Next thing I knew, I'd got another wave of scumbags descending on the shows. And that was when I decided I would seriously have to go to war with this scum. The trouble was, you never saw the cops anywhere. They had their own little game going on. So the way I saw it, it was down to me to police my own shows, to put a stop to those elements that I felt were threatening my business.

Bootleggers, for example. Around the same time as the drug dealers started homing in on us we suddenly had pirates turning up outside the shows selling dodgy, unofficial gear – photographs, T-shirts, any old tat they could get their hands on. As the promoter, I owned the sole rights to sell official merchandising material inside the venues. I would do a deal with each artist and we would split the profits accordingly. But the people on the street arriving for the shows – being confronted by all this hooky gear that was sold out of suitcases – didn't know that of course: they assumed it was all kosher.

Well, I wasn't having that. I saw the pirates as only slightly better than the drug dealers. I decided to tackle both problems the same way – in the tried and trusted manner. Go in hard and hit them where it hurts. Most of the guys selling this stuff were ex-convicts, hard cases. I didn't give a shit. I had always been able to take care of myself. Running a cash-rich business like that always meant having to carry plenty of muscle and by the early sixties I had assembled an impressive array of nasty-looking characters around me: 'security' staff that I always had on standby.

Even the guys in my office looked the part. There was Peter Grant, whom I had recently brought into the office to work as an agent; a guy who had worked with Peter as an extra in a couple of movies and whom I hired to replace him as Gene Vincent's road manager; and Stan Simmons, who was another good guy to have around in a tight spot. We never went looking for trouble but I made it clear I wouldn't hesitate to act if any started, however big or small the problem. In fact, I found that if you dealt with the small stuff decisively it helped prevent the big stuff from happening. People would look at how severely you dealt with a relatively minor incident and wonder what the hell you would do if something really serious occurred.

On the Everly Brothers' tour, for example, George Harrison was backstage one night, talking to my son David. Meeting a Beatle was a big thing for an eleven-year-old boy, even one like David, who had been brought up in the biz. To make him feel at home, George explained how he knew his father, adding that he'd just bumped into me late one night a few weeks before. At which point a journalist butted in and said, 'Oh, Don's always out at that time of night looking for birds!' He thought he was being funny but it upset David, who took him at face value. It embarrassed him and spoiled his moment with a Beatle. Peter Grant, who was stood nearby, was so incensed he told Stan Simmons to take David home, and then he got hold of me and told me what the hack had said. I went berserk. How dare he!

We found him, still trying to crawl up George Harrison's arse, and dragged him outside. It was humiliating: one moment he's talking to a Beatle, the next I've picked him up by the scruff of the neck and marched him to the door. Outside I didn't wait to hear what he had to say, I just walloped him – hard – and watched his feet lift off the ground. He actually landed on top of my car – the lovely white Chevy Impala that Manfred sold me. It was a soft-top and he literally bounced off the roof! So I hit him again for being a cheeky shite and denting my car!

Then we picked him up and drove him back to my place. We carried him upstairs and slung him through David's bedroom door. He was down on his hands and knees crying his eyes out, telling David how sorry he was for telling such awful lies about his father.

As always, you can say it sounds harsh, but I don't believe in farting around: life's too short. And it sent out the right signal: if you gave me a problem, I would give you one back ten times worse. It was with that attitude that I decided to unleash my dogs of war on both the drug dealers and the pirates.

Whichever way you looked at it, they were all scum, all on the make from both the artist and me. If the police wouldn't do anything about it, I would.

My main man for dealing with the pirates was a complete headcase called Mad Tom. We called him Mad Tom because he insisted on it. He even referred to himself as Mad Tom and woe betide anyone who made the mistake of not addressing him by his full title. If you simply called him Tom and he heard you, it was over. He would literally have to be pulled off you. 'My name's Mad Tom!' he used to scream. 'Say it! Mad Tom! Mad Tom!' So everybody called him Mad Tom. Everybody, that is, except me. Because I was his boss, he said. Oh, he was mad all right . . .

It worked like this. I would go out to the front of the theatre first each night and try to talk to these guys quietly to see what their reaction was. But it was always the same: 'We'll fucking do what we want! What you gonna do about it?' So that was that. Having given them the chance to withdraw politely, I deemed it time to send in Mad Tom.

It could be quite comical, actually. At first, he was just one of my guys but he developed such a good routine that he was able to frighten most of them off all on his own. I used to go outside to watch. Tom would go up to them and say, 'My boss says you've got to fuck off.' Often they'd just look at him and start laughing. They thought he was a bit backward, which I suppose he was. But he was built like Frankenstein's monster and he'd soon wipe the smile off their faces. He would ask them again. If they hadn't responded sufficiently after the second request he simply picked the nearest one up and brought him down on his knee, snapping his back like a twig. Sometimes you heard the crack. Then he would pick them up again and toss them into the gutter. Mad Tom used to shell 'em like peas. Then we would 'confiscate' all the merchandise they had been pushing and – if it was any good – flog it ourselves inside the hall.

I made it a rough scene all right, but people got the message – this guy Don Arden didn't mess around: he broke bones – and the pirates soon stopped coming round. Tom had simply done too many of them serious damage. He didn't kill them but, by God, it was close sometimes! He would leave them an inch from death. But they were all ex-cons, so there was no question of getting the police involved.

Eventually I had to get rid of him when he went too far once too often, but he was certainly a character and I don't regret a bit of it. The only shocking part for me was that the police were often just sitting in their cars on the opposite side of the street watching. They didn't do it to any other promoters, just me. I used to laugh about it but inside I was fuming. Why was I being left to do their dirty work for them?

The drug dealers were harder to frighten off – or, rather, they were just as easy to scare away but they always came back for more, no matter how cruel the punishment. Not that that stopped me from dishing it out. At which point, the police decided to make a belated entrance into the story. Not to protect me from these vermin, but actually to accuse me of being in league with them! I could barely believe what I was hearing. Then it clicked: the incident with Jerry Lee when I ushered that little drug slut into his dressing room was still coming back to haunt me.

'Listen, you cocksucking bastards,' I told them the first time they came to question me. It was backstage at one of my shows and I was furious. 'I am responsible for dealing with these fucking whores who come here trying to sell my artists this shit while you lot are sat outside in your Noddy cars playing with yourselves!' I really let them have it. I felt so affronted. They didn't know what to make of it. They had obviously never been spoken to like that before and they went scurrying out of the door again like frightened mice.

The problem was that the cops couldn't figure out why I was so much richer than all the other promoters they were used to dealing with. Also, I was well known, and that used to wind them up too because they couldn't figure out what for. They were all too young to remember me as a singer and of course none of them understood the first thing about rock 'n' roll or the music business. Yet here I was driving a Rolls-Royce, dripping in gold and diamonds worth thousands, and they just couldn't figure it. Then, when they heard the yarn about my welcoming drug dealers to the show, they put two and two together and made five.

What the police couldn't stand, either, in my opinion, was that I was bigger than they were. Too big for my Jew-boy boots – that's what they thought. Too flash. And maybe I was – for pipsqueaks like them. But I was just me being me. This mania Paddles and I had for jewellery, for instance. She was always wearing at least half a million dollars on her fingers alone. It caused comment, and no little jealousy, wherever we went. I didn't care. Paddles was a princess and so I treated her like one – including giving her the sort of jewellery princesses wear.

So the cops started to hassle me. It wouldn't have occurred to them that I was three times more successful than anyone else in the business because I worked three times harder or was three times smarter, or even three times luckier. They just assumed it was dirty money. They started coming by regularly, each time with a new set of 'allegations' against me, or one of my artists. They probably thought they'd eventually wear me down – and that was when I'd slip up and they would walk in on me with a cartload of drugs in my office. That's how stupid the British police were.

I gave them no rating at all and I told them so. 'You're the scum of the earth; you don't even know why you hate me. You just do. Well, go ahead. Take a look around. The only thing you'll find here is money!' That used to piss them off big time. We finished up threatening each other but they never once tried to arrest me.

It certainly wasn't the police I turned to when faced with serious trouble. So when, in 1964, I discovered that my enemies in the drug world were discussing taking a contract out on me, I decided, as usual, to take matters into my own hands.

It began with a series of threatening letters, which began to arrive in Brixton just before we left there in 1963, warning me of the peril I would put myself in if I continued to fight them.

Those letters had about as much effect on me as a fart in a gale. I laughed when I read them. It just showed what amateurs they were. If you're going to do something to someone, you just do it. You don't send them letters first telling them what you're going to do. That's chickenshit stuff. I was pleased, though, because by sending me those things they had played right into my hands. Now, if and when it came to violence, I could show those letters to a courtroom and prove that I was just protecting myself.

Meanwhile, I was busy with more important things. Paddles had become seriously ill with a chest infection that winter, which at one profoundly distressing moment was deemed life-threatening. But the doctors worked on her night and day and, thank God, she eventually got well again – which was when we made the move to Mayfair.

No one outside the immediate family knew yet, though. Paddles was still recuperating and we wanted to keep the new house quiet for her. But, when I got to the office one morning not long afterwards, I found a message offering me condolences on my recent bereavement. There was no signature but I knew immediately who it was from: the same scumbags who'd sent the letters. They had obviously heard about my wife's brush with death and decided to play a little 'joke' on me. Either that or it was a direct threat against me and my family. I couldn't be sure, but it smelled bad. I knew they wanted rid of me. Of course they did. With me out of the way they knew they'd be able to make fortunes out of my artists. But I wasn't going anywhere; I had made that clear. So now they were making personal threats. They had upped the ante. So be it.

First, though, I had to be sure. I raced back to the new house and ran upstairs and there she was, bless her, resting in her room. She was still on the mend and so I told her to ignore the phone if it rang until I got back. Then I went back to the office and got hold of Peter Grant. 'There's more to this,' I said. 'I can smell it.' I sat there thinking it over and it dawned on me that they wouldn't have known we'd moved yet and I suddenly got a hunch. 'I bet you any money there's something going on at the old house,' I said. 'Let's get down there and find out!'

The last thing I wanted was for there to be trouble at the old house. The neighbours were all friends and I knew they would be straight on the phone to Paddles. We came in from one end of the street – and coming straight towards us from the other end of the street was this bloody great hearse! 'There it is!' I pointed. 'I bet that's going to the house!' I don't know why I was so sure – I just knew the way their twisted minds worked, I suppose. The cab screeched to a halt and Peter and I jumped out and stopped the hearse. I asked the driver where he was going and he said, 'To Mr Arden's house.' I explained that I was Mr Arden but I certainly hadn't ordered a hearse and that it was someone's idea of a sick joke. He didn't know what to make of that but we bunged him a few quid and got him out of the street again as quickly as we could.

That's when I decided: enough already. I went for the girl behind it all, a real eighteen-carat nut. She was a self-confessed mental patient who actually used to live part-time in a mental institution. Mad as she was, though, she was the one running everything, from selling stuff to paying off the desk clerks in the hotels where the artists stayed. She used to go in and open her purse or her pussy, whatever it took, and the desk clerks would give her the room right next to Jerry Lee's. It was sick and it had to be stopped, but the police never spoke to her once. She was paying them off, too. I think they even encouraged her to have a pop at me. As far as the cops were concerned I was Dracula, anyway.

I finished her off once and for all, however, when I went down to the mental hospital she lived at and made what you might call an 'unofficial complaint'. I took my lawyer with me and screamed and yelled until I got the top brass all down there in one room. Then I showed them the letters, told them about the drugs, told them about the hearse, then said, 'If this madwoman ever comes near me or any of my family again, or pulls any more fucking stunts, I will personally have her killed. It's that simple. Now what are you going to do about it?'

They said, 'Oh, there's no need for that sort of talk, Mr Arden.' I assured them that it wasn't just talk. And it wasn't. Threatening me is one thing: pulling stunts on my wife is another. That's death-sentence material.

But they assured me that wouldn't be necessary. 'You'll be pleased to know,' said one of the brain doctors, 'that we've examined her recently and she's not going to be allowed out again.' And she wasn't. In fact, I never heard from her again.

The drugs, though, they never went away . . .

Just like everybody else in the business, by 1964 I was on the lookout for my own version of the Beatles. The obvious contenders were the Rolling Stones, but I had stopped working with them after that tour with the Everly Brothers. They had gone with Robert Stigwood instead – a new face on the scene who had recently arrived from Australia with the Bee Gees.

With neither the Beatles nor the Stones to my name any longer, and not yet having found my own version of them yet, I decided to do the next best thing and approach the one artist both those groups always cited as their main inspiration – Chuck Berry.

Berry was another act William Morris warned me against – but this time I would wish I'd heeded them. They wouldn't touch him since he'd been jailed for three years in 1962 for taking an underage girl across the state line. I didn't like the sound of that, either. But, because of all the free publicity the Beatles and the Stones kept giving him, I figured Berry was probably the last of the original fifties rockers I could still build a profitable UK tour around. So I put aside my personal misgivings and, in 1964, set about making contact. Frankly, in the immediate aftermath of the Beatles' effect on the industry, I needed the work. I was hardly broke, but I was hardly busy, either.

Because Berry was still in prison – and it's against the law in the US for convicted prisoners to conduct any professional business while serving their sentences – I made all the arrangements with the guy then acting as his manager: a white guy and a very charming man who died some years ago now and whose name, sadly, I can no longer remember. It was he, though, who really put me in the picture about Chuck. He told me they were letting him out early.

I had flown out to Chicago, where he was imprisoned, to meet him for myself and, sure enough, he was as horrible a guy as you can imagine: surly, arrogant, treating everybody around him like a dog. I hated him from the moment I met him. Yet every time you picked up a music paper you had the Beatles or the Stones praising this prick. Give him a chance, they seemed to be saying. I was ready to walk but the deal was in place and the tickets ready to go on sale. I thought, I'll try this once and see what happens.

He'd never been to Europe before and so, even though I couldn't tolerate him, I got the acclaim for bringing him over, this so-called legend. But it was one of the hardest – and, for me, worst-paid – tours I'd ever done. I'd been negotiating for nearly a year before I was able to get his signature on a contract. I ended up having to fork out a lot more than I had anticipated at the last minute.

To make matters worse, he was a sell-out only in the London area, where his patronage by the Beatles and Stones had made him fashionable. The further north you went, however, the less anyone gave a shit. He did all right, but he wasn't a star out in the sticks – and he certainly wasn't worth ten grand a night.

Another character I had the misfortune to find myself dealing with in the mid-sixties was Ike Turner. I first booked his group, Ike and Tina Turner, just after we moved to Mayfair. I was at a nightclub called Annabel's, where all the younger members of the British royal family went. Despite the fact that they didn't normally invite Jews to become members, my lawyer, David Jacobs, who also represented the Beatles, got me membership there. They had offered membership to the Beatles but they told them they would agree to it only if their manager, Brian Epstein, could also be made a member. Well, they had to swallow that. Everybody knew he was Jewish but they wanted the Beatles, so what could they do?

After that, it was relatively straightforward getting Jacobs and me membership too; it was all done very quickly and quietly. They didn't have the guts to ask us if we were Jewish. We had a lot of fun there, though. As it was practically on our doorstep in Mayfair, Paddles and I went quite often. Then, one night, the owner, a well-known society toff named Mark Birley, came over to our table and introduced himself, then asked me if I'd be interested in arranging for Ike and Tina Turner to appear at the club.

'Sure,' I said. 'I got plenty of other artists who I think would be better but if that's who you want I'll get 'em for you.' He wanted them for Christmas. I warned him I would have to bring them in from New York and that it would cost plenty, but he didn't mind, he said. So I did the deal, arranged to bring them over, and Birley thought it was splendid. 'Jolly well done, old boy. Have some champagne.'

Then a week before they were due in he called me and asked me if they were here yet. I said no, of course not. They were coming over only for this one spot at Annabel's; we didn't need the extra expense of having them here a week in advance of the engagement. But he didn't understand; Birley thought they'd be here for days rehearsing. It didn't occur to him that they spent their entire lives out on the road and that there was no need to rehearse anything: they'd done it all a million times before.

He was disappointed. I think he thought he'd be able to hang out with them. He said, 'I've got the best equipment in the world and I want them to come in and practise every day so they know how to use it.' I thought, This guy's taking the piss. So I explained the facts of life to him. 'Listen,' I said, 'if Ike Turner could hear you now he'd fucking piss all over you.' He didn't know what to say to that because now I was talking the talk.

'I don't know what you mean,' he said. 'How dare you!'

'Listen to me,' I said. 'Unlike you, these people are professionals. They are here not for the fun of it but to make money. That means they get off planes, go straight to the theatre, do their act and piss off again. That is the way they like it and that is the way it should be.'

But Birley had booked them for a week and so I offered to fly them in the day before the first show, let them get a good night's sleep, then get them down to the club the following morning to take a look at all this amazing equipment he had, and to rehearse with the eight-piece band I had put together to back them. But he wouldn't give an inch.

'No,' he said, 'I'm afraid I can't have that. I want them here the week before or the shows are cancelled.'

I said, 'Well, in that case, the shows are cancelled.' And I put the phone down.

I knew that would drive him crazy. He had been telling the regulars for weeks about how he was bringing Ike and Tina Turner to Annabel's for a special Christmas show. He didn't now want to have to tell everyone that it was off. He started sending messages to the house. We had a French maid who kept coming in every half-hour with another one. I told her not to accept any more and the next time he called I told her to tell him to stick it up his arse.

It was like child's play; I was laughing all the way through it. Then he got Jacobs to call me and, of course, once I'd explained everything to him, he was on my side. He said he'd have a word and sure enough we agreed that they'd come and rehearse on the morning of the show. To 'seal the deal' Birley invited me over for a drink.

The first night, Ike and Tina were fantastic. They pulverised the audience! I'd never seen an act perform in a club with such impact and strength before. I looked at Birley's face and he was delighted.

The only thing that really spoiled the Ike and Tina shows for me was the fact that Ike was such a sadistic brute to Tina. I had no idea of course when I booked them. I found out only when Tina came into my office in the morning and showed me her wounds. He seemed to find an excuse to give her some sort of beating every night. Sometimes it would just be a slap and other times it would be a full-on assault.

She had a permanent black eye the whole time she was in London. She used to wear hats tipped over the eye to try to hide it. She was always trying to hide her condition from the public. She had special, very expensive, flesh-coloured sticking-plasters to put over the cuts on her face so people in the audience wouldn't see them. But when she performed she would sweat like an animal and the plasters would peel off and she'd start to bleed. There would be blood running down her face sometimes before she'd even finished the first song. It was nauseating, especially when you knew how she'd got those cuts. I felt sorry for her, but what could I do? They were a husband-and-wife team and, if there's one thing I've learned, it is that you never get between a husband and wife, no matter how bad it may look from the outside.

Nevertheless, when she came in and showed me what he'd done it would make me boil with anger. Tina really suffered. It was a miracle she had the strength to get up on stage some nights. He was such an evil, two-faced bastard that he would hit her only from the neck up because he knew that, if he seriously damaged her stomach or legs, she wouldn't be able to perform. She told me that he would beat her with one of her own high-heel shoes. I asked why, and she said anything could set him off; it didn't even have to have anything directly to do with her. He would simply take out his frustrations on her. Like the time Tom Jones came down to the club and started chatting up one of the Ikettes, their backing singers. Ike was giving her one on the side and he got so pissed off that he took the shoe to Tina and beat her with it.

He made her life hell. Meanwhile, he lived off her, took more money than she did, and cheated on her every way he could. Everybody in the business knew it but didn't know what the hell to do about it. They were husband and wife, so you couldn't legally even call him a thief. It was a very sad situation and I can't say I was too sorry to see them leave.

The Chuck Berry tour had been similarly depressing, if for other reasons. But it had proved to be fortuitous in certain other

Left: Me doing my Jimmy Cagney impersonation sometime in the early fifties. I'd been doing Cagney since I was a kid. Some people say I'm still doing him.

Right: A publicity still of me from the early fifties.

Me and Gene Vincent, London, circa 1960. And you thought Ozzy was crazy...

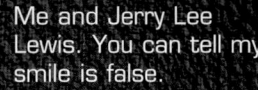

Me and Jerry Lee Lewis. You can tell my smile is false.

At home with the family in Brixton, 1956. Me, my wife Paddles, my son David and my daughter Sharon.

Dinner with the family at the Astor Club, in Mayfair, where we often used to go. This is from about 1970, when Sharon was roughly the same age her daughter Kelly is now — and doesn't it show!

Left: At work in the mid-seventies living up to my reputation as the Al Capone of pop, as the *News of the World* then described me.

Right: Good cop, bad cop. Me and David in the early seventies. Guess which cop I was?

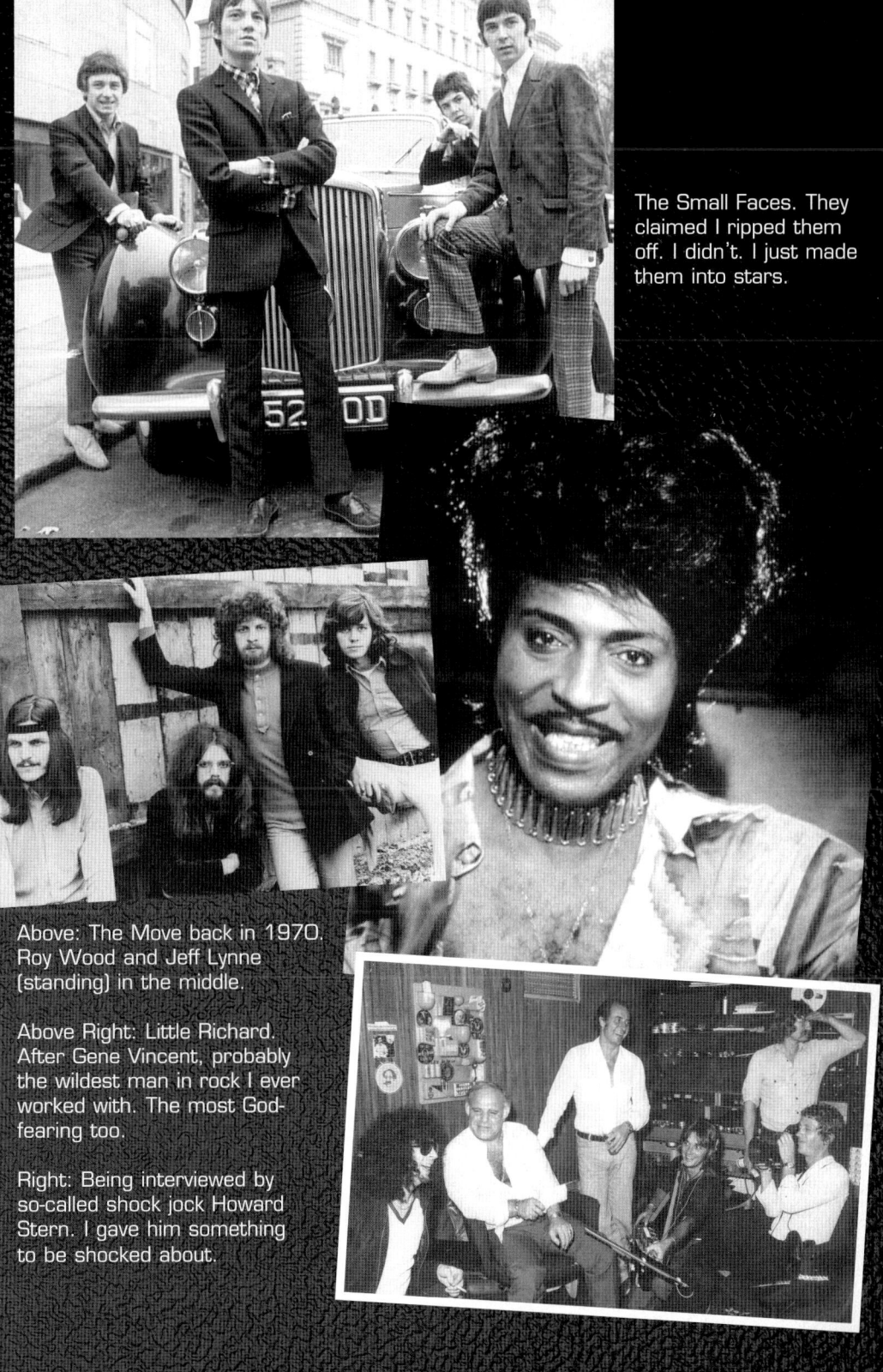

The Small Faces. They claimed I ripped them off. I didn't. I just made them into stars.

Above: The Move back in 1970. Roy Wood and Jeff Lynne (standing) in the middle.

Above Right: Little Richard. After Gene Vincent, probably the wildest man in rock I ever worked with. The most God-fearing too.

Right: Being interviewed by so-called shock jock Howard Stern. I gave him something to be shocked about.

Right: Ozzy on tour in America with Black Sabbath when I managed them in the late seventies.

Below: Me, Paddles and old mucker Ray Chapman at my 50th birthday party.

Bottom: Paddles, Sharon, Ozzy and me. London, 1980.

Bottom right: At Sharon and Ozzy's wedding in Maui in July 1982.

Being presented with yet more gold albums for ELO. By the start of the eighties they were one of the biggest-selling rock acts in the world.

Left: Me and my beloved mum. Without whom...

Below: Me and David with (far left) Air Supply singer Russell Hitchcock and (far right) Black Sabbath guitarist Tony Iommi.

Me now. Older, wiser, but still tough enough to play the part.

Right: Me and Sharon now, at home in Hollywood, where people like us belong.

Left: Sharon and me on good terms again.

Surrounded by rock guitar legends: Brian May from Queen and Black Sabbath's Tony Iommi.

respects. In the short term, it gave me a cheap laugh when Robert Stigwood tried to outbid me for Berry's next UK tour later that year. I had glossed over the poor attendances at the provincial shows and told the music press that the tour had been a huge success. Being based in London, they'd seen only the sell-out shows there and so they believed me and printed it. Bizarrely, though, it was precisely because of those press stories hailing Berry's triumph that Stigwood decided to stick his oar in. When Chuck told me I'd been outbid by Stigwood, I nearly laughed in his face. I said, 'Hey, if he wants to give you more than ten grand a night – good luck.' It turned out that Stigwood had actually offered him close to $15,000 a night! All because he'd read the baloney I'd been feeding the press in London! I phoned him up and said, 'You want Chuck Berry? God bless you, Robert! Take him!' And he did. And the next thing you knew, Stigwood had gone bankrupt! It was a classic!

In the long term, however, the real benefit of that Berry tour was that it helped me launch the group that was to become my first major discovery – the Animals. Fronted by a brilliant singer named Eric Burdon and featuring Chas Chandler on bass (he would later manage Jimi Hendrix) and Alan Price on keyboard (he would soon leave to pursue a solo career and later sign with Jet in the seventies), the Animals were complete unknowns from the northeast of England who had come to me via their manager, a small-time know-nothing shithouse called Mike Jeffries.

Jeffries had been trying to hustle them some gigs down south and was phoning everyone and anyone he thought might help. So far, however, there had been no takers. But on the recommendation of Peter Grant, who had seen them and said they were all right, I thought I'd take a look and offered to audition them at the Scene Club, in Soho. I went down there one lunchtime, watched about three numbers, decided I'd seen enough and offered them a deal to be their exclusive promoter throughout the world. Take it or leave it, I said. They took it. Jeffries would remain their day-to-day manager but from now on I would be the guy overseeing the big picture. To show them I meant business, the first thing I did was stick them on the

Chuck Berry tour. It was invaluable national exposure. Nobody had ever heard of the Animals before that.

As the tour progressed, however, I started getting calls from record shops, asking when we were going to release one of the big songs the Animals did in their set – a cover of an old folk tune called 'House of the Rising Sun'. It seemed that, in every town they played in, the next day people were going into shops asking if they had it. I could see why: it was the highlight of the show. Burdon performed it like an old-style black revue singer: he really put his heart and soul into it, using his voice to jam with the band the way guitarists do. And, if the audience was buying it, he'd go on and on – some nights 'House of the Rising Sun' would go on for about fifteen minutes!

It was a great number all right, but there was no way I was paying for them to release a fifteen-minute single! But the calls kept coming in and I suddenly realised I was being a fool by ignoring them. It was simply a case of supply and demand. The demand was obviously there; all I needed to do was organise the supply. I decided to take a chance and spoke to Dick Rowe at Decca. As always, he offered me nothing but encouragement, and so with Dick's blessing I sent them into the Decca studio in London with a new producer I'd recently hooked up with called Mickie Most.

When I had first met Mickie, in South Africa, in 1963, on that ill-fated Gene Vincent tour, we had got to know each other pretty well in the short time we were together. He had been remarkably helpful in getting Gene safely out of the country, even though it meant he lost money as the promoter on all the cancelled dates. So, when he later asked me if I would consider 'standing' for him as a professional vouchsafe in an application for a work visa from the British immigration authorities, I decided to help the kid and agreed.

As the owner of several successful businesses, I made a statement saying that he would be working for me in a highly specialist field, which was true – and he got his visa. He meant nothing in London but I did him a favour and put him on the bill at every show I had going. He opened up at so many of my shows that I started getting heat for it from the critics. He sang and played guitar and rolled around on his back with his legs in the air. Maybe Gene Vincent or Jerry Lee could have made it work, but Mickie just didn't have the charisma for something like that. He was so bad it was embarrassing. When the Animals came along I saw it as the perfect opportunity to kill two birds with one stone: get Mickie out of the idea of being a performer and get him working in the studio on this other idea – as a producer.

The band had never been in a professional recording studio before but I told them not to worry, that Mickie knew all about it and they were just to do whatever he told them to. I sent Mickie in with strict instructions to ignore whatever the band might have to say about it and get 'House of the Rising Sun' down to under five minutes. When I heard the result a couple of days later I couldn't believe my luck. Mickie may have been a useless prick on stage, but it turned out he was something of a genius in the studio. He had somehow got the whole thing down to about four and a half minutes. That was still long: if you went over three minutes on a single in those days they wouldn't even consider you for radio or TV, let alone jukeboxes.

But there was such a demand for the song that they never bothered about any of that: they just played it to death the moment we put it out. For the next three months you couldn't walk into a pub or restaurant, couldn't turn on the TV or radio without having 'House of the Rising Sun' shoved down your throat. It was fantastic! We shifted more than 250,000 copies of it in the first week alone! That was the most any single had ever sold in its first week. By the end of the following week it was Number 1.

6

Everything happened so fast with the Animals that even I wasn't prepared for it. When 'House of the Rising Sun' then began to get played on American radio I thought I might have another Beatles or Stones on my hands. All I had to do was keep the ship on a steady course. But, instead of sticking with the deal, Jeffries did the dirty on me and went to Allen Klein – and there was nothing I could do about it. It sounds incredible now, but everything happened so fast with the Animals – I had them out on tour within days of meeting them – that I never actually got around to signing them formally to a contract. Then 'House of the Rising Sun' took off all over the world, and before we knew it they were out on their first tour of America.

Also, if I'm honest, I have to confess to a certain amount of naïveté. I should have gone with them on that American tour. But I had my new career in London as a hit maker to think about and so I sent Peter Grant in my place. As the guy who had just transformed them from complete nobodies into international superstars, I never even considered that the band wouldn't want to stick with me. Mike Jeffries didn't know how to get to London when I first met him. Somebody told him there was a train; he went to the station and got on it. That was the extent of his music-business know-how. Later, when I heard he was managing Jimi Hendrix in conjunction with Chas Chandler, I knew it would come to a bad end because Jeffries wasn't interested in looking after his artists. He was there just to take their money, for however long it lasted. He was a cheap crook with no talent who happened to be the right prick in the right place at the right time. When he got killed in a plane crash in the early seventies, I laughed. Good riddance to bad rubbish, I said.

Jeffries didn't even have the grace to let me know that I was out of the picture. It was Peter Grant who broke the news to me. Part of his job as tour manager was to collect the money at the shows and bring it back to me. Yet when he got back to London he claimed he didn't have any. He told me the band had been poached in New York by Allen Klein and that I would need to talk to him.

I was furious. Less so with the Animals, who were just a bunch of Geordie dummies who didn't know their arses from a hole in the ground; more so with Klein. Klein had told them he would make more money for them than I would. And of course they bought it hook, line and sinker. Just sign here, boys . . . I had booked them for a high-profile show in New York, at the Paramount Theater. I had Chuck Berry and Little Richard on the bill as well and with 'House of the Rising Sun' shooting up the charts it was a big success.

When it all came out there were a lot of people who thought blood would be spilled. But this was one war that I decided wasn't worth fighting. I still had the band's agency contract, which I sold to Harold Davidson for something like £40,000, and then cut off all ties with them. I really didn't give a toss, because I knew that without me they'd be dead. They had a couple more hits in the UK but the Animals never really did anything again in America and by 1967 the band were finished. As far as I'm concerned, they got what they deserved.

The next time I was in New York, however, I couldn't resist paying Klein a little visit, just to let him know personally how I felt about what he'd done. I didn't call ahead – I didn't want to spoil the surprise – but just walked in on him one day.

'Hello, Don,' he said, trying to act cool. 'What can I do for you?'

His office was on the 24th floor. I walked over to him until I was very close indeed and said, 'Allen, I just want you to know that, any time I want, I can come in here and throw you out that fucking window.'

He started to wobble then; started to stammer. But I wasn't there to listen to anything he had to say. I had come just to say my piece and go. 'I'm giving you your life back,' I said, 'because I don't give a shit about the Animals. But, if there is ever a next time, you're dead. Do you understand? Dead!' Then I turned my back on him and walked out again. Slowly.

As for Peter Grant, I wasn't angry so much as disappointed by the role he played in that little saga. Peter had become part of the family. Paddles treated him like a son. But when he was put to the test he let both of us down. Paddles was even more disappointed than I was. We both knew it wasn't entirely his fault: it was his wife's. She never hid how pissed off she was that Paddles and I were so much better off than she and Peter were. She'd look at my wife's jewellery and get on to Grant about it. I used to hear her. 'Why can't you earn that kind of money? Why should I have to wear this cheap shit from the high street?'

It was a pity because he had served me well until then. But when it came to the crunch he acted the way a million other guys would have done and took the money. He thought he saw the chance to make hundreds of thousands with the Animals, so he followed them to Klein. I understood. But it was still disappointing. Later, after he became successful as the manager of Led Zeppelin, he tried once or twice to get back in touch. I think he wanted to show the master how well the pupil had done. It was all very friendly, but I wasn't interested.

The wife eventually left him, of course. She ran off with the gardener. Talk about an English farce! I think he ended up living with his daughter. He was actually a very lonely man, though he kept it all very well disguised. He learned from me that you can overcome almost any obstacle in this business if you've got enough front. People love to take things at face value. They see a guy who's six foot two and weighs three hundred pounds and they think he must be a hard case. But, if anyone who knew what they were doing had ever taken him on, he would have died. He may have been the size of a house but he wasn't a well man. It was his size. He couldn't walk more than a hundred yards without having to sit down. You never saw Peter walk anywhere. You always saw him riding around in one of his big cars.

The other disappointment for me, personally, was the part Mickie Most played in that story. Again, this was because everything happened so fast that there hadn't been time to put anything together formally in writing. So when Mickie decided that, as the man who recorded the song, he actually owned the master tape of it, there wasn't much I could do about it – not legally, anyway. And he sold the tapes to Klein for $150,000! After all I had done for that boy! I learned another valuable lesson: help and trust alone did not command loyalty. Only fear and loathing could do that.

Although working with the Animals proved to be a short-lived experience for me, it provided me with my first real insight into how to build a successful new recording group from the ground up. The key, it seemed to me, was to spot your opportunity and make the most of it as quickly as possible – before the fickle finger of fashion moved on again.

I now felt confident that having done it twice – first with Brenda Lee and now the Animals – I could easily make more hit records. As if to prove it, I had recently signed up another new British group – the Nashville Teens – who gave me my third Number 1 in a row with a song called 'Tobacco Road'. I was starting to think there was nothing to this record business. It was like roulette: you just picked a number, spun the wheel and raked in the dough.

It was sweet. And, unlike the Animals, the Teens would stay with me for over twenty years. Arthur Sharp, their original lead singer, carried on working in the office for me years after he had left the group. They were all lovely fellas. Mickie Most had produced 'Tobacco Road' but after he screwed me over the Animals I turned to Shel Talmy, the blind record producer, and he was a lovely fella too. They were all regular party guests at the house in Mayfair. It was a shame the group never became bigger than it did. We must have had half a dozen hits together in the mid-sixties but then the flower-power era came in and suddenly the Teens seemed old-fashioned.

London in the mid-sixties was simply alive with new groups, new fashions, new everything. Something seemed to come along every five minutes; you couldn't afford to stand still. So, while I continued to manage the Teens as well as carrying on my agency and promotion businesses, I was still on the lookout for a new British group that I would be able to mould into something to rival the Beatles.

I finally found them – or perhaps I should say they found me – when a couple of street kids turned up at my office one morning early in 1965 asking to see me. They gave their names to the receptionist – Stevie Marriott and Ronnie Lane – and told her they were from a 'fantastic new group' that I would want to know about. Of course they were. She told them to sit and wait while she phoned through to me.

It was ten o'clock in the morning. They didn't have an appointment and I was busy so I told her to tell them to come back another time. But they were happy to wait, they said. Happy to get out of the cold, more like. I found out later they were homeless at the time, sleeping rough in the park. Consequently, they hadn't washed for days and the smell coming off them was so bad that after a couple of hours the girls in the office started to complain. So I agreed to see them just to stop them hanging round reception, stinking the place out.

I held my nose and ushered them into my office. They looked like what they were: a pair of scruffy street urchins. They told me about their group. When they told me the name – the Small Faces – I had to laugh because that's exactly what they were: two skinny streaks of piss barely out of their teens, as cute and tiny as dolls.

We chatted and it turned out Stevie had been a child actor – he'd been the first Artful Dodger in Lionel Bart's *Oliver!* – and had even been to the same stage school, Italia Conti, as my own children, David and Sharon. I phoned David to see if he knew anything about it and, although he was a few years younger than Stevie, he remembered him well. 'Oh yeah, I know Stevie Marriott,' he said. 'He's great, really talented. Give him a chance, Dad.' So that was that. Purely on David's recommendation I agreed to put them on at one of my shows – just to see what I thought of them.

First, though, I would have to smarten them up and get them some decent stage clothes – not to mention a bath and some food inside them. Although they later became known as clothes-conscious 'mods', they didn't have a clean pair of trousers between them when they first came to see me. Meanwhile, I was the best-dressed man in the business. So I told them, 'If you wanna work for me, you've got to get fucking dressed.' And we arranged for them to come back with the other lads in the group the next day, and I took them shopping.

I had recently moved offices again, this time to Carnaby Street. Famous for its trendy clothes shops and boutiques, Carnaby Street was bang in the centre of so-called Swinging London. As usual, I had read the signs before anybody else and was the first agent to set up office there. I hadn't actually stopped wearing a suit to work yet – that transformation would not be complete until the early seventies – but I had plugged into the sixties 'vibe'. My clothes were still tailor-made but my trousers were now flared, and my hair was creeping down past my collar for the first time in my life. Occasionally, I sported a goatee. That still didn't make me young and trendy and thank God for that – but it did rid me of any lingering traces of that old 'fifties promoter' image. That look was as stale as old cheese in the new era of Twiggy, Mary Quant, David Bailey and the Beatles.

Because of that, I thought getting the Small Faces some decent gear to wear on stage was imperative. They didn't have a clue, so I took them into John Stephen's – then the most fashionable shop in Carnaby Street – and started picking things for them to try on. Most of them laughed and got into it but Stevie kept his mouth shut and got dressed as quickly as he could. He was a little embarrassed, I think. The others were too ignorant to be embarrassed. Once they had the gear on, they began to strut about. They appreciated the difference it made to the way they felt about themselves. It gave them a confidence they didn't have before.

Two days later I had them open the bill at a show I had on in Margate, down on the south coast. Tellingly, I can't even remember who the headliner was now. I vividly recall, however, seeing the Small Faces for the first time. They already had the makings of an image. It was partly the name, partly the trendy new clobber I'd bought them. Mainly, though, it was just the group themselves. There were four of them – Marriott and Lane, plus Kenny Jones the drummer and the keyboardist Jimmy Winston – and they all had the same tiny stature. But, when they opened up, the sound was so big and powerful it knocked everybody sideways. To me, they were already even better than the Animals. With my help, I thought, they can't fail.

I went backstage that night and told them I'd turn them into superstars – as long as they did everything I told them to. They all nodded their heads and said, 'Yes, sir, Mr Arden.' I liked that: polite. Mindful of my previous mistakes with the Animals, I told them to come to my office the next day, where I would have some papers for them to sign. This was one fish that wasn't going to get away – not without a struggle, anyway.

Good as gold, they all came in the next day and signed up, and I started them off on £25 a week each. I also rented them a big house to live in, in Pimlico, and gave them the use of a brand-new Jaguar car and a first-class chauffeur-cum-bodyguard named Bill to drive it for them – all before they'd made a single penny for me.

They all moved into the Pimlico house except for Kenny, who was a bit of a mummy's boy. But once he saw what he was missing he soon cut the apron strings and moved in with the rest of them. It was a big four-bedroom place. I hired a German maid who would fix them breakfast whatever time of day they awoke. When they weren't away on the road the rule was they had to be back at the house no later than eight o'clock every night, when she would have dinner ready for them. After that, Bill the driver took over and they could go wherever they wanted. They were midgets, but cheeky with it, and I knew it would cause them trouble sooner or later. Bill was nearly seven feet tall and had just finished working with the Beatles. I knew they would be safe with him.

I was glad when Kenny moved in, too. I wanted them all living together like that because it made them tighter as a unit, musically, but it also reinforced their togetherness. They all started to look like each other and that – coupled with the 'cool' new clothes – was when their image really became their own. It was mod but it wasn't po-faced like the Who, the other great mod band of the time. It was more cheeky and down to earth.

To help maintain the image, I opened accounts for them at half a dozen trendy clothes boutiques in Carnaby Street and they would go in and help themselves. They didn't get this stuff off the peg, either. The guys in those shops altered everything for them until it all fitted to perfection. As a result, the Small Faces always looked a million dollars.

I was happy to do it for them. They certainly didn't beg me to stop. And the result was that I turned them into stars. But all that stuff costs money – serious money. I agreed to splash it out on their behalf and they agreed to pay me back when the hits started happening – and that was how it worked.

Stevie and Ronnie were the leaders; the others were along for the ride. Stevie was a total sweetheart: a striking voice and a wonderfully funny personality. He was one of those kids who always have smiles on their faces, no matter what. I thought Ronnie Lane, however, was an unpleasant guy, and I'd quickly grow to hate him. He was an evil little man with a massive head on this tiny body and deathly-pale skin. He was supposed to be Stevie's best pal, but you could tell he was nobody's friend, really.

I put those feelings aside, though, as I set about building up the group. In common with so many of my best decisions, at first I received nothing but derision from other people in the business who apparently knew better. Dick Rowe at Decca was the only one who backed me. Just as I had with the Animals and the Nashville Teens, I took the Small Faces to Dick and we did a deal straightaway.

Typically, it was Dick who encouraged me to see the Small Faces as just the next step in a long-term plan to find and develop a whole range of new acts – so much so that he suggested a new type of deal: my own label, Contemporary, over which I would have complete control, but part of the much larger Decca organisation. I would even have permanent use of my own studio at Decca's own London recording complex. As a result, because I now had the machinery behind me to do it, it took me just six weeks from discovering the Small Faces to releasing their first record.

The song – 'Whatcha Gonna Do About It?' – was just something I had lying around on the shelf. The success of 'House of the Rising Sun' and 'Tobacco Road' had demonstrated to me the value of having top-quality material ready made for any number of groups to use. Apart from cover versions, of which there were many, they were the kinds of songs that remained popular on jukeboxes and the radio long after they'd disappeared from the charts. If you owned the publishing, you were minted.

Mindful of that, I had begun paying £25 a week to a couple of professional songwriters, Ian 'Sammy' Samwell, who'd written hits for Cliff Richard; and Brian Potter, a former drummer I knew who would later go to America and pen hits for the Four Tops, among others. It was Ian and Brian who came up with 'Whatcha Gonna Do About It?'. We'd tried getting it off the ground with several other artists before that but there had been no takers. On this occasion, however, I insisted. My determination was rewarded when it smashed into the UK Top Ten, giving both the Small Faces and my new label, Contemporary, a hit with our very first release.

The group later claimed I heavied them into doing it. What crap. I didn't heavy anybody. I might have said something like, 'Do what you're told, sonny, and play the fucking song.' But then I was the guy paying for everything; this was my game, these were my rules. But nobody held a gun to their heads. If they didn't want to do it they could always leave. But they didn't, they stayed, and we made a record that turned a bunch of complete unknowns into a Top Ten act. If that makes me a bully, then I'm a bully and proud of it.

At least I wasn't snide like Ronnie. The first thing he did after 'Whatcha Gonna Do About It?' had become successful was demand that Jimmy Winston be kicked out! It was a rotten thing to do. After Stevie, Jimmy was the nicest one in the group. He cried his eyes out when I told him. But Ronnie was too busy wallowing in his newfound success to give a toss about that. I said, 'Why don't you give him a break? You're in the charts now and he's been with you all the time you were struggling. He gave you the use of his brother's van – at least talk to him.' But no, he didn't want to know. (I was so sorry for the poor kid I took him on for a while as a solo artist, but without success.)

As if that hadn't been bad enough, Lane then insisted on ditching Ian Samwell from the background team, too. He just waved his hand and said, 'I can't play with him, he's no fucking good.'

The whole thing was shameful. The kid they eventually got in – a Scottish lad who got lucky – could barely play keyboards at all, in my opinion. He was all right for tinkling away in the background late at night, but that was all. I couldn't understand it, but what could I do? We pressed on.

Their next single, 'Sha La La La Lee', was another song hand-picked by me. This time, though, it was something I'd commissioned specifically for them. I wanted something like 'Doo Wah Diddy Diddy', which was a Number 1 then for Manfred Mann. So I paid a pal of mine, Kenny Lynch, to come up with some similar-sounding lyrics. Kenny was a singer, actor, comedian, jack of all trades – as well as a pretty good lyricist. He could do it for you to order. Once I had the title and the chorus I gave it to Mort Shuman, who came up with the brilliantly simple but catchy tune.

But when I took it to the group they hated it even more than 'Whatcha Gonna Do About It?'. They said it was corny – and it probably was. But I knew it would be big for them and so I forced it down their throats. I made it clear it was either 'Sha La La La Lee' or nothing, and so, like good boys, they did what they were told. It almost goes without saying that it was another huge hit for them, reaching Number 1 in the summer of 1965.

I felt very proud. I had now had Number 1 records with four different artists, but this one was entirely mine: I made the group, made the song and made the right calls that made it a hit. To see it all come off like that was sweet indeed. The Small Faces never stopped hating it, though, even as the kids used to scream for it . . .

By now I felt I knew something about the record business. As long as you had the right record and knew the right buttons to push to promote it, you had a hit. Having the right record meant having something that was either (a) so unbelievably catchy you just couldn't ignore it or (b) sounded exactly like whatever else was Number 1 in the charts at the time.

Knowing the right buttons to press, however, was slightly more complicated. As the biggest promoter in the country, I had known for years how to phone up TV shows and get artists on them. It seemed to me that the same principles might broadly be applied to getting your records on TV and radio, too. But it was much trickier than that.

Dick Rowe filled in the blanks for me. In order to get your artist's records in the charts, first and foremost, you had to get them played on the radio. In those days, there were exactly three places you could hear pop or rock on national radio in the UK: the BBC, which had an excellent signal but devoted only a small percentage of its airtime to pop music; Radio Luxembourg, which had a terrible signal but at least played mostly rock 'n' roll; and Radio Caroline, who had both – a good clear signal and nothing but great records. As a result, the most important of the three in 1965 was Radio Caroline.

One of the original 'pirate' radio stations, they were mavericks who broadcast from a ship anchored a couple of miles off the coast of Britain, just outside government licensing laws – which meant they didn't suffer 'needle-time' restrictions like the regular BBC radio stations and could play whatever they pleased. Modelled on American radio stations of the time, the presenters were all young and hip and the production style was slick and snappy. As a result, Caroline had the reputation of being trendsetters and having a record played frequently on there meant an almost certain hit.

However, there was more to it than simply knowing the right people to call. You had to have the right money, too. As luck would have it, an old pal of mine named Phil Solomon was the guy in charge of the playlists at Caroline at that time, and it was Phil who put me in the picture.

I had known Phil since the old variety days, when he was a promoter. He'd come up to me after a show in Dublin once and said, 'I've heard you, you're a great singer. Can I buy you a Jewish meal?' I accepted and spent a delightful evening in his company while he regaled me with stories about the business that had me doubled up with laughter. After that we had become friends. We would go out together with our wives. But he was one of those guys who, like me, stand their ground in business, no matter whom they are dealing with, and sometimes we would fight like hell during the day and become friends again at night.

Now he was one of the guys running the show at Caroline. He explained how it worked. The price to get your record played for a week on Radio Caroline: £250. In cash, thank you very much. You paid it on the Friday and they started playing your record on the Sunday right through to the following Saturday. If you wanted the record on a second week, you paid another £250. The idea was that by the second or third week the record would be in the charts and so they would want to play it anyway.

It was a good system and I had no hesitation handing over the dough to get the first records by the Small Faces played on there. Everybody used to do it. To suggest it was somehow 'cheating' is absolute rubbish. I had a saying: you can't polish a turd. In other words, if the record's no good to begin with it still won't be any good after you've wasted your time and money getting it played. All I did was give those records a helping hand; public taste did the rest. The secret was to wait until you knew you had a winner, then drop the money. Otherwise it was all left to chance and it might be weeks before someone played it, by which time the shops would have stopped stocking it and the whole thing would be dead in the water. Get it in quick and make it a sensation – that was my motto.

To that end, another thing I got into doing was bunging a few quid in a bag to the guys on the music papers who compiled the charts every week. Every time I had a record out they would come by my office to pick up their envelopes. That's how I got 'Whatcha Gonna Do About It?' off the ground. I also employed a gang of chart 'fixers' to make sure the records we put out were being bought in sufficient quantities in the 'chart-return' shops – the record shops in which sales of individual records were counted and then passed on to the official chart compilers.

One of the best chart fixers I used back then would go from town to town, zero in on the poorest neighbourhoods, then knock on the doors at random and offer housewives ten quid to go into the right shops and buy the records, sometimes a dozen at a time. Ten quid was a lot of dough to those women and he had a network of them all over the country.

It was the same thing when it came to getting the group on TV. I had people – 'contacts' – on the payroll everywhere. I could phone up anybody you care to mention at the BBC and say, 'Fellas, I want this group on *Top of the Pops*' or whatever show I wanted them on, and it would be done.

Ultimately, though, the reason the Small Faces became popular was that they were a great group. Music-wise and performance-wise, they were unbeatable. After the first couple of hits, I changed tack and encouraged them to have a go at writing their own songs. I knew they were itching to do so and they came up with some top-drawer stuff like 'All Or Nothing', another Number 1, in 1966, which I produced for them myself and which still gets played on the radio today.

They were fortunate because in me they had more than just a manager who could open the right doors for them. It became the popular thing to say over the years that I bought the Small Faces their early success. Well of *course* I did! That was the name of the game and I played it to win. This wasn't some little idea that had taken off by accident. I had done my homework and all the people who played along with me did so for good reason. They were paid sometimes, yes, or I just called in a favour. But everyone who works in this business thrives on hits, on stars. They are what feed the entire industry. Because of that most people were only too delighted to get behind my records.

I even began to receive visits again from my old sparring partners in the police. They were sitting there waiting for me when I arrived at the office one morning. I took it as a sign that my career was in the ascendant again.

They came by a few times. It was a young detective the first time. A schmuck in a suit he hadn't grown into yet. He had a couple of thugs in uniform with him but I ignored them.

'We want to know how you get these fellows on top of the charts,' said the kid in the suit.

I looked at him. 'Don't you understand who I am?' I said. 'What it is I do? I was an artist for twenty years, now I'm an agent, record producer, promoter and manager. I'm in the entertainment business, for crying out loud! I'm not a racketeer. Getting records in the charts is what I do!'

Their response was something like, 'Ah, yes, but . . .'

As usual, the cops weren't interested in the truth. In my view, all they wanted to do was bag a showbiz celebrity. They couldn't touch the Beatles because by then the Beatles were like royalty in Britain. But they had apparently decided they could try it on with me. It's since been said that the police as an institution detested and feared the new rock-'n'-roll culture that was sweeping Britain in the mid-sixties. I think they were just pigs, as the hippies said. They hated what they couldn't understand, and they certainly couldn't understand me. My attitude was: you do your worst and I'll do my mine and we'll see who's still standing at the end.

I told the kid to get out. The next day he came back with his boss – another schmuck in a cheap suit. He tried another tack and opened with, 'What's all this business about you chinning some boys?'

I said, 'It's all fucking lies. What evidence do you have to the contrary?' Of course, they didn't have any – just what they'd heard. So I told him to fuck off, too.

Then one of the top guys from Scotland Yard tried his luck. 'We've heard you're doing deals with housewives up and down the country to buy your own records – is that true?' he asked me earnestly.

'I send lots of different people around the country on errands when my artists are on tour – you wouldn't believe the sorts of bizarre things artists ask for when they're out there performing every night. So, yes, I may have sent people out to buy me some records,' I said, keeping a straight face. 'Is there some law against that?'

'What, your own records?' he pounced, triumphantly.

'Especially my own records!' I replied without skipping a beat. 'Sometimes because I want to see if the pressings have come out correctly, sometimes just because we need extra records to give to journalists or other media people, to friends of the band, friends of friends – you know the sort of thing. Even the police sometimes.' I winked.

He looked at me as if he were going to faint. 'You don't have any friends in the police force!' he seethed.

'Oh, but I do,' I said, tapping the side of my nose.

'I see,' he said, seeing absolutely nothing. He didn't know whether to believe me or not. It was always the same with the cops. They didn't buy me as a goody and yet they couldn't put the finger on me as a baddy. It screwed them up. Well, that was their problem . . .

*

My time with the Small Faces also produced one of the most oft-told stories of my career, where it's said I hung Robert Stigwood by his ankles from a twentieth-floor balcony. As is often the case, the truth quickly got buried beneath a mountain of apocryphal details, new layers of which have been added to by everybody who has ever told the tale. For the first time ever then, allow me to tell the real story of the Robert Stigwood incident. Yes, I threatened to throw him off the balcony of his office. But no, I didn't personally hang him by his boots. I wouldn't have dirtied my hands on them. Here's what really happened.

By 1966, the Small Faces were the hottest new group around. Suddenly everybody in the biz wanted a piece of them. Eventually, Stigwood found out the address of the house in Pimlico and just turned up there on the doorstep one night. It was gone midnight but only Stevie and Kenny were in and they didn't know what to do. They sussed why he was there but they were too embarrassed not to let him in. They offered him a drink and he sat down and chatted to them, but they didn't know what to say to him, so after about thirty minutes he got up to leave. Fine. No harm done.

On his way out of the door, though, he turned to them and said, 'Oh, yes, I know what I forgot to mention. You should get a new manager – and I'd like to be that guy. Why don't you come and see me in my office some time?' And that was his big mistake. Going behind my back to my artists was never a good idea, not if you wanted to stay on my good side. But to try to steal my discovery – that was unforgivable. It had happened to me once with the Animals; it *wasn't* going to happen again with the Small Faces. I would make sure of it.

The boys phoned me the very next morning and told me all about it. We all had a laugh but I was pleased they had shown great loyalty to me by letting me know what happened – unlike the Animals, who bailed out without even having the courtesy to inform me first – and I decided an example needed to be set: to the group and to Stigwood – and to anyone else who thought about trying the same trick.

I put the phone down and quietly seethed. I wanted to kill him, but there are worse things than sudden death, and I decided Stigwood deserved something special for his trouble – something to remember me by. Then I had an idea. I got hold of Stan Simmons and we worked on it. Stan happened to be working at the time as a stuntman on the movie *Caesar and Cleopatra*, starring Elizabeth Taylor and Richard Burton, which they were shooting at Shepperton Studios, just outside London. There were literally thousands of extras on that movie, so I asked Stan to round up some of the biggest, nastiest-looking ones and offer them double whatever they were getting per day on the movie if they would come into town and act out a private little scene for me that afternoon.

A couple of hours later Stan walked through the door with ten of the biggest, ugliest-looking creatures you've ever seen. He introduced them to me one by one and, despite the way they looked, they were all nice, personable guys. I lined them up and I explained exactly what I wanted them to do, right down to the last detail. I had it all planned out in my mind and I rehearsed them through their scenes like a director. Anybody who didn't fancy it could leave right then, with their day's fee safe in their pockets, I said. But anybody who stayed and saw the job through would get a nice bonus at the end. Nobody left and an hour later we jumped into a couple of cars and drove over to Cavendish Square, where Stigwood had his office.

Contrary to legend, it wasn't on the twentieth floor, or anything like it. If you take a look around Cavendish Square, even though it boasts some of London's most impressive-looking buildings, you will find that the tallest are only four or five storeys high. Stigwood's office was actually on the fourth floor. We walked in unannounced, my guys and I, and everybody just froze. Then, just as we had rehearsed it, a couple of my guys locked the front door and took over the phones. I told everybody to stay calm and remain seated and said that we would be gone in a few minutes. Nobody moved.

Then I walked into Stigwood's office, followed by this triangle of guys, and just stood before him, looking down my nose at him. He began trembling.

'Don,' he said, 'what a pleasant surprise.'

'Cut the shit,' I said. 'You know why I'm here.'

'Is it about the Faces?'

I didn't even bother to answer. I just looked at him. Then I said, 'You know, you really shouldn't do things like that. That isn't showbiz, that's just bullshit. You should go out and find your own act, and build them, like I have done. Not try to steal them from other people – and especially not from me.'

I walked around his desk until I was standing over him. 'Now you must promise me you will never, ever, try to do this to me again.'

He was squirming by now. 'No, Don,' he said, 'absolutely not!'

'Because if you do,' I said, pausing for dramatic effect (I was enjoying this), 'this is what's going to happen.'

I lifted him out of his chair and dragged him over to the balcony. He was crying, 'No, Don! No, Don!' I stuck his head over the edge of the balcony rail and said, 'You see that fucking street down there? Well, that's where you're going the next time you fuck with me!' At which point I was going to give him a couple of digs maybe and leave it at that. Job done.

What I didn't know, however, was that my guys had decided to play a little gag on me and rehearsed an extra little scene of their own. Just as I finished my little speech about throwing this guy over the balcony if he ever messed with me again, one of them shouted, 'Fuck next time! Let's sling him now!' And they all rushed forward and took Stigwood out of my hands and lifted him up above their heads. Then they carried him right to the edge of the balcony and made as if to throw him off.

Stigwood must have gone into shock because his body went completely limp. It was as if he'd died. We left him there on the floor, not even moving. He never bothered me again.

Oh, how we laughed about it back at the office! But that was the finish of it, as far as I was concerned. I'd made my point; I wouldn't need to again. But of course, as soon as we left his office, Stigwood's staff, who had all been glued to the walls, got straight on the phones and started telling everybody what had happened – including the cops.

They were knocking on my door within the hour – a whole gang of them. They said, 'You've gone too far this time, Arden!'

I said, 'That's *Mister* Arden to you. And by the way, I don't know what you're fucking talking about. Has Mr Stigwood actually filed a complaint against me?' They had to admit he hadn't personally. It had been a member of his staff who'd rung them. I said, 'Well, you better go round there first, then, hadn't you?' And they left.

I must admit, I wondered what Stigwood would say. I didn't know him well enough yet to know if he was a squealer; I just figured he'd be smart enough to know I'd be back in double-quick time if he did say anything. To his credit, however, Stigwood kept his mouth shut.

And so the cops were forced to climb down again. It had become a habit for them whenever they had to deal with me and if they disliked me before they absolutely loathed me now. I didn't care. The feeling was entirely mutual.

By the time I went out for dinner that night the story of my encounter with Stigwood had gone all over London, but now I'd reputedly single-handedly hung Stigwood out of a window by his ankles. I didn't bother trying to deny it – they wouldn't have believed me, anyway – and overnight I became like the evil villain in a James Bond movie. By the time the story got to America, it was a window on the twentieth floor and I was the Jewish Terminator!

It was just nuts but that story continues to follow me around to this day. It's become the one story everybody knows about me. Even people who have never heard of me or can't remember Stigwood's name know the one about the music-biz guy who hung the other music-biz guy out of the window. I have even met people who have sworn blind that they were there with me the day it happened, because they can see it so clearly in their minds. But to me it was only a minor incident.

I didn't want to hurt Stigwood. I just wanted to frighten him – and get a laugh out of it, too. Otherwise I would have taken the real guys in.

Well, the laughter has never stopped. When I die they'll probably put it on my gravestone:

> Don Arden – Hung Robert Stigwood Out of Window.
> Ha Fucking Ha.

But there were other, far more serious situations I got into on behalf of the Small Faces. Like the time a local promoter of one of their early shows decided to play the old trick of holding back the group's cash as 'expenses'. He then added insult to injury by trying to hold onto £20,000 worth of new equipment that I'd just bought them. Big mistake.

Stevie called me up at home at one in the morning and told me what was happening. I said, 'Don't leave. Lock yourselves in the toilets if you have to but stay where you are. I'm on my way.' I got on the phone as I dressed and got my guys to meet me there. It was a dancehall just outside London. An hour later we met up in the car park. I gave them their instructions and we walked in – me and ten other guys. Not actors this time – these were my real guys.

The group were in the dressing room. I walked in and the boys pointed to a heavy with a bag in his hand – the bag with my boys' money in it.

I moved fast in those days. My motto was always: go in first. I walked straight up to this gorilla and said, 'Do you wanna leave a note? Have you got a son, a wife?' He looked at me, puzzled. 'Because you're dead,' I said. 'You're fucking dead!'

Then I grabbed the bag. He was too stunned to do anything; he just looked at me in astonishment. I opened the bag and looked inside. There was maybe two or three grand in there – in cash. I said, 'My boys were supposed to get a thousand tonight but you and your boss tried to stiff them. Not only that, but you tried to steal their equipment. That is fucking out of order. So now I've come to teach you a lesson. We'll take our grand, thank you – and whatever else is in this bag. As a little bonus for all this hassle you've caused us.'

I called Stevie over. 'This is your fee for tonight, son,' I said, and gave him the bag. Just then the promoter walked in with three or four of his own boys. He must have heard what was going on because one of his guys had a go immediately. A brave guy, but when we finished with him he was unrecognisable. Then the boys set about the rest of them.

I admit I may have overdone it a bit at that particular stage because we battered them until they were barely breathing. But a serious move had to be made. Most managers in that situation crapped out – that's why these guys got away with it. Maybe they'd try to sue them for the money later, but nothing would ever come of it, and the promoters would just go bankrupt the next week. But I wasn't 'most managers'. I was Don Arden, king of the jungle.

So we left these jokers all bloody on the floor, took the bag of money, loaded up our equipment and drove away laughing. The Small Faces put their arms around me and kissed me.

As my dealings with Robert Stigwood, Gene Vincent, Bill Haley and others have shown, I hope, I didn't always go straight for the nuclear option. Violence was only one method I employed to sort out my problems. Intimidation, mockery, even a well-timed gag could all send the same message: don't mess with Don.

By 1966, however, I was able to add a new and even more potent weapon to my personal armoury: my reputation as a hard man. As I was to discover, this could have certain disadvantages over the long term. Over the short term, however, fear became my number-one weapon. That kind of reputation tends to precede you everywhere you go and so people were wary of me before they'd even had a chance to speak to me. I recognised that and played on it. Suddenly it wasn't about what I did so much as what I might do – if you got on the wrong side of me.

When it came to dealing with the parents of the Small Faces, however, my reputation counted for nothing. All they saw – or thought they saw – was a guy in an expensive suit getting rich off the overworked backs of their poor little boys.

I hate to criticise other people's families. Stevie's mother worked, as did his stepfather, so they were never short of a bob or two. They had certainly been able to afford to send Stevie to the Italia Conti. And yet when I met him he was sleeping in the park. The story was that his mother had kicked him out and told him not to come back until he'd found a job.

Ronnie Lane came from a similar sort of background: working-class people who ran their own pub. He lived there with them until he met Stevie and formed the group. He had all the food and clothes he needed at home but again when I met him he was sleeping in the park. In that case, however, I think it was more his choice. He knew it would hurt his parents and I think he got a weird kind of kick out of that. He was a sick guy, in mind and spirit. He never considered anything that was done for him, yet, without first Marriott and then Rod Stewart to piggyback him to success, he would have been absolutely nothing.

As soon as the hits started rolling in, Ronnie, predictably, was the first one to mention money. But he was too chickenshit to talk to me about it himself. Instead, he sent his older brother round to see me. He was a big truck driver and I suppose he thought I would be frightened of him. He said, 'I've come here to talk to you about royalties.'

The conversation didn't last long!

I phoned Ronnie and he said, 'Oh, I don't know anything about it. Tell him to piss off.'

I said, 'I already have. I wasn't ringing you for advice. I was ringing to ask if I should kill him – because if he ever comes here again that's what I'll do.' That was the last I heard of Big Brother . . .

In the end, I held a meeting with all the parents after a piece appeared in one of the newspapers quoting them as saying how worried they were about their kids. 'This fella Arden works them too hard,' they said. 'He takes advantage.' So I brought them all in and told them in no uncertain terms what the real story was.

'Let it be clearly understood,' I said. 'The reason your sons are so tired is not because of all the fantastic work I put their way, but because they have parties every single night of the week. How do they manage it? Because they're all doing this . . .' I mimicked sniffing stuff up your nose. They all looked at each other in bafflement. They didn't know what on earth I was talking about.

'It's not just the drugs, though,' I said, ramming the message home. 'It's the girls, too. They're the ones that keep your sons up till dawn every night. All I do is feed them, clothe them, put a roof over their heads and earn them a decent living. So please can you stop saying all this stuff about me in the press?'

They just sat there looking at me like sheep. 'What about the money?' bleated Mrs Marriott. I thought, They're not even listening. I don't think it even sank in about the drugs. Well, that was their lookout. They were the ones who had expressed 'concern' when they spoke to the newspapers. So I told them how things really were with their precious little boys. But did they care? No, they didn't. The only thing they cared about where their sons were concerned was money, money, money.

Once that became clear I decided to put them all on exactly the same wage as the band had been on when they first started – £25 a week. The parents all later emphatically denied this, and said I was the most evil man in the world who had never paid a penny to them or their precious darlings.

The end came unexpectedly suddenly when, in 1967, I received a letter out of the blue from their new lawyer informing me that the group wished to dissolve the professional relationship between us. I suppose I had seen it coming. I had almost sold them to Brian Epstein before he died. He had come to me and told me he thought they could be even bigger than the Beatles. I didn't know about that but I did agree to talk to him about it.

We were still talking about it when he died. According to David Jacobs, he committed suicide. It didn't say that in the papers, but I can't say I was surprised. I was one of the last people in the business Epstein spoke to and it was clear to me his mind was clouded with despair. He had me to dinner one night just before he died and asked me if I would be willing to help him 'get rid' of Allen Klein. Epstein's contract with the Beatles was due to end and he thought Klein was going to 'steal the group' from him. I told him I would think about it. He was obviously in bad shape mentally and I wanted to help him but I wasn't sure what sort of help it was he really needed.

Then the day that Epstein was supposed to come back to me with an offer for the Small Faces, David Jacobs phoned to tell me he'd been found dead. According to him, Brian simply decided he didn't want to live without the Beatles. It's very sad that you give up your life for a poxy group. So, when the Faces sent me that lawyer's letter saying they wanted out, I took it philosophically.

Why did they want to leave? There were many reasons, probably. The main one, I think, was that they simply wanted their creative freedom. They were like kids ready to leave home. I had turned them into a hit-making machine but they saw themselves as more than that now. They wanted to be like the Beatles and the Stones and be recognised for albums, too. But this was in the days when you had to sell only thirty thousand copies of an album in the UK to have a Top Ten hit. We were always too busy putting out singles and EPs that sold ten times that number to worry about albums.

Not that they mentioned that in the lawyer's letter, of course. The main reason they gave there for wanting to leave, and the thing that still sticks in my craw today, was that they couldn't stand by any more and watch promoters getting beaten up. What can you say about that? I had risked life and limb for them. I could have gone to jail. At the time they never stopped telling everybody how wonderful I was. Yet that was one of the excuses they used in their lawsuit against me.

I don't deny that, when the chips were down and the call came, I was always ready with the appropriate measures. But they tried to paint me as a gangster. I was never a gangster. I didn't turn up at meetings surrounded by heavies. But of course the myths had built up by then and so everybody believed them.

Well, if that was how they felt, so be it. I washed my hands of them. Within a week I had paid everybody off and dissolved Contemporary. There were no artists on it other than the Faces. Within a few days of that I had sold their recording and management contracts for £40,000 to Harold Davidson. Harold was marvellous about it. He said, 'Here's your cheque, love,' and gave me a kiss on the cheek. Then we shook hands and arranged to go out for dinner later that week, and that was that. Problem solved, as far as I was concerned.

What was funny, though, was that Harold couldn't stand them. His scene was so different. Harold had Sinatra and Sammy Davis Jr. He ruled that world as I ruled the rock-'n'-roll world and we ended up doing quite a few things together over the years. But he didn't know how to handle these flash young kids at all. He would phone me up every day after he had taken them over, asking for advice. In the end, I had to get my secretary to tell him I was out!

What became of their finances after that was nothing to do with me. It was only after we split that they made all the accusations about me ripping them off. Like the Stigwood incident, it's the type of story that continues to follow me around to this day, and it pisses me off because it's simply not true. When I walked away from the Small Faces and wound down Contemporary, after all the bills had been paid, the group were owed precisely £4,000 in unpaid fees – which, although they never saw a penny of it personally, *was* sent. Four grand may sound like a low figure, but what the band have always conveniently chosen to overlook was just how much money they were getting through in their heyday. They may have looked and sounded like a million dollars when they were with me but they certainly never made anything like that as a group.

The money you actually earned as an artist from hit singles was relatively small once the few shillings a single sold for had been split various ways between the four boys in the band and all the people behind them like me who had made it a hit. Unless you had a million-seller every time, hit singles certainly didn't make you rich. 'Whatcha Gonna Do About it?' sold maybe half a million copies, but there were also records – like the *My Mind's Eye* EP – that probably sold only about fifty or sixty thousand, despite being a Top Ten hit. The biggest-selling record the Small Faces did with me was 'Sha La La La Lee'. I think that eventually sold over a million. But they didn't write that, of course, so they missed out on the song-writing royalties.

None of the hits they had with me in Britain were big hits abroad, either. The group managed only one hit single in America, for example, and that was 'Itchycoo Park', which came out after they'd left me. So we're not talking about millions of dollars in unpaid royalties here. The Small Faces probably didn't even earn into the hundreds of thousands. And what they did earn only paid off the enormous bill they had notched up with me.

Apart from the escalating costs of keeping a big band like that on the road, there was also the studio time to pay for and the wages of all the people they now had working for them. And then there was all the money for the clothes. Kenny Jones alone had almost a hundred suits, and he was just the drummer! When on one tour they started getting into the habit of throwing their jackets out into the crowd at the end of the show – the kids were killing each other to get one – I had to put my foot down. I said, 'Do you know how much those fucking jackets cost? Christ! If you'd told me you wanted to throw stuff into the audience I could have got you a nice deal on some monogrammed handkerchiefs. But whole suits? Gimme a break!' They just laughed at me.

And then there were the things they didn't want to know about, such as the money I laid out to get them in the charts. They didn't even want to talk about that, of course.

The lawyer they hired to get them out of their contract with me was Victor Gersten of the firm Gersten Nixon. Gersten struggled to build a convincing case against me. I didn't do anything to the Small Faces that any other top manager wouldn't have done back then. I might have done it more capably but that didn't make me a liar or a thief.

For the most part I just laughed and shrugged it off. Nevertheless, it was a black mark against my name and it has caused me great concern through the years. You could call me a ruffian for the way I dealt with those who threatened my livelihood, and I wouldn't disagree with you. You could say I played fast and loose when it came to getting my records in the charts, and I would take it as a compliment. But, whatever you do, don't call me a thief. I didn't *take* money from the Small Faces: I *made* them money. I took them from the gutter to the top of the charts and showed them a lifestyle they had only ever dreamed about. They should have been kissing my feet but instead they have spent years whingeing about me. So much rubbish has been said and written about those times.

And then you had bullshit artists like Tony Calder chipping in with their own little stories. Tony Calder was Andrew Loog Oldham's partner at a new record company Andrew had set up called Immediate. Calder was the one who started the story of my selling him the Small Faces' contract for £25,000 – delivered in a brown paper bag, because I needed the dough and didn't want the taxman getting his hands on it. Complete and utter bollocks!

The truth is, the Small Faces were then signed by Immediate Records. I liked Andrew and, despite his once telling me he couldn't see the commercial potential in the group at all, I wasn't surprised when he later went for the Small Faces. They were an established hit-making act: just the thing to get a new label off the ground. He was also smart enough to acknowledge his mistake and rectify it. To me, that showed he was someone I could take seriously. He wasn't just another money man: he was into the music and the clothes, too. He knew what the kids wanted because he was still just a kid himself – but he was also talented and astute and brave enough to do something about it.

There are so very few people in the business who were ever artists themselves. That's why I always felt I had an edge. If I made an observation to an artist it was because I had been a successful artist myself for two decades. Andrew hadn't been an artist – at least, not on stage. But he understood performance and image and music better than most people who had been performing for years. He also produced the early Stones records, told them how to dress, what to play, how to think. To me, he was an artist from head to toe and I always enjoyed talking to him whenever we met. We never argued about anything, never had a false word together. He always appreciated my talent and I appreciated his. We used to compare notes and piss ourselves laughing.

The fact that the Small Faces ended up with Andrew lessened the blow to me personally. I knew at least that they would be in good hands. And they were, whatever they may say now. They had more hits with Andrew and Immediate, including two of their most famous: 'Lazy Sunday' and 'Itchycoo Park'. But simple success was no longer enough to keep them happy: they wanted recognition. When the album that was supposed to give it to them, *Ogden's Nut Gone Flake*, failed to capture the critics' imagination on its release in 1968, the group collapsed. I heard that Stevie actually walked off stage halfway through a gig and didn't return.

Of course, that wasn't the end of them: Stevie went on to form the heavy-rock band Humble Pie, who did very well in America in the early seventies; and the rest of them went off to back Rod Stewart in the Faces, who did even better in America. But the fact that neither of those groups lasted very long shows how wrong they were to splinter the original line-up, which, frankly, made better records than either of them.

Indeed, if they had stayed with me I believe the Small Faces would still be around today. Ronnie died a few years ago of multiple sclerosis, but I doubt he would still have been in the group, anyway. I don't wish to speak ill of the dead but he was a poisonous little man. The more Stevie loved me the more Ronnie loathed and detested me. Sooner or later it would have been him or me – and then we could have got a new bass player in. A good-looking one who didn't bitch and moan about everything.

It was a different story with Stevie. Even after we split he always had good things to say about me, as did Kenny Jones. Whenever Stevie saw me he would run up and jump on my back and we would mess around for half an hour. It was an entirely different scene with Stevie than it was with the rest of them. Jet – the label I set up in the seventies – actually released the last couple of albums he made. But they weren't very successful. He was floating at that stage; his career was near its end. It was all very sad.

You couldn't keep him down for long, though, and he ended up playing in pubs and clubs with a pick-up band. He was still full of himself, still winding people up. I remember having dinner with David Gilmour of Pink Floyd not long before Stevie died. Dave said he'd recently been to visit Stevie and was worried about him. When he got there he'd found his front door smashed in. When Dave asked him what had happened, Stevie just smiled and said, 'Oh, Don Arden came round. He was pissed off with me and so he blew the door off its hinges!' It wasn't true of course. It was obviously just something he had said off the top of his head to divert attention from whatever the real reason was. But Dave believed it and was very upset with me and it took me about half an hour to make him realise it was just another one of Stevie's wind-ups. Stevie knew I would never do anything to harm him.

When Stevie died tragically young in 1984, after a fire at his home in London, a journalist called me and asked, 'Would it be true to say that Steve Marriott would be alive today if he had listened to you back in the sixties?' The answer I gave was, 'Yes, I believe it is, because I would have looked after him if he had. I always did.'

It's very hard to convince the public that their idols are just people who waited around for somebody to come along and mollycoddle them and make it happen for them – the way the Stones did with Andrew or the Small Faces did with me. They had the talent but lots of young groups have talent. They were stars because we made them so. We did everything for them.

When Stevie died it was because there was no one there to look after him, no one there to put his cigarette out when he fell asleep with it still alight in his hand. Say what you like about my methods, but, if he had still been with me, that wouldn't have happened. It's as simple as that.

7

Not having the Small Faces around any more freed up my time considerably. Not just my time but my thinking. I had proved I could take unknown new groups like the Animals and Small Faces and turn them into stars. Now I felt I was ready for anything.

My son, David, now accompanied me to most of my meetings. Even Paddles had briefly got involved in the business again when she managed John Lee Hooker for a few months as part of the Paviron Company that I had recently set up. Paviron – like the Davron management company I also later formed – was a name I invented composed of letters from all the family's names: the 'PA' from Paddles, the 'VI' from David, and the 'ron' from Sharon. (Likewise, Davron was simply David's and Sharon's names intertwined.) In the case of my wife, she had been involved behind the scenes in my business since the beginning, anyway, and she did great with John, who even had a belated hit single with 'Boom Boom'.

With David, and later Sharon, it was a case of showing them the business, teaching them the tricks of the trade. We all thought that John – one of America's original blues legends – was a terrific artist. Like most of them, though, he had his ways. I had breakfast with him once and watched him cut his bacon and eggs into little pieces, then scrape them into his bowl of cornflakes and eat the lot like that with a big spoon. And, like Chubby Checker, he was hardly leading-man material, either, but the women couldn't keep their hands off him.

That kind of luck with the ladies could be a double-edged sword, though. I went backstage one night at a gig I'd arranged for him at Oxford University and was accosted by one of the most beautiful girls I'd ever seen. She had a big, ornate-looking leather autograph book in her hands and so I asked if she was a fan. Silly question. 'Oh, I adore him!' she gushed. 'He's just the most wonderful singer in the world!' She was one of those. So I took her to the dressing room and when she finally came face to face with him I thought her eyes were going to pop out. 'Oh, my darling!' she cried. 'I have followed you everywhere!' John looked at me. He knew what I was thinking. Here's one of the most beautiful girls in the world and here's John Lee Hooker, an old black guy who looked as if he hadn't slept in a year, which he probably hadn't. I mean, you could understand the dolly birds swooning over Stevie Marriott – but this guy? Then she pulled out her autograph book, flung her arms around his neck and simpered, 'I want you to write something really nice to me!' I thought, He's had it now. John could barely write his own name. But he had been there a thousand times before, of course, and he just smiled.

'Well, darling,' he said, 'you're the most beautiful girl I've ever seen, but I can't write a message to you because I believe it ain't lucky.' Slick. But he wasn't completely off the hook.

'Oh, well,' she sighed. 'If you would just sign your name then . . .'

There was no way out of that. He took the book in both hands and held it up close to his face, then he took the pen and set to work. It must have taken him five minutes to finish the job. It felt like five years. By now, you might have thought she would guess what the problem was, but the silly bitch didn't get it at all. When he finally handed her back the book she thought he was taking the piss. She took one look and said, 'This is pathetic!' She looked at me. 'It's pathetic,' she repeated.

John just beamed at her. 'Yep, that's me all right,' he said. 'I is pathetic!'

The silly old sod thought it was a compliment. She stormed off. 'Nice kid,' he said. 'I wonder if she'll be back after the show.'

It took me days to get over that one!

It was also in the late sixties that I decided to branch out and bring over some non-rock-'n'-roll stars from America. The first was the movie star Jayne Mansfield. Jayne had been so popular back in the fifties that when she turned on the Blackpool Illuminations in 1959 more than 25,000 people turned up to see her do it – the largest crowd the event had ever attracted. Ten years on, her film career had nose-dived but I heard she now did a cabaret act, and I decided to take a chance and bring her over for some shows. Jayne was a nice enough woman, warm, friendly, funny. But she was also the typical mad Hollywood movie star. Her manager was Sam Brody, a lawyer who was also her boyfriend. They used to fight like cat and dog but somehow they seemed made for each other. The fights were like part of their sexual thing: they'd fight, then go to a room, lock the door and shag for two days. I walked in the dressing room on one occasion and she was on her knees combing his pubic hair. When they later died together in a car crash it was a tragedy of course, but somehow I think they might have wanted it that way, going out together like that in a blaze of headlines.

I had sold Jayne into the clubs for a small fortune, but unfortunately she didn't go down that well. She couldn't really sing, bless her, but then it was hardly her singing voice, or even her acting talent, that had made her so popular. She knew it and halfway through the act she'd always make a point of going down into the audience to sit on a few of the old boys' laps, flashing her gigantic tits at them. They loved it of course, but their old-biddy wives would get the needle and the show would go downhill from there.

Unfortunately, not all of my new ventures panned out quite so amusingly. Another non-rock-'n'-roll project I embarked on in the late sixties was an idea to bring the hit Broadway show, *Milk & Honey*, to London. A musical about Israel (the biblical 'land of milk and honey') it had a typically 'radical' sixties twist to it in that the story revolved around a boy dressed as a girl. I had seen it in New York and loved it, and so, when Larry Parnes came to me with the idea of bringing the show to London, I jumped at the chance. I had known Parnes since the fifties, of course. He used to tell people what great friends we were but I'd never liked him. I didn't like his crappy British artists like Cliff Richard and Billy Fury, and I didn't like the fact that he was always telling me what a mistake I was making getting involved exclusively in rock 'n' roll. But I had agreed to get involved on one condition: that we be equal partners and that everything – from the responsibility for making it happen to sharing the glory and the profits afterwards – would be split fifty-fifty. He said fine and we shook on it. Not that a mere handshake meant anything to an old operator like Parnes. He wasn't interested in honour: he was just interested in indulging himself. He was part of that homosexual showbiz clique that was obsessed with young boys.

Unlike someone like Brian Epstein, however, Larry was never particularly discreet about his sexual proclivities. For example, he was wealthy enough to live anywhere in London. He could have been living the high life in Mayfair like me. But no: heaven for Larry Parnes was an apartment on the Cromwell Road in what was then regarded as the downmarket end of Kensington. He bought it because it was directly opposite Baden Powell House, the headquarters of the British Boy Scouts. From his lounge window he could see into the little boys' changing rooms. He even bought a telescope to help him do it, the dirty pervert.

He loved gambling, too, and was hooked on the ponies. A day off for Larry meant sitting at home all day with the curtains drawn watching the racing on TV. He owned his own bookmaking firm and he'd sit there all day with the phone in his hand, making bets. All this was interspersed with little trips to the telescope to see how his 'lovely boys across the road' were getting on. David went there on an errand for me one day and Parnes hit on him immediately. He invited him in, poured him a stiff drink and asked him if he was interested in horseracing. As it happened, David did like a little flutter now and then, but as soon as he said so Parnes offered to open an account for him at his bookmaking firm, allowing David to make bets of his own for anything up to a grand. Not wanting to seem a schmuck, David had gone along with it. Big mistake. Imagine giving a teenage boy a grand to gamble with now. Back then, it was like giving him *ten* grand.

David went wild and before you knew it he'd spent the lot! That was when Larry made his move, chasing David on the phone, telling him to come over to Cromwell Road where there was 'more than one way to settle a bill'. But David ran a mile and wouldn't return any of his calls. So now the old queen was getting pissed off and had started calling me, demanding his money. When I found out what had gone on I wrote him a cheque and told him to get lost. Then I got hold of David and told him I'd strangle him if he ever put me in a position like that again.

Partly because of that, but mainly because Parnes and the writer started fighting over changes to the script that Larry had suggested behind my back, *Milk & Honey* never did come to London. I was furious. I must have made five trips to New York in the course of trying to put that deal together – only for Parnes to ruin the whole thing. I never spoke to him again.

I got my own back, though, when not long after that I released my own single – a cover of 'Sunrise Sunset' from the musical *Fiddler on the Roof*. Nobody in the business knew what to make of it. I think they thought I was off my head. I knew most of them did anyway, so what the hell! I did it very strait-laced, as it's supposed to be done, brimming with pent-up emotion. But it was all a huge joke. I did it simply to piss off Larry Parnes. There was a giant billboard on the corner of his street that you could see from his bedroom window. When 'Sunrise Sunset' came out I booked an ad for it on the billboard, which ran every day for two weeks, just so Parnes would have to see my smiling face when he woke up every morning! I used to imagine him pulling back the curtains every morning and screaming!

A rather more successful acquisition that I made back then was the Galaxy Entertainment agency, which I picked up as a job lot from an old pal named Ron King. Ron was great guy, he was an old-time promoter to whom I rented space in my Carnaby Street office so that he could set up a new agency in the sixties – Galaxy. I gave him the Small Faces as his first clients. Galaxy had a whole raft of acts, mostly second-division ones. But they did have the management and the agency contracts for Amen Corner, already a Top Ten act, and the agency contract for the Move, who were managed by Tony Secunda, another old pal from Brixton days. Both were Top Ten acts in Britain at that time, so I decided to get involved on the management side with Amen Corner personally, while I got my son, David, to liaise with Secunda and the Move on the agency side.

The rest of the existing Galaxy roster I turned over to my staff. By then I had so many acts vying for my attention it wasn't like the days of the Small Faces where I could give them all my personal attention. As a result, not all of them became stars. But that was no crime. Most of the acts I inherited from Galaxy were so ropey they were lucky I didn't just drop them in the river. But I didn't: I kept them working for as long as there was someone out there ready to cough up the dough. As long as the successes you do have are significant, the failures are soon forgotten.

Occasionally, as in the case of Neil Christian, a talented singer I looked after briefly who should have made it but quickly disappeared, I have to hold up my hands and say, 'You know what? Maybe I could have tried harder.' Sometimes, though, one just had to strike out. For instance, I picked up an act called Johnny Neil and the Starliners. They came to my attention when they won Hughie Green's popular TV talent show *Opportunity Knocks*. I saw them on the show one week and liked them so much I decided to sign them. I thought they had a future. They did – playing in pubs.

Another Galaxy group who should have made it but didn't – through no fault of their own – were the Attack. They were a good live band who had the right image for the time; they just didn't have any original songs that sounded like hits to me. I decided to give them a new song I had just picked up called 'Hi Ho Silver Lining' – a cracking tune I had discovered on a recent 'fishing' expedition to New York. I had been to the famous Brill Building on Broadway – a hugely important centre of American songwriting during the middle of the twentieth century – where I'd hooked up with Helios Music, a song-publishing company whose main writer then was Scott English. I took David with me for the experience and he fell in love with the place.

This was when the Brill Building still had all the great songwriters – names such as Scott, Neil Diamond, Neil Sedaka and so many others. Scott also wrote 'Brandy', which Barry Manilow – another former Brill songwriter – later recorded and had a hit with as 'Mandy'. Scott had played me two new songs he'd written: 'Bend Me, Shape Me' (which I gave to Amen Corner, who had a massive hit with it) and 'Hi Ho Silver Lining'. I did a deal with him for the sub-publishing on both of them and he gave me the finished acetates. What I didn't find out until later was that Mickie Most went there a week later and also got hold of an acetate of 'Hi Ho Silver Lining'. He was told I had the sub-publishing for the UK but he didn't care. Like me, he knew it was a hit and he wanted to record it with Jeff Beck.

Meanwhile, I had taken the Attack into the Decca studio, where they recorded 'Hi Ho Silver Lining' in a single session. It was a great version and I was sure it was going to be a big success. Then I discovered Mickie Most had done it with Jeff Beck and suddenly there was a race to see who could release their version first. As it turned out, both records ended up being released the same week and the whole thing quickly escalated into a war to see whose version would go the higher in the charts.

I did what I had to do to get it played on radio. As the publisher of both records, I got the sales figures back for both of them and, sure enough, for the first week they showed we were comfortably outselling the Beck version – but it was the

Beck version that was higher in the charts! I put more money behind it but the second week it was the same deal: on paper, the Attack were outselling Beck by nearly 2–1 but he was the one shooting up the charts. Clearly, even more money was being put behind the Beck version. At that point, I threw in the towel on the Attack record. One of the keys to success is knowing when to call time on a deal that's gone bad. Besides, I was in the comfort zone on this one – because I owned the publishing on both I couldn't lose. When Beck's version of 'Hi Ho Silver Lining' went to Number 1 – and stayed there for what seemed like an eternity – I even threw a party to celebrate!

It was also around this time that I had the misfortune to become one of the first promoters to bring Sly and the Family Stone to Britain. They were hot at the time – one of the first multiracial groups that combined rock and soul – and I'd been told they were a phenomenal live act. But the whole thing was a disaster from the word go. The opening night of the tour was at the Tottenham Royal, in London. But just before they went on Sly turned around and said, 'Hey, we haven't got two Leslie speakers for our organ. We've only got one.' It was an oversight, yes, but hardly one of earth-shattering proportions. It was too late to do anything about it now anyway, but we could get another one in the morning. Oh, no. This guy actually refused to do the show. Or, rather, the group went on stage, Sly said, 'Sorry about the equipment' and they started to do 'Dance to the Music' a cappella style, shaking tambourines. The audience didn't know what to make of it. Then some kid shouted, 'Ah, fuck off, ya black bastards!' And that was it: the group walked off.

It got worse. I actually had them booked to do a second show that night down the road with a local promoter I worked with sometimes called Irish Jerry. Jerry was a real character, a face. He must have been seven feet tall at least – and nearly as wide. When Sly insisted the band wouldn't be performing at his club either, Jerry lost his temper and dragged them out of the van by their hair and threw them onto the stage. 'I've got a club with a thousand kids in it!' he roared at them. 'And I don't let kids down, do you understand?' They shat themselves and did the gig, but the next day they'd hopped it, vanished, never to be seen again.

Other than the Move, the only consistently successful act to come out of the original Galaxy stable was the one whose management I had also inherited: Amen Corner. The singer and leader of the group was Andy Fairweather-Low, who would later become a sideman in Eric Clapton's band, among others. Even though he was hardly the most charismatic frontman, I acknowledged his talent, and he had the hits behind him to prove it. But there was always something between us that wasn't quite right and at first I couldn't put my finger on it. I just saw the potential and decided to go for it.

Just as I had with the Small Faces, I put them all up at their own house and I set about building their career, starting with 'Bend Me, Shape Me', which was their biggest hit to date. The more I did for them, though, the more distant Andy seemed to become. Then, one day, he and the group stopped returning my calls. I couldn't figure it.

It was also around this time, however, that I became aware of a new threat to my livelihood. It seemed that a certain group of misguided fools in London had clubbed together to form a loose association. According to my spies, apart from goosing each other, their main preoccupation seemed to be how to get rid of me.

I was tipped off by one of Phil Solomon's boys, another big Irishman. Big Jimmy, as we called him, had red hair and looked like a boxer but was really a lovely soft Irishman – though he was as mad as they come. It was Jimmy who told me that this group had taken out a contract on me. He said it was because they wanted to take Amen Corner from me. At first I was nonplussed. Like most Irishmen, Big Jimmy liked to embellish his stories and I didn't know how seriously to take this sudden news flash. But I had been around too long and made too many enemies to be sure, so I took precautions and immediately surrounded myself and the family with a few extra boys. Not just the usual crew, either, but friends of Big Jimmy's, some Irish boys. Suddenly, things were getting out of hand. Meanwhile, Amen Corner appeared to have done a bunk and I was convinced it was because one of those scumbags from that group had got to them. This, for me, meant an act of war. So now we're all tooled up in Denmark Street with the IRA on our side, and even I knew maybe this was going too far.

Then David came up with a good idea. He knew a promoter on the Isle of Wight named Wilf Pine, a bit of a heavy but nowhere in the same league as the IRA. He was someone we already knew of old: David used to book the Move and Amen Corner with him. The acts – particularly Allan Jones from Amen Corner – always liked Wilf. So David called Wilf and he agreed to come to London and help patch things up between us and Amen Corner, which he actually managed to do for a while. I liked Wilf as soon as I met him, and he had some good boys working for him – wonderful characters like Canadian Dave, Jinksy and Big Arnie – and so I moved them all into the top-floor rooms at Denmark Street and started to phase Jimmy and the rest of the Irish lads out of the picture.

My problems with Amen Corner didn't end there, however. I went to pick them up one day for an important TV appearance. It was a big deal that I'd gone to a lot of trouble to arrange for them and so I got to the house early to make sure everything was running smoothly. When I rang the doorbell, though, there was no answer. They were obviously out. I didn't like it. Even though I was early, they should have all been there, getting ready. I walked around the back of the house and – luck! – there was an open window. I climbed through it. As chance would have it, the room I found myself in was Andy Fairweather-Low's bedroom. I looked around. The walls were covered in pictures and other things. Not pictures of the group, though, but something else. It took me a few seconds to take it in. Then I realised what it was and nearly collapsed: the walls were covered from top to bottom with political memorabilia that I found personally offensive. I stood there, trembling with rage, and the doubts I'd always nurtured about him suddenly all made terrible sense. As far as I was concerned, that was it, no more second chances: he was out. I just said goodbye and did another sale – at which point the rest of the band left him too. They formed a new group called Judas Jump – which I then began managing in 1969.

They took on a new, much better-looking singer called Adrian Williams – who would later become head of promotion at Sony – and I signed them to EMI. Meanwhile, another band over whom I clashed with the group was Skip Bifferty, fronted by Graham Bell. Graham had been up to the house a few times with Sharon and David, so he was already part of the family, I thought, and I encouraged David to take control of the day-to-day running of the band. He treated them well and we got them a very nice deal at RCA. But that was one band we were wrong about. We thought they were destined for huge stardom but it just wasn't meant to be. Before I was to figure that out, though, I heard they'd also been approached by the group and the next thing I know they'd done an Amen Corner on me and vanished off the scene! My first thought was to hunt them down then go in all guns blazing, but David talked me out of it. David favoured the softly-softly approach and he persuaded me to let him go and talk to them first – and, if that didn't work, then go in with the heavies. I reluctantly agreed and it was the start of what would become our good-cop-bad-cop routine. Just to be on the safe side, though, I sent a couple of the boys with him – Canadian Dave and Jinksy – not tooled up, but just to be a couple of extra bodies there should David need them. David found Graham and the lads in some squat in south London and Canadian Dave and Jinksy waited in the car while he went inside to see them.

The band all liked David – he was like his mother in that everybody always liked him – and so they sat down and talked. They told him that, basically, they didn't know what to do, that they were frightened of me and the group. David told them not to worry, that I bore no grudges against them, and that whatever they decided would be all right with me – but just to let me know where I stood. They were just starting to come round to him when there was a knock on the door. It was the police. By now it was almost midnight and the cops had seen Dave and Jinksy sitting in the car outside and thought something funny was going on. So they went over and asked them what they were doing there. When they said they were waiting for David, the cops had gone to the house to check. Needless to say, this totally freaked the band out, and they now thought David must have been about to call in the heavies when the cops spotted them and inadvertently spoiled his plan. He tried to explain what was really going on but most of them were so out of their heads that they all thought they were about to die or something.

David left in despair. He went back to the car; the boys apologised, and then dropped him back home before heading off back to Denmark Street. When we got to the office the next day, however, both the guys and the car had disappeared off the face of the earth. For two days we looked for them. It turned out the cops who had stopped them earlier had been waiting for them outside Denmark Street, where they'd nabbed them and charged them with 'possession of dangerous weapons' – in this instance, a juggler's club they'd spotted on the back seat of the car. The cops had not allowed them to make a call, just got them straight up to Great Marlborough Street court, where they were put on remand and sent straight to Brixton Prison. It was unbelievable. Why such a big deal for a couple of small-time heavies who weren't actually doing anything? I got the lawyers involved and it turned out there was a police sergeant from Peckham, south London, who had a hard-on for me that wasn't going to quit. It was the familiar drill: poor little pop groups, big bad Jewish guy ripping them off. He was one of those schmucks who like to get into the papers and make names for themselves.

On the lawyer's advice, I told David to get his hair cut, then come down with me and the legal eagles to Holborn police station, where the boys had been charged. The cops took their time but really they had nothing to pin on them other than this bloody juggling club! So I said the club was mine.

'I use it to exercise with,' I said.

'Are you taking the piss?' one of them said.

'Certainly not, officer,' I said. 'I used to be a performer too, you see.'

God, they hated that. But what could they do? Canadian Dave and Jinksy left Brixton nick a couple of days later free men. Justice had prevailed again. After that, I began to hear less and less about the so-called group. They might have talked about sorting me out but the truth is they didn't really have the stomach for it.

At this point in my career, I found that I was at the receiving end of some annoying publicity, courtesy of a guy called Billy Gaff. To this day, I have never actually met Billy Gaff face to face or done any business with him. Yet the way he acted, you'd have thought I'd murdered his grandmother! It all stemmed from the fact that he had taken over the Small Faces after Stevie had bailed out and they'd persuaded Rod Stewart and Ron Wood to join them. Because of that, Billy always had this thing about me and how I supposedly screwed the Small Faces out of their royalties. That old story again. It was pathetic. He believed every word the group told him until he'd built up this monstrous picture of me in his mind. Eventually, he went to the journalist Paul Foot, who was then working for the satirical magazine *Private Eye*, and got him to do a so-called 'expo' of my business dealings. The nephew of the future Labour Party leader Michael Foot, Paul went on to become a well-respected campaigning journalist and author, and when I spoke to him years later he more or less apologised for the story.

'I was young then,' he said. 'I didn't know how the music business worked and that you hadn't actually done anything that unusual.'

As far as I was concerned, the *Private Eye* thing was no biggie. It was an irritant but very few people actually read the magazine, anyway, so it didn't really matter. What did piss me off, though, was that Gaff then raised the stakes by going to the *News of the World* – the biggest-selling Sunday tabloid in Britain – and persuading them to do the same story, but in even more lurid detail. That was when I said, 'Enough! If this prick wants to fight dirty, I'll show him dirty.' And that was when I turned the tables on him and did the famous *News of the World* article on 2 July 1972 with the headline THEY CALL ME THE AL CAPONE OF POP.

It happened like this. The paper had originally put two of their top investigative journalists, Trevor Kempson, who's now dead, and Ray Chapman, onto it and they started going round talking to people about me, both on and off the record. They did the rounds, though, and got nowhere. Sure, they got plenty of people badmouthing me but no actual evidence of criminal activity. And that was when I spotted my chance, made contact with them, and offered to give them an exclusive, as long as it was told from my perspective and to hell with Billy Gaff – and they agreed. It was great, in exchange for a no-holds-barred interview with me, the journalists – without the paper's knowledge – gave me copies of all the tapes they had compiled, openly and surreptitiously, of people talking about me, including one of Gaff saying things like, 'His wife goes round dripping in diamonds and mink coats. I'll have those mink coats off her!' I thought, Well, if that's what they think of me, I'll give them what they want. And in the story I let every arsehole I could think of have it. Billy Gaff, Tony Secunda – they all got what was coming to them as I proceeded to make myself the most infamous music-business figure in the land.

Before the article appeared, though, I decided there were one or two faces that weren't well known enough to be damaged in that way, but which I felt deserved some sort of response from me nonetheless. For example, we sometimes used an independent publicist called Keith Goodwin. Keith was a lovely guy but he had an assistant named Mike. One of the tapes the *News of the World* had given me was of Mike slagging me off, saying that my acts were all terrified of me and that he would have nothing to do with me – this at a time when I was actually employing him! So I asked Keith in for a meeting and told him to bring Mike with him.

When they turned up I played it cool. I looked at Mike and said, 'Look, tell me what I've done to you.'

He said, 'What do you mean?'

I said, 'Well, I must have done something to you because I heard you've been going round town badmouthing me.'

He feigned astonishment. 'No, Don,' he said, 'you know that's not true! I fucking love you! I tell everybody you're the greatest!'

At this point I turned on the tape recorder and we all sat there in silence for a few moments while we listened to Mike slagging me off. I kept my eyes on him the whole time, watching the blood drain from his face. Then I turned the tape recorder off again.

'You say I've done nothing to you,' I said. 'Well, I have now!' I leaned over the desk, picked him up by his hair and cracked him a good one right in the mouth. 'Now fuck off,' I said.

I didn't touch Billy at that point: I just left him to stew over the *News of the World* article. Things didn't end there, though, and a couple of years later he tried to mess with me again. At the time I'd just done a deal for ELO with Warner's – whose label the Faces were also on – and ELO wanted to bring a bassist named Mike Albuquerque into the band. Mike had previously been in a group that Gaff had once looked after. The next thing I knew, Gaff had sent a telex to Warner's office in London saying he represented Mike Albuquerque and threatening them with legal action if they tried to use him in ELO without his permission. It was bullshit, but it caused me no end of trouble until I assured the label that I'd sort it out personally with him.

Oh, I'd sort it out all right. After everything I'd already been through with him this was the last straw. I decided it was time to pay Mr Gaff a visit at his office. I took an associate with me. I remember Paddles telling him to stick with me and when it was all over to point me in the right direction for the exit. She knew that when I got upset I could never find the door. So we went round there, charging in, demanding to see him. But they said he was out. That only made me madder, and I began tearing the place apart. I turned the desks over, smashed everything I could get my hands on and threatened to do the same to anyone who tried to stop me. Once I was satisfied he really wasn't there, my associate got me out of there again and I went back to my office. Within an hour, Warner's had, as I intended, received another telex from Gaff's office saying that actually it would be OK for Mike Albuquerque to join ELO after all. Years later, when we were living in LA, David told me he was in a club one night when he saw Gaff walk in and take a table. David sent him a note: 'Hi Billy, baby. Sorry to see you're still not big enough to fit my mum's fur coats.' He said Gaff literally got up and ran out of the door!

The biggest group I took on after the Small Faces – and the group, though none of us could have known it then, who would eventually transform all our lives beyond recognition – were the Move. They were a good little outfit from Birmingham whom I had first come across on the Midlands ballroom circuit a few years before when they were known as Carl Wayne and the Vikings. Like the Small Faces, the Move would never be as big as the Beatles or the Stones. But they had a wonderfully flamboyant image and a consistently winning way with a pop melody, which saw them notch up an impressive string of hits in the late sixties, including such Top Ten classics as 'I Can Hear the Grass Grow', 'Flowers in the Rain' and 'Fire Brigade'.

Off the back of that, their manager Tony Secunda had built them into a £300-a-night act. Not major money but better than most. That was as far as Secunda was ever going to take them, though. Tony was a familiar face from Brixton days, and I had always thought of him as a nice, polite young guy. I didn't think that any more. I found him virtually unrecognisable from the happy-go-lucky kid we used to know. Now he was a screwed-up middle-aged monster who couldn't manage a piss-up in a brewery. He had such a crummy attitude that no one wanted to do the group a favour. He was starting to hold them back.

He even got them into trouble with the prime minister, Harold Wilson, when he mailed out dozens of copies of 'Flowers in the Rain' in a sleeve with faked pictures of a naked

Wilson on it. As a PR stunt it certainly got them on the front pages – but for all the wrong reasons. Wilson had been furious and actually sued the silly bastard. Secunda was even forced to give up all the publishing rights to the song. As a result, he lost them hundreds of thousands of pounds. The problem was, like so many people by then, he was just totally wrecked on drugs the whole time. I kept being told by starry-eyed young dickheads that drugs were 'mind-expanding'. All they did for Secunda was turn him into an arsehole. That was why the group eventually wanted to get away from him. Not that he could see it.

It was like when Mick Jagger eventually got rid of Andrew Oldham and Andrew asked why. 'Too much of this,' said Jagger, tapping his nose. He meant drugs and he was right. Andrew was doing too much of everything by 1967. He accused Jagger of hypocrisy, pointing out that he never stopped taking drugs. Jagger didn't deny it but pointed out that he was the artist – 'therefore I can do what I want'. But Andrew was supposed to be the manager and therefore had to 'see that everything is right'. Andrew had no answer to that because there wasn't one. Jagger was right. You can't all act like musicians; someone has to lead the line. But at least Andrew had the satisfaction of knowing he had taken that group and turned them into something truly special, something history-making. With Secunda, all you had was another schmuck who won the lottery. But, instead of making the most of his luck, he shoved it all up his nose. He got himself into such a terrible mental and physical state that everything he did for the Move turned rotten – which is how they eventually ended up coming to me.

When I became indirectly involved with them through my acquisition of their agency contract with Galaxy, Secunda became distinctly worried. He knew Charlie Wayne adored me and that it was only a matter of time before he would start talking to me about the group. Initially, though, I had nothing to do with them personally. It was David who actually booked them for the agency. He was seventeen and determined to prove himself to me, so he worked his arse off getting them some plum TV bookings and getting their fee up to £500-a-night. David felt he could take them even further than that – if only the group would also start producing credible hit albums. Whether Secunda saw it like that, I don't know, but he certainly didn't appear to encourage them in that pursuit. Once they became famous, I don't think he really did anything for them other than collect the money.

Then, one day, Charlie came to see me with Roy Wood, the singer and writer of most of their hits. They came straight to the point. 'We've got a new record coming out that we think is our best yet and we don't think Secunda's going to be able to do it justice for us. We want you to manage us, Don.' I asked to hear the song. As soon as they played it I said yes. The record was 'Blackberry Way' and Roy wasn't exaggerating: it was fantastic, as catchy and inventive as anything the Beatles were coming up with. I could see why they were concerned. Secunda was a washout by then, while I was still king of the hill – the guy Secunda used to run errands for.

So we came to an agreement. The record came out before we could even get the papers signed but as an act of good faith I began work on it immediately. Needless to say, it smashed straight into the charts on its first week of release, and the group all came rushing round my office to celebrate. When I shoved a contract under their noses they couldn't wait to sign it.

When Secunda found out, he went insane. He was already the type of person whose jealousy could easily cloud his vision and he hated the fact that I had known him when he was an eager kid looking for a break. When he then lost the Move to me, he took it personally and started walking around telling everybody how he was going to 'do' me. I heard on the grapevine that he'd gone as far as looking into taking out a contract on me. He was going to hire this cheap East End hood known to everybody. So I had him warned off. Once it became clear that if anything happened to me he would be dead himself within the hour, he decided to see sense and never bothered us again. I never stopped hating him, though. I still hate him now, even though he's dead. He was the type of Jew who gives Judaism a bad name. He committed suicide in the end and I like to think he did it because he finally realised what a bastard he was. I was sorry when I heard, though.

Tony Secunda got off lightly compared with what I did to Clifford Davis, who was then managing Fleetwood Mac. Clifford Davis was one of those tossers who think smoking a cigar makes you a big man. He was also foolish enough to think he could interfere with the Move and get away with it. The Move were doing *Top of the Pops*, when Davis made the fatal error of approaching Charlie Wayne and telling him that he should manage them – and that he'd certainly do a better job than that schmuck Don Arden. The next day, when Charlie called me and told me what had happened, I decided a little visit to Clifford's office was called for.

I took Wilf Pine with me and turned up there unexpectedly later that same day. I walked in, straight past the secretary and into his office. He was sitting behind his desk with a big cigar in his mouth, playing the big guy. He had seen me come in and didn't move, tried to play it cool. He started going on about how he came from a tough old family from the Elephant & Castle, a rough area of London, as if that was supposed to impress me.

'Just remember, Don,' he said, 'I know where you live.'

But the cigar in his mouth was so big you could barely make out what he was saying. He was so corny that he was laughable. But I didn't laugh. I just looked at him.

'What did you say?' I said. 'I can't understand you.'

'I said I know where you live,' he repeated.

I walked over to where he was sitting and stood for a while looking down at him.

'No, sorry,' I said, 'I still can't hear you properly. Here, let me help you.'

I took the cigar out of his mouth with my right hand and grabbed him by the back of the head with my left, all in one easy movement. Then, holding him tight, I drilled the lit end of the cigar into the middle of his forehead. He struggled of course but I was too strong, too intent upon my work, and I held him there for a long time until he went limp. I wanted to see if I could actually penetrate his forehead with that thing. Eventually the crushed embers of the cigar fell down between his knees and burned a hole right through his trousers and into the leather chair he was sitting on. I started to laugh.

He was upset, of course, crying and moaning and all this sort of thing. But by then he didn't even have the strength to lift his hand to brush it off. In the end I was laughing so hard I had to stop. When I left there that night I felt so good I dismissed my driver and decided to walk home. Stuff like that made you feel alive.

Then later – out at a club maybe, drinking champagne with Wilf and David and the boys – we'd all piss ourselves laughing as I told them the story, celebrating our success and toasting the demise of our enemies. They were great days to be alive. The funny thing was that Davis's partner, Peter Walsh, rang me the next day to complain I'd burned a hole in his chair! 'You'll have to pay for it!' he sobbed. He wasn't worried about poor Clifford sitting there with a bloody great cigar sticking out of his head. But that was Walsh for you, a born grocer, always counting the pennies.

By the early seventies I had moved office yet again, this time to a flat I had bought in Berkeley Square. The family had also moved, down to a large mansion house in Wimbledon. We also had the beachside flat down in Minnis Bay near Margate, which Paddles and I still used as a summer house, and the early years of the seventies found me up to all sorts of new tricks – among them the legendary rock group Grunt Futtuck! Sometime early in 1971, Andrew Loog Oldham had come to me for help. He had made a huge initial splash with his label Immediate but had bailed out when things started to become too much like hard work – Andrew was a creative genius, not a nine-to-fiver.

Now he was strapped for cash. He needed a lump sum to start up somewhere else again and so he came and asked me if I would help him raise some readies.

Andrew was family to me by then and so of course I agreed, and together we cooked up one of the maddest schemes ever. Andrew knew I was friendly with Freddie Bienstock at the publishing company Carlin Music. He suggested we go there and ask for a deal.

'For who?' I asked.

'I don't know,' he said. 'We'll just blind 'em with science.'

As it turned out, Bienstock also had his own small-label deal with EMI, so I called him and he arranged a meeting for Andrew and me with the guy who was running the label for him. By the time we arrived, Andrew and I had it all planned. It was simple: we had discovered a great new band and out of the goodness of our goddamn hearts we wanted to offer Freddie's label the chance to release their first single. The guy was only too delighted.

'Great! Great!' he said. 'Let's hear it!'

So Andrew pulled out this tape – God knows where he got it from – and stuck it on. It sounded like the most awful heavy-rock bollocks to me, a horrible, tuneless noise from start to finish. But this fellow who was running the label for Freddie was not a prick: he was a *gigantic* prick! He started going into rapture. 'Oh, Jesus Christ!' he enthused. 'This is fantastic, absolutely fantastic! I must have this!' Andrew and I were looking at each other, trying desperately not to laugh. Then the tape finished and this schmuck says, 'Jesus, what do you call this group?' Andrew just looked at him very calmly and, in a voice as quiet as a whisper, he said, injecting a little drama into his delivery, 'Grunt . . . Futtuck.' This guy almost had a heart attack. 'Oh my God!' he cried. 'What a brilliant name! Pure genius, pure genius! Grunt Futtuck! Yeah!'

Then it was my turn for some fun. We knew he would be only too well aware of our reputations and that he would be nervous about discussing money. We played along and acted as if we were too big to bring the subject up. But of course he couldn't let us walk out of there without some mention of it, and, as we got to the door, he was clearly unable to contain himself any longer, and, grabbing me by the arm, he said, 'How much do you think I'll have to pay for this?' It was only a one-off deal but I held up all ten fingers – meaning ten grand, a fortune for a single in those days (people made albums for less). 'Pounds?' he said. I turned very serious. 'Of course,' I said.

We received the cheque for £10,000 the next day. He was so keen not to lose out on the Grunt Futtuck deal that he couldn't wait to give us the money. It was fantastic, the easiest deal I ever made. Talk about cutting out the middleman! I thought, If only you could do all deals like this – without having to worry about some fucking band! It wasn't as if we took them completely, either. We gave them the tape they'd paid for and they released it. The top brass at EMI said: 'Gee, who did this?' When they were told it was this new group from Don Arden and Andrew Oldham they said, 'Jesus, we must get behind this!' It was all red hot.

Yet, to this day, I still don't know who it was on that tape. I think it was probably just Andrew playing around on his own, drunk one night in the studio. Eventually, of course, it all came out and caused an enormous stink. But, since he was the sole beneficiary of the deal, I left that part for Andrew to handle. God knows what he said but Freddie Bienstock never forgave me for it.

I last saw Freddie in the early nineties and he was still upset with me over it. We bumped into each other somewhere and started chatting and I noticed that he was a bit cool. I said, 'What's the matter with you, you old cunt?' He's Viennese and he said in his accented English: 'Well, you know, Don, I like you, but sometime I remember, you sold me a group that did not exist.'

I said, 'Fucking hell! Is that all?'

Ten grand to Freddie was like ten quid to anyone else. But he never forgot it. In fact, the longer I spoke to him the more broken-hearted I realised he still was over it. But then Freddie wasn't beyond pulling a few strokes of his own back then; like anybody who makes it in showbiz, he had his fair share of 'luck' too.

Another what you might jokingly call 'semi-fictional' singer I had great fun with that year was the world heavyweight champion boxer, Joe Frazier. I brought Joe over to Europe not long after he became the first man ever to beat Muhammad Ali, in their legendary 1971 fight at Madison Square Garden. I brought him over not as a boxer, though, but as a singer. I got the idea of approaching him when I read that he'd actually done a couple of shows at a nightclub in America. I was intrigued and thought other people would be, too, and so I offered to put on a tour for him.

I got on the phone and spoke first to his people and then to him. I think he was unsure at first, but they explained who I was and once he realised I was perfectly serious he thought it was a great idea. He arrived in London about a month later. I had never actually seen him perform before, except on TV as a boxer, and I didn't really know what to expect. I just figured his status as world heavyweight champ would ensure ticket sales. But Joe was actually a pretty good singer and dancer, and it was an impressive revue-style show he had brought with him. There must have been forty different people in it: musicians, backing singers, gorgeous dancers, the full nine yards.

We toured the UK for about six weeks and I had him doing TV, radio, newspapers – the whole thing caused a big splash. Then we set out on the Continent and, if anything, he made an even bigger splash with shows in Hamburg, Paris and Vienna. What I liked about Joe most, though, was his character. I admired him for what he had achieved in the ring, particularly against the seemingly omnipotent Ali. But, after I got to know him, I also found him to be a genuinely good and intelligent person and I respected him enormously as a man.

You don't necessarily expect heavyweight boxers to be the sharpest knives in the box, but Joe was shrewd. Like me, he could size people up in a second. He'd learned the hard way how to separate the goodies from the baddies. And, while he was very serious about his work, he also had a wonderfully understated sense of humour. People who hadn't spent any proper time in his company – like the press – would miss it completely. They just didn't get him at all. But I did. He was a poor guy from the slums who had used his brains as well as his brawn to fight his way to the top – no matter how many times people told him he was wasting his time. In some ways, it was like looking in the mirror.

On one occasion we were on a plane and he said, 'There's a guy sitting behind us, big fella, and when he's plucked up enough courage he's going to approach me with some silly questions. He wants to know just how tough I am. When that happens you're gonna have to be there to deal with it for me, OK? I'm considering it your job because I know you can handle it – and because I can't. When you fight for your living you can kill somebody with a punch and I don't wanna kill nobody.'

No sooner had he spoken than this chap got up to approach him. I moved fast to intercept him. 'The champ's trying to sleep,' I said. 'Go back to your seat.' And I gave him one of my coldest shark-eyed stares and put my hand into my jacket pocket as if to reach for something. He immediately sank back into his seat, where he stayed for the remainder of the flight.

Later in the tour, in Sweden, I had booked Joe into a huge nightclub in Stockholm. It was very plush: everything was red, gold and black. It looked more like a whorehouse than a nightclub with a stage at one end, circled by tables and chairs, where you could have dinner, and a large dance floor in front of it. Joe took one look at the place and told me to be on 'special alert' that night for 'jealous husbands and boyfriends'. Sure enough, as I was watching from the wings that night, I spotted a young couple towards the front who seemed to be working up to something. The guy was yelling in her ear but the girl was ignoring him and just staring at Joe. You could tell she was fascinated by him, but the more she stared the more uptight the guy was getting. I thought I'd better go down and have a closer look.

Being heavyweight champion of the world – with the physique that goes with that mark of distinction – Joe did a nightly routine in which he got the audience to persuade him to take off his shirt. He had just got to that part of the show as I got to within a few feet of the unhappy couple. They were still rowing, but now she was really giving it to him.

As Joe took off his shirt, I heard her say, 'Wow, look how strong he is, how beautiful!'

This was obviously the last straw for the poor schmuck next to her. 'I'm stronger than him!' he screamed.

I could see what was coming next but before I could get my hands on him he'd already started to make his way up onto the stage, heading straight for Joe. I pushed everybody out of the way and chased after him but by the time I got on the stage he already had his hands round Joe's throat. To his credit, Joe never moved a muscle. He could have killed this lunatic with one blow to the side of the head but he never even raised his hands. He saw me coming and that comforted him, I think. I had actually just had a cartilage operation on my knee and was still recovering, so I had a walking stick with me, and I used that to knock this raving idiot out. He was so intent on strangling Joe that I was able to take aim. I clubbed him good, once behind the ear and a second time across the back of the head as he was going down – just to make sure. Once I was certain he was out cold, I signalled for the boys in the wings to come and carry him off. Joe apologised to the audience for the 'minor interruption', everybody cheered and the show resumed.

It was actually quite a good night after that. This was a Joe Frazier audience, after all. A bit of blood and guts just added spice to the show. As we travelled together, Joe would tell me old boxing stories about Joe Louis and Sonny Liston and I would tell him stuff no one knew about Sam Cooke and Little Richard. And, of course, we talked about Ali and his fight with him. He knew there would be at least one more fight between them and Joe wanted there to be so he could beat him again and prove that the first victory wasn't a fluke. (As things turned out, Ali would defeat Joe in 1974 and again in 1975.)

But he didn't hate Ali in the way people say he did. He didn't even appear to dislike him whenever we talked about it. Maybe beating Ali had taken the sting out of his Uncle Tom taunts. But it seemed to me that Joe rather liked Ali. He just didn't respect him any more. He thought all that Black Muslim business (Ali had changed his name from Cassius Clay some years before on joining the movement) was totally fake, and again I had to agree with him.

Just as the sixties had ushered in a new era in music that not all of us who had first made our mark in the fifties were fortunate or clever enough to survive, the dawn of the seventies saw the start of another new chapter in the story of rock 'n' roll. Like the decade it reflected and perhaps helped shape, rock had become self-absorbed for the first time as albums overtook singles as the main focus for most major artists, many of whom hardly even released singles now. Rock had lost its innocence and suddenly everything was exaggerated – the music, the clothes, the hair. Nothing was simple any more. All the drugs that swamped the music scene in the late sixties had seen to that. Now music had to mean something deep or it wasn't worth a dime. At least, not in the albums market – and the albums market was where you wanted to be if you intended to play the game seriously in the early seventies.

As ever, the wind of change was something I responded to positively. If anything, changing the rules had got me interested in the game again. I looked at the success in America of British groups like Led Zeppelin and Cream and thought that here was a new way to play the game that I hadn't proved I could master yet, and I badly wanted to give it a go. It was then that I first became involved with the two groups who would, in a roundabout way that still has echoes to this day, have a profound effect on my life like no other artists before or since: the Move, who were about to metamorphose into the Electric Light Orchestra, or ELO, as they soon became known; and Black Sabbath, featuring a complete nutcase on vocals called John Michael 'Ozzy' Osbourne. I first saw Black Sabbath play live in

London, in 1970, at the Marquee club in Wardour Street. They had just released their first album but it was the first time they'd ever been to London and no one in the biz knew anything about them yet. At the time, I was trying to get the first Judas Jump album off the ground, but, despite getting EMI to shell out a fortune on promotion, we weren't really getting anywhere. However, I noticed that an album by another new band – Black Sabbath – had gone into the charts without any promotion whatsoever. I thought, Who the hell *is* this? I'd never heard of them, which was unusual for me then.

I told Wilf Pine to look into it for me and that was when we found out about the Marquee show. 'Heavy' rock – or 'heavy metal' as it also later became known – was the new 'in' thing at the time, and Sabbath's music was very much in that style. If anything, it was even darker, more convoluted than what else was out there. I wasn't sure how much I liked it but I had to admit that it was exciting. You certainly couldn't sleep through it!

The band had a good name, too. It conjured up an image in your mind immediately, which they played on by wearing crosses and adopting a very serious manner. The whole package was just there. They fitted right in with what was going on in that scene, but, like all the greats, they also had a little bit of something no one else had.

Ozzy, the singer, looked like a genuine mental case. He howled and hooted and ranted and raved – I couldn't understand a single word of it but he never stopped moving, never stopped communicating with the crowd, getting them going. He was obviously mad but absolutely brilliant with it. To me, Ozzy was so obviously a star from the word go. He may not have been the greatest singer in the world, but as a performer he walked away with everything. He was a winner. I decided there and then that Black Sabbath would be my next signing.

There were several other faces I recognised there that night from the biz, all sniffing around, as I was, all watching each other out of the corners of their eyes to see what everybody else thought of this phenomenon. So I deliberately played the whole thing down, yelling in one of my corny old gangster voices, 'Fucking hell, boys! What's this load of old crap?' Meanwhile, they were standing there, these nobodies, saying, 'Ooh, yes, Don! Quite right, Don!'

Then, as soon as they finished their set, I went backstage and introduced myself. 'Boys,' I said, 'you are superstars and I am going to make you a million dollars!' They all just looked at me as if I were crazy. I was so excited I told them I'd get their records to Number 1, put their faces on giant billboards, take them to America – everything. But the whole thing backfired on me. They were just kids from the sticks who'd never seen a ten-pound note, let alone a million dollars, and I scared the living daylights out of them. In the end, they just didn't believe me.

Years later, Ozzy told me, 'We thought you were mad. People coming through the door and saying they're gonna make you millionaires only happened in the movies.' They didn't know yet that my whole life was like the movies! So, instead of signing with me, Ozzy and the boys did something they regretted for the next twenty years: they signed with another so-called partner of mine, Patrick Meehan! Patrick was an old duffer who had been with me for years and I couldn't believe it when it came out that he was the one who had stitched me up over the Sabbath deal. What made it worse was that he took Wilf Pine with him. I had considered Wilf a good friend until then.

We'd had a meeting the morning after the Marquee show, in which it was decided to make a formal proposal to take over the band's management. Until then, they were looked after by a small-time local guy, Jim Simpson, who was looking for a payoff, which was fine by me. But, within a month, Meehan left the company suddenly. I was surprised: he was a doddery old git and I couldn't see where he'd go without me. But he said he was leaving to take part in a new venture with his son, Patrick Junior. I shrugged and wished him good luck. A few weeks after that, however, Wilf also left the company. The Sabbath deal was dead anyway by then, though I still couldn't figure out why. Then, when Pine left, I found out he'd teamed up with the Meehans, and that was when I started to get the picture. Of course, if you talk to Ozzy and the guys now, they will deny that that was what happened. But they were only the artists, just kids. What would they have known about this business? I decided not to interfere. The group had made their choice; they would have to live with it.

Ultimately, none of them had anything to do with the success of Ozzy and Sabbath – that band would have been big no matter who managed them. For the time being, then, I filed them all in my mind under the heading: 'unfinished business'.

8

On paper, becoming involved in ELO was a much more straightforward proposition than trying to take control of a totally unknown new group like Black Sabbath. Born from the ashes of the Move, ELO already belonged to me, whether I liked it or not. And at first, I wasn't sure that I did. In fact, following my little set-to with Clifford Davis, I became briefly disenchanted with the Move. It felt like the Small Faces all over again. Despite a string of hit singles, we could never quite get an album off the ground with them. They'd release one and it would sell, but no one really took it seriously, which is what they were after of course: critical acclaim. Meanwhile, most of the guys with critical acclaim would have given their right arms to have the sort of chart success with their singles that the Move had. It was the same old story: the grass is always greener on the other side of the fence.

Now I had started to feel the same way, perhaps. And so I did something completely perverse and phoned Peter Walsh and said, 'I'll tell you what: you and Davis want the Move? Write me a fucking cheque and you can have them.' He couldn't believe his ears. At first he was suspicious, but I made it clear I wasn't joking, he wrote me a nice fat cheque, and I let him and the walking cigar have them. Looking back, I think I wanted to make a point, to teach them all a lesson. I knew they'd soon regret leaving me. Whatever anyone said about me, when I represented artists I looked after them. They would be treated like kings wherever they went; everything was laid on. Let Davis and Walsh see what it was actually like to try to fill my shoes. Getting an artist from me was like accepting a curse.

Sure enough, the Move lasted less than a year with them before they came running back to me. Charlie Wayne had left and come back to me after just three months. I got him a huge solo deal with RCA. Charlie was then swanning around telling the Move how great he was doing now he was back with me, and that just twisted the knife even more. Finally, the inevitable happened. Neither Davis nor Walsh stood in their way.

They did only one more album as the Move, however, *Message from the Country*, which was released early in 1972, and from which came their final British hit, 'California Man'. And that was it. It was over. I was on tour with Joe Frazier when David called me to tell me they were breaking up. I was aghast. 'California Man' had been in the Top Ten in Britain and I had just done a new deal for them in America. But that's showbiz for you. Here today, gone later today. Little did I know it, but the break-up of the Move proved to be the catalyst that would transform them – or at least some of them – into one of the biggest acts in the world.

As people, the group were all right, I suppose, for a bunch of moaning Brummies. I don't know if it's that lilting, melancholy Birmingham accent, or the fact that they really are just a lot of miserable bastards in the Midlands of England, but Ozzy and Sabbath, who are also Brummies, were exactly the same when I later worked for them – the glass was never just half empty, there was no glass!

There had always been two singers in the Move: Charlie, who had started the group back in the early sixties as Carl Wayne and the Vikings; and Roy Wood, who wrote and sang pretty much all of the hits. Now there was also Jeff Lynne, who had replaced Charlie in the group and had previously been in a bunch of nonentities called the Idle Race. Jeff wrote, too, but nothing that would get the milkman whistling, and at first he was happy to take a back seat to Roy. When the Move broke up, though, the balance of power between them began to shift subtly as they embarked on a daring new project – a group that crossed rock music with classical. I admit, I thought they were out of their tiny minds when they first told me about it. Then they played me some of their early demos and that was when I knew for sure they'd lost it. It sounded like a classical orchestra gone mad, with this awful, distorted heavy-rock guitar thrown over it. It was all very deep and meaningless.

But they eventually scaled the idea down a notch or two, musically, until what remained was essentially a pop group augmented by a classical string section – not a million miles, in fact, from what George Martin had done for the Beatles in the late sixties – and I began to warm to the idea. Then Roy played me the demo of the song that became the first single, '10538 Overture', and I was sold.

'Progressive' rock – which also made claims to borrow ideas from classical – was the in thing at the time and what Roy and Jeff were doing in their new group fitted in well, even down to the pretentious name, the Electric Light Orchestra – a mouthful quickly shortened to ELO. There was one crucial difference: ELO's music wasn't nearly as self-regarding or overindulgent as the stuff then being churned out by groups like Yes and Genesis. These may have been the 'serious' album-oriented artists that Roy and Jeff originally sought to emulate, but Roy couldn't help but make whatever he did so melodically right that you found yourself tapping your foot no matter how weird or wonderful he'd made the songs sound.

I decided to go for it. As hoped, '10538 Overture' came out in August 1972 and was an immediate Top Ten hit. I got them on *Top of the Pops* and several other TV shows and the record was all over the radio. Everything looked set for their first tour. I had wanted them back in the studio to record a follow-up but the single had become a hit all over Europe, so I decided we should cash in while we could, make some headlines and maybe win over some new fans, then do a new record. But the tour was a disaster almost from the start. The trouble was that Roy still saw himself as the leader but Jeff was no longer prepared just to tag along, as he had in the Move. Jeff saw ELO as his group too. It was only a matter of time before it all ended in tears.

All in all, from the day Roy first came to see me about the new group to the day he told me he was leaving, the whole thing lasted just six months. The last thing Roy did with ELO was a show in Italy, when his stupid bickering with Jeff almost resulted in a riot. We'd sold every seat in the venue and I was chatting to the local Italian promoter at the front of the house when all of a sudden we heard the crowd go silent – something you never heard at a rock gig, let alone an Italian rock gig, where the crowds were known to go crazy. We went back in to see what had happened and found them on the verge of tearing the place down. It seemed an announcement had been made saying the group were unable to perform and that the show was cancelled. What the hell was happening?

We rushed backstage. My first thought was that something terrible must have happened to one of the boys. But when I got there I couldn't believe it. Jeff and Roy were refusing to go on until it was decided which one of them would actually walk out first. I told the theatre manager to go out and make another announcement, assuring everybody that the group would be playing. Then I closed the dressing room door and grabbed both of them by the hair, one in each hand.

'Listen,' I said, 'if you don't go out there right now I'm going to beat the living shit out of you! Do I make myself clear?' They looked at my face and saw that I meant it. Terror began to fill their eyes. 'After that, I'm gonna let them Italians out there get their hands on you and they're gonna rip you limb from limb. That's if there's anything left after I've finished with you.' Then I took hold of the two of them by the backs of their necks, shoved them out of the door and marched them down the corridor towards the stage. 'Now get out there and play, you fucking wankers!' I yelled and pushed them out there. The rest of the band meekly followed.

Well, they did the show and the crowd were ecstatic. But as I watched from the wings I noticed that Jeff and Roy would not even look at each other. When they both came to see me separately in my hotel room afterwards and said the same thing – that they just couldn't work together any more – it came as no surprise. OK, I thought: Lynne is easily replaced. But when Roy turned out to be the one who bailed out – leaving Jeff to front the band – I wondered how we would manage. As far as I was concerned, Roy was the talented one; the one who came up with the hits. Until then, Jeff had always been just the other guy.

I asked Roy what he planned to do now. 'Oh,' he said, 'I've got something better than this in mind.' I doubted it. Nevertheless, I was heartened to learn he wasn't thinking of throwing in the towel completely. I wished him well and told him to get back in touch when he had something to play me. A week later he was back in my office telling me all about his new group – Wizzard. He didn't have any music to play me yet, he said, he just had the idea. It would be the greatest group ever. He talked for hours. I wasn't really listening. Of course it would be great. I've never met anybody yet whose new group wasn't going to be the greatest. It didn't matter: Roy was a proven hit maker, so I was always ready to take a punt on a guy like him.

Sure enough, his first singles as Wizzard were a phenomenal success in Britain and several other territories. The one everybody always remembers now, of course, because they still play the damn thing every year, is 'I Wish It Would Be Christmas Every Day'. But 'See My Baby Jive', which was Roy's homage to Phil Spector, was miles better and remained at Number 1 for what seemed like forever.

He had a fantastic new image, too, completely different from the student, hippie vibe of ELO. Glam rock had arrived in the shape of flamboyant new stars like Marc Bolan and David Bowie, so suddenly Roy had green hair, red hair, shit-coloured hair . . . And he would dress in all kinds of different way-out costumes. He looked like the original mad-Viking-alien-from-hell. The rest of his band dressed no less bizarrely. It was as if the circus had come to town every time you saw them on TV –

something that appealed to everyone from little kids to the album-buying Bowie fans.

The trouble was, by then Roy was acting as eccentrically in his personal life as he appeared to be on TV in Wizzard. Perhaps the pressure of being what was virtually a one-man band in the studio had got to him. It all started to fall apart in 1973, when Wizzard took to the road on what should have been one of the most successful tours of the year. But Roy, seemingly exhausted after months of seclusion in the recording studio – or perhaps just freaked out at the idea of performing live for the first time without the safety net of the guys in the Move – gave some of the worst performances I'd ever seen. It was terrible. Every night, people would besiege the ticket office, demanding their money back.

He'd totally lost it and kept turning up the volume to try to compensate. Within about fifteen minutes the noise was so appalling that people were leaving the building holding their ears. I was there one night, and I swear he took away 50 per cent of my hearing! I tried talking to him about it but, no matter how many times I thought I'd got through to him, the very next show would take us back to square one.

Nevertheless, the hits continued for a while longer and the offers kept coming in, including some interest from America, where Wizzard had picked up a cult following. Despite my misgivings, the timing was right. If ever Roy was going to crack America, right then was the time to do it with Wizzard. So I booked them a tour – nothing too arduous, just some showcase dates in the major cities. It could have been the jumping-off point for Wizzard to conquer America the way ELO would later do. Instead, it was another disaster – and that was when I bailed out.

It didn't help that his Brummie accent was so thick that the Americans couldn't understand a word he said. Unless they were from Birmingham, even British people often had trouble understanding that accent. I told him, 'Don't waste your time talking to people – they can't understand you, anyway. Just give them what they've come for – the music. Stick to that, kid, and you can't go wrong.' But he wouldn't listen. We did the Roxy in LA and he went down pretty well, but afterwards the manager of the club asked me in all seriousness, 'Does Roy have a speech impediment? Or is he just on something? We couldn't understand a word he said.'

That was the finish for me. I did make one last-ditch attempt to get him to take speech therapy – if he was going to insist on talking to them, at least let him learn to do it properly like a normal human being – but it was useless. Roy Wood was a terrific musician and he wrote some fantastic songs but he let himself drift off into fantasy land, and after he left me his career just dissolved. He stopped being a star virtually overnight. It was terribly sad. He was one of those acts who seem able to come up with million-dollar hits every time you put them in a studio. He should have been the biggest star in the world. But he just destroyed his chances, wouldn't listen, didn't care, was maybe even scared of it. Who knows? He wouldn't be the first. Whatever it was, I had decided it would no longer be my problem, and I let him go.

As for ELO, when Roy suddenly jumped ship the whole thing fell onto Jeff's shoulders. It was sink-or-swim time and I have no doubt whatsoever that both he and ELO would have sunk without trace had I not been there to save them. But I was, and I did. By then I had seen the huge potential of the group, and so I rebuilt the whole thing around Jeff, who didn't really know what was happening. It didn't matter. He didn't have to know anything any more now that I was in charge. All he had to do was stand there and sing.

When Jeff Lynne took over as the main man in ELO, he'd been in the business for nearly eight years and yet he didn't have a pot to piss in. After Roy left him holding the baby, I thought he might bottle it. But I told him, 'Don't worry about a thing. You concentrate on the music and leave the rest to me.' He was happy with that and from then everything that was done for ELO was done by me, personally. The only thing I didn't do for them was write the songs, and even there they still needed my help. Jeff had been writing songs for eight years and had never had a hit. That all changed when I took over.

It took a lot of thought and a lot of forward planning. Jeff was not what anyone, including Jeff, considered a natural-born frontman. He became a great singer in ELO and a great leader, musically, in the studio. But, apart from that, he was too quiet to try to build a big image for himself the way Roy had in Wizzard, and I realised the new ELO would need a lot of nursing. Fortunately, I had some help from an unexpected quarter: Mike Stewart, then head of United Artists Records in America.

In Britain, the Move had been on EMI. Consequently, when they split, EMI picked up the options and now had both ELO and Wizzard. At the same time, I had recently done a deal for the Move in America with Mike at United Artists (UA), and so again when they split Mike simply took up the option to have ELO in their place. Mike was a bit of a fan of mine, and would probably have signed them just to do me a favour. But it was more than that. Mike was one of the first people in the business to agree with me about the potential of ELO. He put his faith in them and me from day one and for that I shall always be grateful. To help get us off the ground, Mike did deals with me that gave us much more money than I'd have got for a new British act anywhere else in America – which also gave us enough cash to help finance them at home in Britain, where support for them was not nearly so strong initially.

After Roy left, I had bundled the group back into the studio to record a new album. It was important to get something out quickly, to prove that the loss of Roy didn't necessarily spell the end of ELO. To cover for the loss of its main hit maker, I had encouraged them to release their version of Chuck Berry's 'Roll Over Beethoven' as the second single, replete with droll da-da-da-dah! classical intro. It was a wonderfully inventive stopgap, which also served to prove that having this extra 'classical' element to the band didn't make them boring. Sure enough, in January 1973, it became their second Top Ten hit. It was perfect. It kept the band in the public eye – and bought us enough time to find out whether Jeff had it in him to come up with some hit material of his own.

To everyone's relief, he did. Jeff had always been able to come up with decent tunes. But there's a difference between a good song and a sure-fire hit. Though he would never admit it, I think it was the time he'd spent with Roy, absorbing how he did things, that gave Jeff whatever element it was he'd been missing from his songs prior to that. Now, finally, it seemed as if he'd found the magic formula. Even as I was helping Roy get back to the top of the charts with Wizzard, I was listening carefully to what Jeff and the boys were up to in the studio, and the music they were now starting to make spoke for itself. You would have had to be a real greenhorn not to realise you had something great on your hands. Critics liked to say he got his ideas from others for early hits like 'Showdown' (Marvin Gaye), 'Ma Ma Belle' (the Rolling Stones) and 'Can't Get it Out of My Head' (the Beatles). But it was never that easy. Jeff wrote so many hits for ELO that by the end of the seventies they were one of the biggest bands in the world. You don't achieve that kind of popularity by being mere copyists. Jeff was a genius. He didn't just write hits: he fashioned each and every one of them in the 'classic' ELO mould – an incredible achievement in itself and something he's never really been given proper credit for.

Certainly, he surprised us all with how amazingly prolific he did become. It was like when Phil Collins took over from Peter Gabriel in Genesis: on the surface, you had lost the flamboyant frontman and replaced him with an anonymous-looking guy with no obvious charm – except an uncanny ability to come up with hit after hit. Jeff's image was that he didn't have an image. He was so shy he always wore tinted glasses and hid the rest of his features behind a mop of shaggy hair and a beard. Yet rock was going through a very theatrical stage again, and it wasn't enough any more just to stand there and play. That was when I devised the idea of building a show that would divert the audience's attention away from the musicians themselves. Every time they went out on tour, the shows would have to be bigger, more spectacular, than the last.

In America, Mike Stewart listened patiently and signed the cheques – and his faith was paid off as ELO quickly started to make a name in the US as a top live attraction. Back in Britain at EMI, however, it was a different story. Despite two Top Ten singles, neither of the first two ELO albums sold particularly well. I blamed the label. I always double-checked everything. So if EMI said they were going to do a promotion or have the records in certain stores on certain days or whatever, I always checked to see if they had followed through on their promises. And EMI weren't especially good at following through on anything, it seemed to me.

By then David and I had perfected our good-cop-bad-cop routine. Whenever I wanted something someone didn't want to give me – usually more money for promotion or a tour or whatever – as a last resort, I would go in and shout at everybody and turn their desks over. Then, while they were still recovering from that, David would come in and quietly smooth things over. By then they'd be ready to give him anything he asked for just to stop me from coming back again. Meanwhile, I'd be waiting downstairs for him in the car laughing. It never failed.

Things hadn't quite reached that stage with EMI yet and I had no wish for them to do so. All I wanted was for them to do their jobs and everything would have been fine. But they finally pushed me over the edge one day at a meeting with the managing director, Roy Featherstone. David and I had arranged to see him one day in 1973 to talk about how we were going to promote the third ELO album. I saw it as a make-or-break album for the band: if this one didn't catch fire then maybe none of them would. So I took the meeting very seriously and turned up brimming with optimism and plans for the future.

Unfortunately, Roy was expecting the Don Arden who hangs people out of windows and he was so keyed up he began shouting at me practically every time I opened my mouth. It went that way for me now with lots of experienced guys in the biz. Mo Ostin at Warner Brothers was the same when I first met him. They'd prepared themselves so thoroughly for the Don Arden of legend that when a completely different Don Arden walked in they would be so keyed up that they couldn't help themselves, and would just launch into the bullshit regardless.

That was how it was that day with Roy. I knew what was happening so I was actually quite patient to begin with. But every time I tried to make a suggestion he'd shout me down. 'Don't you come in here telling me what to do! I'm not scared of you!' All that crap. I lasted about fifteen minutes before finally cracking and giving him what he wanted. I didn't harm him. I just went off like a bomb in his face and told him exactly what I thought of him and his two-bit record company. 'You can fucking kiss goodbye to ELO, too!' I yelled at him.

David had to get me out of there. I was more upset than angry, though. Why do they get you to act like an animal just to get them to do their jobs? We went home that night and sat down and talked about it – and that was the night David and I came up with the idea of starting our own record company. Although we didn't have the name yet, that was the start of Jet.

Obviously, it takes time to start up a record company – time *and* money. And not just *any* record company. I had something bigger in mind than the kind of outlet the old Contemporary label had provided for me back in the sixties. That was just an imprint belonging to a much bigger company, Decca. Now I wanted to have my own genuinely global company able to handle the biggest acts in the world.

While I was laying the foundation stones for that to happen, I started shopping for a new deal outside America for ELO. I had meant what I'd said to Featherstone. I didn't bother with lawyers or any of that nonsense. I just took them. They were my group, they belonged to me. I could do just what I liked with them. And that was exactly what I told Roy. 'Fuck your contract,' I said. 'They've had a better offer.' They caved in straightaway.

I left them Roy Wood as a solo artist (though not for long) and took ELO to Mo Ostin at Warner Brothers, who released their third album, *On the Third Day*, in December 1973. Yet again, however, despite having two hit singles from it with 'Showdown' and 'Ma Ma Belle', the album didn't generate a lot of attention. It sold respectably, made the charts – but there was no fanfare. The critics disliked them; they seemed to find the concept confusing. And in a seventies Britain that still only had three TV channels and one national pop radio station, what the critics had to say had a huge bearing on album sales.

Once again, I largely blamed the record label. They simply weren't working hard enough. When the next ELO album, *Eldorado*, came out in October 1974 and did the same – made the UK charts but not in nearly the big way it charted in America – I decided we were out of there. In America, *Eldorado* was ELO's breakthrough album. Both it and the single from it, 'Can't Get It Out of My Head', were Top Ten smashes and for the first time in my career I had a group who seemed capable of emulating the success in America of the Beatles.

Back in Britain, however, the single and album barely made the Top Twenty. I was outraged. I went to see Mo Ostin and told him I wanted the band off the label. Unfortunately, Mo was another of those guys who had it in their minds how they wanted to 'handle' me, and Mo didn't want to be seen to be giving in to me.

Once we got to know each other, we actually became friends. You couldn't fight with Mo: he wasn't that kind of guy. He had artists who had been with him for thirty years because, like me, he looked after them. But back then it seemed as if we were on a fast track to nowhere over ELO. The problem was that Mo never really liked ELO. He just wanted Roy Wood as a solo artist and thought – correctly – that if he signed ELO he'd eventually get Roy. I had signed Roy to Warner's not long after the ELO deal. Now he had what he wanted, why wouldn't he give me what I wanted and let ELO go? Partly, it was jealousy: he knew the group were not going to stop being a success and he didn't like the idea that some other label might look as if it had lured them away from him. Mainly, though, it was because by then the American arm of the company wanted to sign them too, so that Warner's would effectively have ELO for the world. Our contract with UA was about to expire and, with the vast majority of ELO's huge sales now coming from America, Warner's wanted in. They felt they had the crummy end of the deal having them on the label everywhere but America, and they wanted to fix that.

I might have been tempted – indeed I met with the guys from Warner's in the States several times to discuss exactly that – but by then I had my own plans. Meanwhile, I didn't care what poxy little corporate games Mo was caught up in, I wanted ELO off his label and I wanted it yesterday. But no matter how much I leaned on him he just wouldn't give.

Then something funny happened: the Warner's offices in Greek Street burned down. Arson was suspected, though never proved. But within two or three days of that their whole attitude had changed and suddenly ELO were free to go – at a price. In this case, $2.5 million. I paid up. The group's freedom to sign a new contract with another major label was worth far more than that, both figuratively and metaphorically. What changed their minds? Putting two and two together and making five, they thought it was I who had set fire to their building. Did I do it, though? Well I was away in America at the time and so I couldn't have, could I? Of course not . . .

It was at this point that the dream of having my own top-drawer record company started to become a reality. During my battles with Mo I had actually become close to his right-hand man, Des Brown. Des was a great guy, very smart, but like me completely disillusioned with the setup there. He had actually been about to leave to run a label for Paul McCartney. But he liked us better. It was a bit more rock 'n' roll for him I think. I invited him over to the house in Wimbledon for dinner one evening with the family and we talked long into the night, at the end of which I offered him the chance to come in and help us put the new label on a truly international footing. Des accepted and we immediately started laying plans.

We talked about names and Des said he wished we could have used the name he and McCartney were going to use for their label – Jet (after the 1974 Wings hit of the same name). I agreed it was a great name. I said, 'Let's get it checked out – maybe McCartney never got round to registering it.' So the next day that was what we did and to our delight and astonishment he hadn't – so I did! Thanks, Sir Paul!

Jet Records was designed to be a big company, ready to handle the biggest acts. By the time I was able to add ELO to the roster in 1975, both David and Sharon were also working there and it was a very exciting and creative time for us all. Jet lived up to its name by getting off to a flying start. The first single we released in the UK was 'No, Honestly' by Lynsey De Paul, which went to Number 1. Lynsey was a lively blonde singer-songwriter whose previous Number 1 had been 'Sugar Me' three years before. But I had got her the gig writing and performing the theme tune to a new TV comedy show called *No, Honestly*, and suddenly she was back in the charts in a big way.

Personally, I found her a nightmare. I made Sharon her tour manager because I thought she'd appreciate having another woman around. Big mistake. The two of them fought like cat and dog. The final straw, though, was when Lynsey turned down my offer to get Jeff Lynne to produce her next album, maybe even write a couple of hits for her. She hadn't managed to follow 'No, Honestly' with anything nearly as successful, and, with ELO now a proven hit-making machine, I thought she'd jump at the chance (as Olivia Newton-John did when she teamed up with ELO in 1980 for 'Xanadu', and had one of her biggest-selling hits).

But instead Lynsey just pulled a face as if she'd just trodden on a dog turd. 'Oh my God!' she exclaimed. 'I couldn't have ELO producing me! They're outdated!'

I looked at her. If a man had said that to me I'd have chopped him in half. ELO were so 'outdated' that every album they did was now selling 5 million copies. But she couldn't see it and turned down a golden opportunity that I thought she should have snapped up. I didn't know if she had guts or just couldn't see it, but I walked away fast before I did anything I wouldn't regret later.

It was strange how it worked. Some of the acts we signed in the early days of Jet, like the rock group Widowmaker, were great guys to work with, honest and talented. Yet you couldn't give their records away. As a result, we said hello and goodbye to a lot of acts at Jet in the seventies. I didn't care. I saw myself as the creator. I created opportunities for people, opened doors for them – if they were too vain or too stupid to walk through them that was their lookout.

The actress Britt Ekland was another one. Her movie career was in the doldrums but she had recently become Rod Stewart's girlfriend and had managed to get her voice onto one of his hits, 'Tonight's the Night', moaning and groaning in the background as though he were giving her one. Suddenly people wanted to know about her again, and so I did a deal with her for one record: a single called 'Do It To Me (Once More With Feeling)'. She told me she had always wanted to be a singer first and an actress second. It wasn't a bad record, either – there have been a lot worse – but there was no hope, really. During the first couple of weeks we worked it fairly hard, but there was no reaction whatsoever. It was a dud.

So I got her acting work again, where she was at least well known through her early films with Sean Connery and her former husband, Peter Sellers. The only problem with Britt was that she was always in everybody's business. She became a big pal of Sharon's for a while, during Sharon's 'wild child' phase, but I just got tired of hearing from her.

Of the other artists we had on Jet in the seventies, the ones I remember best are people like Alan Price, who had been the keyboard player in the Animals. Now he was a successful singer-songwriter. We had a few hits with him in Britain and Europe. But it was never really going anywhere. He saw himself as a sort of Geordie Bob Dylan. Just what the world needed, obviously.

David Carradine is another I always think of from those days. He was the star of the massively popular TV show, *Kung Fu*, which I used to love. ('Ah, Grasshopper, when you can shove your dick up your own arse you can leave the temple . . .') Like a lot of actors, David really wanted to be a rock star, so I signed him to Jet for an album that, sad to say, was total hogwash.

Some of the other acts I still remember well from back then were guys like Adrian Gurvitz, whose band, Baker-Gurvitz Army, was going to be 'the new Cream' – until the former Cream drummer Ginger Baker bailed out just as we were about to release the album; and Carl Perkins, who had reinvented himself for the seventies as a singer-songwriter. Or Chopyn, who should have made it with the talent they had but seemed to turn everybody off with their personalities; and Raymond Froggatt, a truly talented singer-songwriter whose album simply got lost amid the turmoil of our protracted departure from Warner's.

One of the acts that I could and maybe should have signed to Jet back then was Queen. In the mid-seventies, the group were tied to the Sheffield brothers, who owned Trident recording studios in Soho. Queen were at their height at the time. Every album they did was selling 4–5 million copies worldwide, and yet they appeared to be penniless. They didn't even have a car between them. Freddie Mercury and the rest of the guys in the band were friendly with David and Sharon, and so they asked them if they would ask me for some advice. I told David and Sharon my advice would be to get their coats on and fuck off!

Queen were signed to EMI, but the deal the label had done had been via the brothers' own production company. It was the same with all the deals the band made: nothing was signed directly to them but to the brothers' production company. As a result, the brothers not only owned their management contract, but owned their recording contract and their song publishing, too. They were earning money hand over fist. I almost admired them.

The Queen boys sat there and told me all this after I had agreed to meet them at David and Sharon's request. They were living in a dingy place with no real furniture, no food. They had a roof over their heads and an old van they travelled in when they were on tour. I couldn't believe it. It was as if they'd never sold a record. I said, 'Well, what do you want me to do?' They said, 'We want you to manage us, Don.' I said, 'OK, get your lawyer to send me a letter confirming your intention to come to me and I'll go and sort these fucking guys out for you.' We shook hands on it and the very next day I drove up to Soho to see the Sheffields.

I didn't actually bother making an appointment, of course. As usual, I just turned up. But this time I went alone. I thought it important to show how little I was intimidated by the likes of them. Sure enough, when I walked into their office and announced myself, it scared the hell out of them, you could tell. They began talking very fast, chattering away about how they'd just been shopping with their wives, buying them jewellery. They were starting to make me sick, so I looked at my watch and said, 'Well, we've done with the niceties. Now listen to me very carefully. I'm not here to talk about your fucking wives. I'm here to inform you that you no longer represent Queen. It's over, OK? *Finito*.'

They looked at each other. Did they have the balls to take on Don Arden? No, they didn't. They couldn't even look me in the eyes. They were worried about what was coming next. Would I have a go? Maybe. But I wasn't evil to them, I didn't have to be. I told them that if they agreed to walk away right now, this instant, they would get a cheque for £100,000 for their trouble and they would never have to see me again. I pointed out that if they didn't agree, however, the group would still be gone but they wouldn't get any money at all and they'd have me to deal with. They sensibly took the money. 'As of now you no longer have anything to do with these boys, do you understand?' I added. 'You take the hundred grand and you give up everything: management, recording contract, publishing, everything.' They agreed, we shook hands, and I left again.

I walked out of Trident feeling good, but my day wasn't over yet. I left the car and headed across Oxford Street on foot towards Manchester Square and the offices of EMI. When I got there I demanded an impromptu meeting with the various heads of department and told them straight: if they wanted Queen to remain on the label then as of right now there would have to be a new deal, which I would be negotiating on the group's behalf. 'Any questions?' I asked. 'No? Good.' They were so relieved I didn't say I was going to do an ELO and just take them away that they were ready to give me anything I asked for, including an immediate advance of £500,000. I said the band were starving and needed the money and that I wasn't leaving until they assured me I would have a cheque for exactly that amount in my hand the following day. And that was exactly what happened. Or should have happened.

When I got back to the office that day and told them what I'd done they literally wept for joy. They were hugging me and kissing me. But then I never heard from them again . . .

I couldn't figure it. It wasn't until some weeks later that I found out what had happened. In America, Queen were signed to Elektra, which was being run at the time by David Geffen. Even though the band were now huge in the US, I knew that Geffen was still paying them an advance of $40,000 an album, a trifle compared with what a group like that should have been earning. If they had been signed to me I would have been getting them $3 million an album easily, and one of the first things I was going to do when we'd signed the contracts and sorted out the situation in London with EMI was go to Geffen and renegotiate the deal. But then Geffen got wind of what was happening from Mo Ostin and he got one of his friends to call the band and say, Don't go with Don Arden, if you don't do what he says, he'll fucking kill you! Yeah, right. Like all those other dead musicians I've worked with. But the group believed him and ran away and hid from me.

So be it. I knew they wouldn't be able to remain invisible for long – not with that half a million burning a hole in their pockets. Sure enough, I was at a party with my wife about a month later and guess who else was there. Bold as brass, Freddie came straight up to me and said, 'Ooh, Don, it's so lovely to see you!' I had to hand it to him: he didn't lack front. He said, 'I wonder if I can have a coffee with you. I'd like to explain.' I said I wasn't sure if I was interested in anything he had to say except maybe an apology. He said, 'Oh, I know, my dear, and I can't tell you how sorry I am things went the way they did. But how about we get together and have a chat?'

I laughed and agreed to meet him the next day and that was when it came out about Geffen. I was furious, but there wasn't much I could do about it now. Or was there? 'I thought maybe you might take us back,' said Freddie. 'God knows we need a good, strong manager.' I admit I was tempted, if only just to get my own back on Geffen. But, having walked out on me once, they weren't about to be given a second chance. I'd been through that situation so many times before – but it wasn't like those days of the Small Faces and Amen Corner any more. I didn't want to go through it again. And, with ELO now busting out all over the world, frankly, I didn't have to.

So I turned him down. But I did recommend someone else to them: Elton John's manager, John Reid. 'Great idea,' cooed Freddie. 'I never thought of that.' So I called Reid up, made them an appointment, and he signed them. I never saw a penny.

After finally getting them released from their Warner Brothers contract in 1975, my next move was to get ELO officially signed to Jet. I had allowed ELO's contract in America with UA to expire, at which point I had toyed with the idea of having them on Warner's worldwide. But, once we had left the label in London, that plan was scrapped and I went back to UA and did a new deal with them, which would give them back ELO – and also make them the distribution company for all Jet products in America. By then, ELO were a major hit act in America and needed better support than a new label like Jet could give them at that point, and I needed a US distributor I could trust for Jet, so UA seemed a safe bet on every level.

In Britain and the rest of the world, however, where I was convinced I could do a better job than the entire staff of Warner's and EMI put together, ELO would henceforth release their records and tapes on Jet. Originally, I did a deal with Polydor to distribute us outside America, and things went well. But then, in 1977, I came up with a better plan and did a new deal with UA to distribute Jet products worldwide.

I told everyone it was just a case of putting everything under one roof but actually I had an ulterior motive. ELO were the only act UA had in America that you could call major: without them they were nothing. As a result, ELO had been keeping UA afloat almost single-handed throughout the seventies. I thought it only right that we now get a larger slice of the pie. In fact, I decided I should own all the pie, and the real reason I did the new deal with them for Jet was because I planned to buy UA.

A guy called Artie Mogul had now taken over from Mike Stewart. Artie was a wheeler-dealer, lovable guy who'd done all sorts of things to all sorts of people. But everyone always forgave him – or nearly always. Artie was in on it with me, but then he bought the label himself with a guy called Jerry Rubenstein.

So that soured it for me and UA. If I couldn't own the label I would simply divest them of their biggest assets: ELO.

It was time to do another deal . . .

Meanwhile, however the fortunes of our other artists fared at Jet in the seventies, one thing we could always rely on was the success of ELO. Both the *Face the Music* (1975) and *A New World Record* (1976) albums had sold in their millions in America. And with me now looking after them at Jet, they had finally cracked it everywhere else in the world. Indeed, by the late seventies, ELO were not only the most successful group I'd ever managed, but the one I was most proud of, the one with whose success I had been intricately involved every step of the way. It was a unique concept that, through Jeff's impeccable ear for a melody and my vast business know-how, we had turned into gold dust.

Not that it was all plain sailing. I always had a way of dealing with the worst you could throw at me. But this was America, baby. Here everything was bigger – the success, the money and the shit you had to go through to get it. The American pirates, for example, were much harder to frighten off than the types I had busted up in Britain back in the sixties. These guys were organised, had their own fleets of trucks and carried weapons and walkie-talkies. I sent in the heavies and they roughed up some of them. But then they retaliated by shooting off the tyres of two of our trucks carrying official ELO merchandise. It was a war.

The biggest threat to my authority in America, however, came early on in ELO's rise to stardom, in 1974, when the band arrived in New York for a big showcase gig at the Palace Theater for all the East Coast record company bigwigs and media. The Palace was a secondary venue that held only a couple of thousand, halfway up from the clubs to the Garden. *Eldorado* was about to go into the Top Ten and everybody knew ELO would never play anywhere that small in the city again, so the place was packed.

I was standing at the side of the stage watching when three guys I'd never seen before suddenly appeared out of nowhere. One of them said, 'Hi, Don. Glad to see you.' I said, 'Oh, yeah? And what can I help you with?' But I already knew. You didn't have to be a brain surgeon to figure it out. Three heavy-set, Italian-looking guys immaculately dressed in tailor-made suits . . .

The guy who was doing the talking just smiled and said, 'What can you help us with? Well, you're gonna help us with our group.'

'Oh, yeah? Who's that?'

'ELO,' he said.

'Oh, no,' I said. 'You've made the wrong call there.'

'No, no,' he smiled, 'my friend, he got the group now.'

'No,' I said, turning deadly serious. 'What you mean to say is your friend *wishes* he had the fucking group!'

'Come with me,' he said, no longer smiling. I looked at him and the other two. 'What are you worried for?' he said. 'Come on, we just want to talk.' I glared at him.

'I ain't fucking worried,' I said. 'You wanna talk to me, OK, let's talk . . .'

I followed them into a room backstage that I had never noticed before and one of them bolted the door behind us. I should have been scared but instead I was filled with self-righteous anger. 'Right, that's it!' I thundered. 'Unlock that fucking door or I'm leaving right now!'

They unbolted the door. 'Relax,' the talker said. The rest just looked at me. 'We're just here for our friend.'

'Oh, yeah?' I said. 'I don't know what fag sent you – but I don't give a fuck. I know all about you guys,' I continued. 'I'm a player. You think I travel the world and don't know what's going on? I know all about you but here's the deal – I ain't interested. This is my group, end of story.'

'You don't know what we can do,' he said.

'Bullshit!' I said. 'You don't know what *I* can do!'

'What do you mean?' he said.

'Well, for one thing, I know you've got a lot of British stars – but you ain't got one American star. Why is that? I'll tell you. Because all the American stars know you're Mafiosi. So you come to England to find talent. Well hear this – I rule England! I own London! Fuck with me and you'll never see an English act again. I'll personally make sure of it. Now get out of my way, I've got a show to see to.'

That threw them because it was true. The Mob did come to England to pick up talent. I knew I had turned the tide when they started jabbering to each other in Italian.

'I'll repeat this one more time,' I said, interrupting them. 'Fuck with me and you can't ever go to England again because nobody does anything in London without my permission. Now go back to your boss and tell him I ain't selling.'

They held the door open for me as I walked through it. 'So long, fellas,' I said. 'Have a nice day.'

I had been nonchalant but I had a feeling that wouldn't be the end of it.

Thankfully, I never heard any more about it until about three months later, when Wilf Pine, of all people, called David one night to tell him he'd just saved my life. He said that when his 'godfather' in New York had been told I'd called him a fag he was going to take a contract out on me. But Wilf had managed to talk him out of it at the last minute, sticking up for me as a man of honour and saying that there must simply have been some misunderstanding.

But Wilf was the type of guy who loved to tell stories, of which maybe 70 per cent were usually pure fantasy. He loved to boast about all the hoods he knew. So when he came up with this guff about his so-called godfather, David and I just laughed it off. It wasn't until a couple of years later that I discovered he had actually been telling the truth.

It all came out after I bought from Wilf the management contract of a promising young black singer. It was a great deal. The only loose end I would have to tie up, he said, involved a Mafioso who had put $75,000 into the singer. I was told that the next time I was in New York it would be a good idea to go and see this guy just to reassure him that if the singer did ever make it he'd definitely get his 75 grand back. I was given a name – Joe Pagano – and a phone number and I realised my old associate Wilf had been telling the truth. I checked into it and it turned out that Joe Pagano was the head of one of the biggest Mafia 'families' in New York.

So, a few months later, I went to meet Joe Pagano for the first time. It was a place on 77th Street and Second Avenue, a lovely, old-fashioned, family-run Italian bar, just like you see in the movies. I took David with me and when we walked in they were all there, these guys in their suits. And in the middle of it all was this wonderful little man, old but sharp with it, with the little hat, smoking a cigarette. It was all very friendly and charming. Chairs were pulled out for us to sit down at the same table as Joe and drinks were poured and toasts made. David and I loved it. We both loved Mob movies and this was almost like being in one. We talked about the singer, and Joe just waved his hands. 'Sure, sure,' he smiled. 'I know I'll get my money back. But it's nice of you guys to come down here and tell me so personally.'

Then Joe asked David if he'd mind if he and I went over to another table for a few minutes on our own. 'There are a couple of things I want to discuss with your father,' he said. 'You understand.' David could hardly refuse, so off I went with the old man to another table. I wondered what was coming. He didn't keep me waiting long. He asked me if it was true I had really called him a fag. At first I was confused. I couldn't think what he was talking about. And then I remembered the phone call to David from Wilf and what I'd said to the Mob guys at the ELO show two years before – and suddenly the pieces all fell into place.

So the hoods waiting for me had been Joe's men.

Now Joe asked me to my face: was it true? Yes and no, I said. It was true I had called *someone* a fag but, in fact, I had wrongly assumed the men had been sent by someone I'd done business with and fallen out with in the past – who *was* a fag! When I explained who I had in mind, we both started to laugh and it was the start of a long and enduring friendship between us. When David and I left there that day, having spent several marvellous hours in their company, eating and drinking and telling each other stories, it was all kisses on the cheek and slaps on the back. 'Next time you come to New York,' said Joe, 'let me know and I'll send my car for you.' And he did – a fifty-foot-long limo I think he must have had specially built. It was probably bulletproof.

Although I heard that he and his brother, Pat, who was later rubbed out himself, had carried out more than 150 Mob killings between them in their younger days, the Joe Pagano I got to know in the late seventies and eighties was one of the most charming, intelligent and genuinely caring men I have ever had the pleasure to know. What he did or didn't do in his business – well, that was up to him. We were civilians, so it didn't affect us. Those old-time Mobsters had a code about things like that and, if you were their friend, they really looked after you.

Over the years I actually became closer to his son, Danny, than I did Joe. I still loved and respected his father but Danny was a bit more like me. Joe once said to David, 'The trouble with your father, he wants to kill everybody.' Well, Danny was the same. As I write this, he's just finishing a six-and-a-half year stretch in the pen. Danny was tough and I loved him as if he were my own son.

My real son, David, however, actually became closer to old Joe. They were very alike – calm, wise. Rushing in wasn't their style. They both liked to think everything through very carefully first – then take action. Joe also treated David like a son. When David's daughter, Charlotte, was born prematurely in 1980, it was touch and go for a few weeks as to whether she would survive. She did, thank God, but every single night while she remained in hospital Joe would call David on the phone to check on him. This was before mobile phones and if David hadn't come home from the hospital yet, Joe would keep calling back until David got home and he could talk to him, no matter how late at night it was or what state of mind David was in. He was just unbelievably supportive.

Joe also did us some wonderful favours in our business. Once ELO began raking in the big money in America, there was more than one promoter who made the mistake of thinking we wouldn't notice if they took more than their fair share for themselves. Usually I handled it myself. But out there in the Midwest almost everybody carried a gun and sometimes I simply didn't have the firepower to match them. That was when Joe would get one of his guys to make a call and suddenly the promoter would be on the phone telling me there had been a big mistake and that he was sending me a cheque – express delivery.

The big thing Joe really helped me with, though, was the pirates. With ELO getting bigger every tour, I was now plagued with so many Mafia-connected merchandise pirates I was swamped with bad guys. I couldn't fight them all on my own and they were stealing millions from me and the group. Joe saw what was going on and, though he couldn't be seen to come out on my side, he offered to 'mediate' between us. Eventually he was able to cut me a deal. 'Look,' he said, 'you'll never keep them away for ever. Let them sell a certain amount; we'll set a reasonable limit. That way they're off your backs and at the same time it keeps the small fry away from the business.

Whaddaya say?' I said yes. All-out war with the pirates was averted and we all went back to making serious money.

Being friendly with Joe Pagano and his associates didn't make me a Mob guy, though. For a start, I'm not Italian, and then there's the fact that I didn't *want* to become a Mob guy. Nor, I have to say, did Joe or anyone else ever approach me about becoming one. They never once came to me with any sort of business proposal. It was always a strictly social relationship, which both of us enjoyed, I think, because we were similar sorts of people.

Yes, they were murderers, but there was more to them than that. To me, they were true, blue-blood Americans. They would never turn anybody away. If you needed money they'd put their hand in their pocket and bring out a wad. They had big mitts and big wads of money, but if you couldn't pay them back you'd get mashed up. If, after that, you still couldn't pay, they bumped you off. The way I see it, though, a deal is a deal and anybody who dealt with those guys on that level always knew that.

One of the things they loved about me and ELO was that it was very much a family-run organisation, too. With both Sharon and David working with me, everything had a very personal touch. And of course that treatment extended to the Paganos, whom we treated as part of the extended Arden family, as we did all our friends. Whenever ELO played New York, for example, we always made sure Joe and his family were given as many tickets and VIP passes as they needed, a couple of hundred at a time if necessary. We'd invite them to all the backstage receptions and after-show parties, too, of course, and they were the happiest people in the world. I discovered that the greatest thing in the world to a Mafioso was to be able to step out of those surroundings for a while and go out and have dinner or a party with some straight people. And to be *seen* doing so. They didn't want to bust the joint up and scare the hell out of everybody: they simply loved life and didn't want to deny themselves any of its pleasures. As a result, whenever ELO played New York you'd get about a hundred of the best-dressed people in the city turning up, all different ages, all waiting to thank me as I walked in. Joe literally made them stand in a line, waiting to kiss my hand in appreciation of my hospitality. I was always very touched by the gesture.

Of course, not everybody saw it that way and the first time they turned up at an ELO show at Madison Square Garden I got an urgent message from the chief of police asking to see me. He had been backstage as part of the normal security presence and when he saw Joe and his family all greeting me he nearly had a seizure.

He took me into his office and said, 'Why didn't you tell us you were of the same blood?'

I said, 'I ain't "of the same blood". I don't know what you're talking about. These people are just my friends.' But of course he didn't believe me. In fact, I later found out the cops in New York spent the next couple of years fruitlessly investigating my so-called 'involvement' with the Paganos. To this day, I still don't think they entirely believe it. But that's what we were – great friends.

Meanwhile, the ELO show just kept getting bigger and bigger – on every level. The wonderful thing about the success in America of ELO was that it came to the group so naturally. People in America loved ELO like nowhere else on earth and it was the most tremendous time for all of us – me, the band and all our families. By the late seventies, every new ELO album had already sold a million in advance orders in the US before it was even shipped to the stores. It would then sell another million as soon as it was released. We had so many orders for ELO albums that we had the presses working round the clock to meet the demand for them.

It was the same frenzied atmosphere on tour: tickets were always like gold dust. There were no cheap seats but I made sure we always gave value for money. Of all the spectacular shows I devised for them over the years, though, the most memorable has to be the one for the 'Out of the Blue' world tour of 1977–8 – the one that became famous for the huge spaceship that 'flew' above the stage. Of course, it cost a fortune, but nobody spent the way I did on ELO. There were many bands in the seventies who threw hundreds of thousands into putting on a show. But with ELO I was now spending over a million dollars per tour on their stage show.

The idea for the spaceship first came about from the UFO-like smudge on the cover of the previous album, *A New World Record*, which was expanded on the cover of *Out of the Blue* to a full-on flying saucer. *Star Wars* was the big hit movie of the year and suddenly science fiction was fashionable again. So I sensibly decided to cash in. I said, 'I want that fucking spaceship built. I want it to open, I want it to land, take off – and I want them in it!' Making the whole thing work was one of the most incredibly fulfilling moments of my career. The first time the band actually saw it was the day before the first show – and they all loved it.

With the album at Number 1 in both the British and American charts, the 'Out of the Blue' world tour began in suitably over-the-top style with the band headlining nine consecutive nights at Wembley arena in London. All the media were invited to the opening night. The Duke and Duchess of Windsor were there and, to top it all off, I had the actor Tony Curtis come out to London to introduce the show.

When I later moved to California, Tony lived nearby and we became good friends. I grabbed him one day and said, 'Hey, do you wanna come to England and be recognised again?' Tony had been the star of a hit TV show in Britain in the early seventies called *The Persuaders*. But when his co-star, Roger Moore, left to become the new James Bond, the show was cancelled and Tony had returned to America.

'Oh, I'd love to!' he said. 'What do you want me to do?' I told him I wanted him to introduce ELO on stage at Wembley. 'Oh, I'd love to do that!' he said. 'What do you want me to say?'

'Nothing,' I said. 'Just walk out and see what happens.' But he wasn't buying it. 'I can't do that,' he said. 'I've gotta be introduced properly.'

But I was insistent. 'No, that would be too corny. This is a rock show, not a fucking Oscars ceremony. They're not expecting to see an old fart like you up there so when you walk on they'll all freak out. It'll be great, trust me.' I had thought about it for some time. This was the seventies. Sarcasm and in-jokes were now as much a part of the social fabric at a rock show as coke and marijuana. 'I think they'll get a kick out of it,' I said. 'And so will you.'

He still wasn't sure, but I eventually got him to see it as his chance to connect with the new, switched-on seventies audience and he reluctantly agreed. I offered him a nice fat fee, too, but he complained he'd have to pay too much tax on it. So I sent Sharon out to buy him a gift instead and she came back with some jewellery for him and his wife as a thank-you. Some thank-you – the jewellery cost ten times what his fee would have been!

In retrospect, however, it was worth it. Tony came to Wembley and did exactly what I asked of him. He walked out there without any introduction whatsoever – but as soon as the crowd realised who it was they actually stood up and applauded him. My instincts had been proved right again. Then, when the lights came on and the spaceship started to take off, the crowd went bananas! Then the applause turned to gobsmacked silence again. It was like that scene in *Close Encounters of the Third Kind* when the alien ship finally lands – they all rushed forward as if to greet it. Then they just stood and gawped. There must have been a full five minutes of that, no music, just the crowd trying to get their heads round how it was done – and not getting it all. It was fabulous.

It was like that every night of the tour. Thousands of people would just become transfixed by this giant spaceship. The size of it was incredible. When I heard Mick Jagger going on about how fabulous the new Stones show was I would think, Pass the sick bag. Nothing but cheap, sleazy rubbish compared with the show I put on with ELO that year.

As a result of all this, financially, the success of ELO took me into another dimension. At the height of their fame, they were selling out football stadiums, playing to 85,000 people a night. Factor in our share of ticket sales, merchandising, song publishing and the huge lift a show always gives current and back catalogue sales, and you're talking about serious money. We were literally making millions of dollars now every time the band went near a stage.

I may have been rich before, but I was now mind-blowingly, filthy, stinking rich. And that was when I decided to move to America full time – to Hollywood, to be exact. Where else for a full-blown showbiz personality like me?

9

Despite the enormous success of ELO, there was still a bit of business I needed to tie up before my wonderful new life in America would be complete. When Artie Mogul thought he'd pulled the rug from under me, in 1977, by buying United Artists, as far as I was concerned, he had also signed his own death warrant. ELO were by far United Artists' biggest-selling act, and, by taking them away, I would effectively slash the value of the company to the bone. It might even be the finish of them, I thought (as it turned out, they were sold at a bargain-basement price to EMI just a few years later). And so that was what I did, told Artie he could stick his label up his considerable arse and put ELO – and Jet – out there on the open market again.

Of course, Artie demanded a huge amount of money from us for breaking the contract, but that was the least of my worries. ELO were the hottest band in the world that year and I was convinced I could get even more money from whomever I did my next deal with. Sure enough, there was a feeding frenzy of activity in New York, London and Los Angeles, when news broke that ELO and Jet were both up for grabs. Having already walked away from both EMI and Warner's, I realised that it now came down to a choice between CBS, where we were negotiating with their US head, Walter Yetnikoff, and Ariola Records, whose then chief, Monty Luftner, was a pal of mine. Both sides wanted ELO for the world. I said they could have them, as long as they also agreed to distribute Jet Records, too. That way, ELO's records would all carry the Jet label but they would still essentially be pressed and distributed by the parent company. Both CBS and Ariola agreed and ended up putting identical offers on the table of $5 million.

I chose Ariola. The reason: I couldn't stand Dick Asher, who was then head of CBS for everywhere in the world outside North America, and who had already made it clear he didn't want to work with me back in the early days of Jet. Back then, Dick had been head of CBS in the UK and I had gone to see him with a view to getting CBS to front Jet some start-up money. I think I asked for £50,000. I played him a tape of 'No, Honestly' and he agreed it sounded like a hit. I went through the whole spiel, told him we'd also be bringing ELO to the label in the future as well as others. He listened patiently then uttered two words – 'No, thanks' – followed quickly by 'goodbye' and that was that. I was perplexed but figured, What the hell! It was his loss.

About a year later, however, Jet was up and running, 'No, Honestly' had been Number 1 and ELO were bigger than ever, and I'd gone back to him to talk about the possibility that CBS might distribute Jet in the UK and Europe. This time I asked for what under the circumstances was now a fairly modest advance of £150,000. 'No, thank you,' he said. Now I'm confused. But what the hell! You meet all sorts in this game.

Fast-forward another year or so, the aptly named Dick is now the head of CBS Records for the world, excluding America. I wasn't going to have anything to do with him again but it was just after I'd taken ELO from Warner's, and while I was happy for them to remain on UA in America, I toyed with the idea of having them on another major label similar to Warner's throughout the rest of the world. That meant CBS. So against my better judgement I went to see Dick Asher – again.

This time I asked for a quarter of a million. Peanuts compared with what the band were going to be worth over the next ten years. 'No, thank you,' he said. Now he's making me sick. What the hell was wrong with this guy? Didn't he like making money? I decided I would never again ask Dick Asher for anything. (Years later, when I became friendly with Maurice Oberstein, who eventually replaced him, he told me Asher was simply terrified of me and that was why he acted as he did. Jesus Christ! All he had to do was say yes and he would have been sitting in clover for the rest of his days.)

Now I had Walter Yetnikoff at CBS desperate to do a deal for the world – but that would have meant dealing with Asher. 'Fuck it,' I told him. 'In that case I want six and a half million!' I was fairly sure there was no way they'd go for that but I didn't care. While I liked the idea of having the enormous CBS machine behind me in every part of the world, I wanted to make my point about Asher and maybe stir some heat up for him, too – it didn't look good for him to be the guy who had turned down ELO when they were going for peanuts.

In the meantime, Monty was my man. His five million was as good as anybody else's. To my utter astonishment, however, Yetnikoff's lawyer, Marty Machat, came back to me the very next day and said, 'OK, we can do that – six and a half million it is.'

Fuck! I hadn't seen that coming. Now what was I to do? I called Monty and explained the situation. He asked me to give him 24 hours, which I did. Lo and behold, he came back the next day and said, 'OK, no problem. We'll match their six and a half million.'

Unbelievable. So the next day I go into the CBS offices to meet with them all, and to tell them that Monty at Ariola had matched their offer and that because of Dick Asher I was going to go with them. At first they were dumbfounded. Then Paul Russell, their head of business affairs, came up with one of the best lines ever: 'That fucking Monty Luftwaffe!' he cried. I had to laugh.

So we sat down and had a bit of a chuckle about that but at the end of it I was insistent – if the money was identical and the choice was Monty or Dick Asher, I was going with Monty. At which point Yetnikoff exploded and said, 'Look, if we give you eleven million can we fucking close the deal?' They didn't just climb to seven or eight: Walter just went bananas and said, 'Fuck it, we'll give you eleven million, that's it. Now can we close the deal today?'

Well, what can you say? We did the deal.

For the next few years, I lived the sort of life that Reilly could only have dreamed of. In 1977, I bought my dream house. Actually, I don't think even my dreams ever stretched quite as far as something like this. It was actually the house that Howard Hughes had designed and built for himself back in the forties. This wasn't just another Hollywood mansion: this was a self-contained world. I bought it from Charles Boyer, the French actor. Altogether, I paid $7 million for about eight acres of land and all the fabulous property Hughes had built on it. I then spent another $3 million renovating it. Of course, it caused a lot of envy among certain people. I remember the first time Walter Yetnikoff came by, sitting there looking around at the place almost in disgust. 'What do you need a joint like this for?' he asked.

'What do you fucking think?' I replied. 'To live the way I want to live.'

As a kid I had always loved tennis but where we came from they'd call you a poof and give you a kicking if they caught you with a poncy tennis racket in your hand. Now I had my own tennis courts. I used to have the pros from the nearby hotels over every Sunday and we'd play for $20 a game. I used to kill everybody at tennis; I was so proud of that. I used to play three-hour matches against kids half my age and beat them.

And I was always giving parties there for the people who worked for us: the staff at Jet and CBS – not just the heads, either, but the secretaries too, everybody, right down to the guys who ran the warehouses and pressing plants. I wanted them all to feel important and appreciated. I used to invite them to the house as my personal guests and tried to make them feel a part of the family. And they liked it that way. It gave everybody a buzz. We had so many parties that the guy living in the next place along started pestering me to be invited too. He was a Hollywood doctor who fancied hanging out with celebrities. But when we wouldn't let him in he turned nasty and started calling the cops and complaining about the noise. In the end, I went to him and said, 'You know what? I'll buy your fucking house. Now fuck off!' Fortunately for him, because my next offer would not have been so generous, that was what I did. I didn't want anyone spoiling my fun.

The biggest and best party we ever had at the house, though, was the one I threw to celebrate the CBS deal in 1977. We had enough champagne and caviar to feed an army of millionaires and it went on for about three days. We put everybody in the atrium, because it had a big retractable roof. It was like something out of James Bond. You just pushed a button and there was the sky. Then the day after the party finally ended I took Paddles on a round-the-world sea cruise that lasted three months. David joined us for a couple of weeks when we were in South America and the whole thing was fantastic. I was 51 that year and had been working since I had won that talent contest when I was fourteen. That's 37 years of taking care of business. I figured I had a little break coming. I also needed to be out of the country for a few months, anyway, as part of my tax situation. With David and Sharon there to run things while I was gone, everything worked out nicely.

They say America is the place to reinvent yourself. But by the time I came to live there, in the mid-seventies, my reputation was already well established. It was generally known that I had cracked a few skulls in England on my way to making millions with ELO. Now, because of my friendship with Joe Pagano, something I never tried to hide, there were more than a few people in the US music business who were wary of 'the English Godfather', as I became known. I didn't take it seriously but it didn't appear to do me any harm with those who did.

Were the Mafia involved in the US record business, though? Of course. The Mafia are involved in every branch of the entertainment business and have been all our lives. Everybody knows it but what can you do? Every now and then the government makes a fuss – like the high-profile FBI investigation into Mafia involvement in the record business in the early nineties, where that scumbag Morris Levy was finally caught. But it was a ritual sacrifice. Something to keep the media happy. These things never go away. There's no need for them to. Levy was then head of Roulette Records but he had been involved with the Mob all his life. The FBI would have to be dummies not to know what was going on, the millions floating around in un-accounted-for pay-offs. But they were in on it too; they were all getting a present. Either they were told to retreat or they did their own deals, take my word for it.

Was I up to any shenanigans, though? Actually, no. Because advance sales on each ELO album alone were up to 3 million in the US by then, there was never any need for me to try to manipulate the charts the way I once had in Britain. What was the point? We'd already made our money back – and then some – before the albums had even been released. For once, I was clean as a whistle.

By the late seventies, however, it was no longer just ELO and Jet Records I was looking after but Ozzy Osbourne and Black Sabbath, too. After seeing them waltz off with Wilf Pine and the Meehans in 1970, I thought that would be it, that I would never hear from them again. But the guitarist, Tony Iommi, had remained friendly with David and Sharon and had become a frequent visitor to the house in London whenever Sabbath were in town. Then, when the Meehans' company, World Wide Artists, closed down in 1974 and things turned bad for the band, they came knocking at my door again. Or, rather, Tony Iommi did.

Although Ozzy was the front man in public, behind the scenes it had always been Tony Iommi who cracked the whip in Sabbath. Which was fortunate for the rest, since Tony was the only one of them I had any time for back then. Having once turned down the opportunity to work with me, nobody else would ever usually have been given a second chance. But Tony was a good sort and I could see he was in trouble, and so I agreed to take a look into their affairs. What a disaster area!

Everything they thought they owned, they didn't. Not their houses, not their cars, and certainly not their money. They didn't even own their own songs!

In the four years they'd been together, Sabbath had released five albums, all of which had not only been Top Ten hits at home in Britain but had all gone gold in America (the highest accolade attainable in those pre-platinum days). But instead of being millionaires they were penniless. Oh, the Meehans had put a few quid in their pockets and got them all the rock-star extras they'd needed. But, once the management company went down, it had stopped paying their bills – including the mortgages on their houses. One of the guys literally had the bailiffs come to his door one morning with papers to repossess the house. He was sitting there with the family having breakfast one minute, and the next minute they were all out on their ear, totally destitute.

I thought I'd seen everything by then but this was unbelievable. The music business is full of bastards who would sell their own grandmothers to get a hit – so what? That was hardly news to me. But what happened to Black Sabbath was staggering. Sabbath weren't the only ones who got shafted, either. The number of bands who stuck bankruptcy notices on WWA once it went belly up was incredible.

Because of that, a lot of people in the biz assumed I would go after the Meehans. But no: I now had the band – what did I care what happened to them? There is, however, a small postscript to this story – a little memory I gave them to cherish me by – specifically, the son, Patrick Jr, who I felt needed taking down a peg or two. I was happy to oblige.

Much to my chagrin, Sharon had had a brief affair with young Patrick in the early seventies. I didn't like it but what could I do? I just hoped that eventually she'd come to her senses – and thank God she did. But then I heard an ugly rumour that Patrick had secretly made video tapes of himself and Sharon making love and that he enjoyed playing them to people, even going so far as to talk to a newspaper reporter about them. I didn't know how much of it was true but the fact that people were even saying it was bad enough for me. I decided to pay Patrick a little visit . . .

As ever, I just turned up unexpectedly at his office one day. He was talking to Tony Calder when I walked in. I didn't say anything, just pulled up a chair and sat down next to him. They both looked at me in horror. Patrick went to say something, then stopped as I pulled a gun from my jacket pocket and laid it down very carefully on the table. There was nothing in the gun: I had taken all the bullets out in case somebody made a grab for it. But they didn't know that. They just saw my face like thunder and then that gun on the table – and they just shat themselves.

I looked at young Meehan and said, 'This is just a warning, to tell you to leave my daughter alone. From this moment on you don't know her, you don't speak to her, you never even say her name again. Do you understand? Otherwise, the next time you see me I'll be pointing that gun at your head. This is what I do to slags like you who upset my family – I kill them.'

I sat there looking at him, waiting to see what else he might have to say for himself but he was out of words. He started to shake and sweat and that was when I stood up and walked away. Slowly.

After I left, though, he kicked up an awful stink. He actually called the cops. They came to the house in Wimbledon with a search warrant for the gun, but luckily David was quick on his feet and he palmed them off with an old air gun. I ended up having to go to court, though. But the judge, who was obviously a wise old bird, sussed it for what it was – a bit of argy-bargy between old 'friends' – and stopped the trial before it even got started. 'No case to be answered,' he said.

It didn't end there, though, and we had another run-in at Midem, the music-business festival held annually at Cannes, in 1975, not long after I'd taken Sabbath on again. David was on tour in the States with ELO, so I took Sharon with me. We were in the casino when we spotted Patrick at one of the tables. Sharon got the hump of course and started winding me up about it. In the end, just to shut her up as much as anything, I went over there and went off at Patrick again. Then this Italian guy he had with him – who I later found out had just done fourteen years for murder – did a flying head-butt at me and knocked me sideways! So I went crazy, my guys jumped in, Sharon jumped in, and the whole thing became like a saloon brawl in a cowboy movie: bottles smashing, chairs flying through the air, the lot.

It was after that that I decided this little schmuck had to be dealt with once and for all. I got hold of Joe Pagano on the phone and told him about it. He and David tried to rein me in and get me to forget about it but I wanted that troublemaker dead. In the end we reached a compromise. Joe sent his guys to see Patrick and put him on an official warning. One more false move and it would be his last. Just to reinforce the point, though, the following year at Cannes I had half the Mob out there with me – Big Frankie, Danny Pagano, Bobby Bomps, the whole team. They were all tooled up, too. We got the tools from Germany and it was some show we put on. But then I've always been a crowd-pleaser.

It was after that, though, that people started saying I always carried a gun. It wasn't true but as usual I saw the value in the PR and allowed the suckers to believe what they wanted. I used to encourage them. On the invitation for the annual Jet Records Christmas party that year we had a picture of me on it standing in front of a Christmas tree holding a gun, with the words HERE'S AN OFFER YOU CAN'T REFUSE emblazoned across it.

When I first took Ozzy and Sabbath on, in 1974, my number-one priority was to get them some money. That meant going to the record company – Vertigo in the UK and Warner's in America – and making them understand that the band were still viable and that, moreover, they were now in good hands. I told both labels to forget about the previous mess, to leave everything to me. This was exactly what they wanted to hear and I got a nice big advance from them and used it to put the band back in the studio to make another album. The reasoning was simple: I wanted them to stop worrying about money and start thinking about music again. Most of all, I wanted something new out there that they *did* earn royalties from.

The aptly titled *Sabotage* album came out in 1975 and the band were soon back on the road to promote it. The result: another gold record in America and another chart hit in Britain. As Ozzy never tired of telling me, 'If it hadn't been for you, Don, I'd have been a hotdog salesman by now.'

They weren't the sort of band who, like ELO, would sell a million albums straight off the bat. They never had any hit singles to speak of. But they would sell a million maybe over the first six months, after they'd been on tour and the word-of-mouth promotion had begun to spread. This was pre-MTV, pre-Internet, and so you had to take the show to the people. But, because the Sabbath show was so good, all the albums they released with Ozzy in the seventies have continued to sell steadily over the years. As you read this, I guarantee you there is a fifteen-year-old boy walking into a record store somewhere in the world right now looking to buy his first Black Sabbath album. The name has become a brand – the sign of a major, major artist. Even if you've never heard their music, you've heard of the band.

After I'd got them out of the shit they were in, they should have been set fair for years to come. Instead, they went and blew it completely – but this time they had no one to blame but themselves. By then the drugs and alcohol and the years of touring had left all their personal lives in tatters. It wasn't just Ozzy: it was all of them. But Bill Ward, the drummer, and Ozzy were the worst. They were a team. The 'Drug Commandos', we used to call them. They would never come through a door when a plate-glass window would do. Tony Iommi and Terry 'Geezer' Butler, the bassist, did their fair share of drugs, too, but they weren't loud about it like Ozzy or Bill, and they tended to treat them as the oafs of the band, which in fact they were. Tony wrote the majority of the music and Geezer supplied most of the lyrics, and by 1978 they were both starting to feel that Bill and Ozzy were holding them back.

And that was when they made their big mistake: they decided to get rid of Ozzy. I asked why and they said he just wasn't contributing anything musically any more. 'He's not even bothering to show up at the studio most days,' Tony said. 'And when he does he's so out of his head you can't get anything worthwhile out of him. We've got to get rid of him or the band's gonna break up.'

I was shocked. I knew full well what a pain Ozzy could be to deal with and that what they said was true. But this sounded like cutting off your nose to spite your face. I said, 'But you can't! Ozzy's been with you all your lives. What the fuck are you talking about?'

But they already had a plan. Tony said, 'It's OK: we've got Ronnie James Dio lined up. He's a better singer than Ozzy and much more reliable.'

I was appalled that things had deteriorated so badly they had actually contacted another singer. I said, 'Look, this is a huge thing you're asking. At least, before you do it, give Ozzy one last chance. Give him the tracks you've been recording on a cassette and see if he comes up with anything first.'

They were reluctant. But I wouldn't let it go and so they eventually agreed and sent Ozzy a tape. I hoped and prayed that Ozzy would do the right thing and at least come back to them with *some* ideas for the vocals, but we never got a chance to find out. A few days later Bill Ward came to see me on his own and told me he thought giving Ozzy another chance was a terrible idea. 'No fucking way am I working with Ozzy again,' he moaned. 'Fuck giving him a tape. We want Ronnie Dio!'

Bill was so determined that he even offered to be the one who would actually break the news to Ozzy – which was exactly what happened. I make a point of mentioning this because it always makes me sick whenever I see Bill on one of these TV documentaries now going on about how sad he was when Ozzy left and that they were never the same after 'the others' got rid of him.

Ozzy regarded Bill as his best friend in the band back then and he was absolutely devastated when it was Bill who told him he was fired. He literally locked himself away in his hotel room for weeks, crying his eyes out. I felt like crying, too. I knew it was a mistake, but there was nothing I could do. It's easy now to say I should have been stronger and told Bill that if he didn't like it *he* should be the one to leave. But the others felt the same way: they couldn't wait to start over with Ronnie Dio – and in the end you have to let the artists themselves make those sorts of decisions. You can tell them what you think but you can't stop them falling out of love with each other.

So it was that early in 1979 Ozzy was booted out of Black Sabbath and Ronnie James Dio was drafted in. Trying to be as positive about it as I could, I hoped that it might develop into a similar situation to when Roy Wood left ELO – that I would effectively have two major artists where previously there had been one. Double the money? Maybe, but that was no guarantee. Double the trouble, though? Undoubtedly. But I gave it a shot for a while.

The trouble with Sabbath was that I just couldn't see Ronnie Dio fronting the band. Ronnie had been the singer in the former Deep Purple guitarist Ritchie Blackmore's band Rainbow, with whom he had enjoyed a couple of medium-sized hit albums. There was no doubt, either, that he could sing. Technically, he was superior to Ozzy in every way. But that didn't mean he was right for Sabbath. For a start, he was only about five feet tall and looked like one of Snow White's dwarves – Grumpy! I told them, 'You're Black Sabbath. You're supposed to be the heaviest, scariest band in the world – you can't have a fucking midget fronting you!' But they wouldn't listen. They would spend all day telling me what a terrific singer he was but I would go to sleep every night thinking, Yeah, but he's a fucking midget.

Finally, it came to the crunch and, not long after they had ditched Ozzy, I decided to ditch them. There was no big drama: I just said I'd had enough, that I didn't believe in them and that it would be better for them to work with a manager who did. So I did another deal and sold the band's management contract to Sandy Pearlman, who also managed Blue Oyster Cult. They took it reasonably well on the surface. But the fact that I stuck with Ozzy was not overlooked, either.

The trouble with Ozzy was that by then I also had him living at my house. He ended up living with me and the family in LA for over a year. Can you imagine what that was like? Having Ozzy as a permanent house guest for a year?

As anyone who knows him will tell you, Ozzy is one on his own, he really is. That funny, fucked-up guy you see these days on TV in *The Osbournes* is the real Ozzy all right, but that's as he is today: a true survivor who's been through it all and come out the other side shaking – but still laughing. Imagine, though, what he was like back in the late seventies, when drinking and drugging and screwing anything that moved was now normal behaviour among so-called civilised people, let alone stoned-crazy rock stars. I'd got ELO selling out everywhere and yet it was Ozzy I had in my face night and day.

He simply had nowhere else to go, though. No one else wanted him at that point. He was just *too* over the top. People got up and left the room when they saw him coming. Thankfully, Ozzy has always been a funny guy, which is why I always ended up forgiving him. The 'happenings', as we called them – Ozzy didn't have to move a muscle for crazy things just to happen around him – were often hysterically funny. But it made home life chaotic, to say the least.

Everything we tried to arrange for him, whether it was rehearsing with his new solo band or just turning up on time to meet somebody from the record company, we always had to plan it around those increasingly rare moments when Ozzy wasn't completely out of his brain. It would be, 'Quick, get him in the studio!' That would be fine for a couple of hours, then the band would take a break but when they came back they'd find Ozzy had gone through a bottle of brandy and a bag of coke and would be lying on top of the mixing desk unconscious. Work over for another day.

Ozzy didn't care whether it was coke or laxatives: he just took whatever was put in front of him. Mainly, it was booze that was the problem. Ozzy could go weeks at a time without drugs if he had to, but he could never go a single day without a drink. Not back then. It wasn't just a case of social drinking either: it was a case of 'Let's get fucked up!' You'd agree to have 'just the one' with him and, the next thing you knew, you'd been slumped there for five hours and he'd pissed himself three times and set fire to the carpet. But Ozzy was never evil. He doesn't have a bad bone in his body. He only ever looked to have fun when he was with me. As such, he became more like a son than a client and because of that we've always been friends, no matter what trials and tribulations I might have gone through since with Sharon.

By the same token, living with the Ardens was unlike any life Ozzy had ever known before. For the first time in his life he was living among people who had better, more interesting things to do than getting shit-faced every day. I think that's ultimately what saved him. He was seeing a side of life he never even knew existed before. He saw how we found solutions to problems and then acted on them, often in ways other people in the business wouldn't even think of or dare do. He saw how we made it possible to come up with the impossible, practically on a daily basis.

Ozzy was like Humpty Dumpty while the family and I were 'all the king's men', trying to put his shattered ego back together again. History is full of singers leaving to become solo artists, then flopping miserably while the group they left behind goes on to even greater success. The obvious example is Pink Floyd, who lost not one but two lead singer-songwriters in the course of their career – first Syd Barrett, then Roger Waters – only to go on and have even greater commercial success each time. The same thing had happened to Deep Purple in the early seventies when their singer Ian Gillan left – his solo career died while they went on to even greater glory with David Coverdale. And the same thing would happen again a few years later when David Lee Roth was replaced by Sammy Hagar in Van Halen – their first album with Hagar, *5150*, was their biggest seller yet, while Roth's career went into a nosedive from which it never recovered.

At first, it looked as if it might happen that way with Ozzy and Sabbath. The band's first album with Dio, *Heaven and Hell*, had been released in the summer of 1980 and had become their biggest hit since their mid-seventies heyday. However, I had a feeling the novelty of seeing a midget fronting the band would soon wear off. Meanwhile, I was convinced I could turn things around for Ozzy – and so it proved.

Rock critics write now about how Ozzy's initial solo success was down to the wonderful new guitarist we had found for him to work with – a young whiz kid named Randy Rhoads. Randy was a great player, for sure. But there are a lot of great kids out there blasting away on their guitars. There has only ever been one Ozzy Osbourne, though, and, after a year of living with me, he was ready for anything. I wasn't playing around either, I wanted to go for it big time. The result: almost instant success. Ozzy was on $5,000 a night at the start of his comeback tour in 1980. By the end of it he was making $100,000 a night.

Good though his first couple of albums were (nearly 25 years later, his live show is still primarily built around the songs on them, with 'Crazy Train', his first ever solo single, being hilariously revamped as the theme tune – done lounge style – to *The Osbournes*), the trigger for his huge newfound fame was an entirely nonmusical one. With Ozzy, it always came down to more than just the music, anyway, and when you've got an image as strong as that you can play with it – which was how one of the most infamous incidents of Ozzy's strangely incident-filled career came about, when he bit the heads off two live doves.

Although his first solo album, *Blizzard of Ozz*, had been a Top Ten hit when it was released in the UK in September 1980, the album was released in the US at the start of 1981 to mixed reactions. It sold OK but it didn't look as if it was even going to make the Top Twenty let alone go gold. With Sabbath having proved they could go on to even greater success without him, the feeling in America was that Ozzy was now little more than a sideshow. Meanwhile, I was pulling out all the stops, trying to get anyone and everyone I could in America interested. I had signed Ozzy as a solo artist to Jet, now distributed worldwide by CBS, so I organised a special get-together between Ozzy and all the various heads of the most important departments at CBS in Los Angeles. It was meant to be a semiformal meet-and-greet, at which Ozzy could demonstrate that he was not really the lunatic he was portrayed as in the press but in fact a smart, talented guy with a great solo career ahead of him. I wanted them to get to know him, see his bright side, and really want to get behind him. Well, we certainly achieved that, though not quite in the way I had planned.

I had written a little speech for him to give, some old bollocks about how he did all this for love, not money – again, just to try to shed this image he had as the monster from the blue lagoon. At the end of the speech, he was supposed to pull out some white doves we had stashed in his jacket pockets, and release them into the air. I thought they would take off flying around the room, and everybody would go, 'Oh, how wonderful!' That sort of malarkey. Unfortunately, Ozzy had already polished off a bottle of brandy in the car on the way over there. Then, as soon as we walked in, the PR woman began jumping all over him. She started talking and she didn't pause for breath again for half an hour. It was like throwing petrol on a fire, and he started drinking heavily again. Finally, before he'd even had a chance to make his little speech, the PR woman was driving him so nuts he lost it.

'Do you like animals?' he asked her suddenly.

'Oh, gee, I *love* animals!' she cried.

At this point, Ozzy took two doves from his pocket and bit their heads off, one after the other, just like that. Then he spat them up into the air.

The PR woman screamed and collapsed on the floor. Pandemonium broke out. Everybody was going crazy. Security was called and Ozzy was escorted from the building, and I was told in no uncertain terms that CBS would never work on any of his records again. Oh, my God! I thought. What had the silly bastard done now? I really did think that all my best-laid plans had just gone flying out of the window. By six o'clock that night, however, it was one of the main items on the evening news on TV. All across America people were talking about it. Within 24 hours it was news all over the world. And that was when the first album took off in America. We shifted about 500,000 copies of *Blizzard of Ozz* in the week that followed Ozzy's headline-grabbing, dove-decapitating episode. Suddenly, Jet had another major Top Ten hit on its hands in the US and – lo and behold! – suddenly all this bullshit about CBS never working with Ozzy again was quietly dropped as the money started to roll in.

We had already recorded the follow-up – *Diary of a Madman* – in the lull between the UK and US release dates of *Blizzard*, and when it came out in November 1981 it was an even bigger smash, making the Top Ten of every major record-buying market in the world. Suddenly, the game was on again.

And so it might have continued, had things not taken a sudden, unexpected turn when Ozzy began having an affair with Sharon – a situation that would lead to such dire consequences that she and I went from being a close and loving father and daughter to being such bitter enemies that for years she would actually tell her own children I was dead.

Two years younger than her brother David, Sharon was educated in private and theatrical schools (including, for a spell – like David – the Italia Conti). She never went to a normal school, which is something I now regret: if she had, maybe she would have grown up a bit more 'normal' herself. Instead, she went to school with people who were half crazy. She'd come home every day and tell me some new story about the shenanigans going on. She'd do all the voices and act it all out for me.

She was cute and smart with it – but she was also a little too headstrong. You never had to look for trouble with Sharon: it was more a case of, 'Oh, God, what now?' Whenever she became sick of a particular school, which she always did sooner or later, she'd come home and tell me some horrible story about the place. I knew she was having me on but sometimes she was so convincing that I took the bait. For instance, there was the time she claimed she'd been brutalised by a woman teacher. Enraged, I drove down to the school the next morning to confront this bitch who had dared lay a finger on my daughter. When I got there, though, I found that the teacher in question was actually a frail old biddy with a walking stick. She must have been ninety if she was a day! And that was when I realised I'd fallen for one of Sharon's fairy stories again. 'She hit me, Daddy! She's evil! Please don't send me back there! No, no, no, Daddy!' I'd have her voice going round in my head all day. One thing about my daughter, she has never lacked persistence – or imagination.

It was no surprise when she left school at sixteen and came straight to work for me. Her first job was in reception, answering the phones. Then, when I thought she'd been sitting on her backside long enough, listening in to the calls and seeing how we went about things, I brought her inside the office and gave her a job booking some of the acts. I gave her a few names to get hold of on the phone and that was how she started – booking gigs and learning about the business from the ground up. She was great at it, too, and by the time she was 21 she was ready to take on a new challenge, and so I made her the tour manager for Lynsey De Paul. It wasn't exactly a marriage made in heaven. They had row after row, but unlike most tour managers, Sharon wasn't about to turn the other cheek. In the end, she just stormed off. But she didn't write her a resignation letter: she just went to Lynsey's room, found her best suitcase, and crapped in it.

Oh my God! I never heard the last of that one! I had to laugh, though. Sharon was shaping up to be a tough cookie, just like her old man. But she was still going through her wild-child phase and I was worried that if she wasn't careful she would get into trouble. So not long after that I made her the tour manager for ELO. Jeff and the boys weren't exactly known for their wild on-the-road behaviour and I hoped that would keep her quiet for a while. Sharon hated it, of course. She would phone me up and complain that the guys in the band were 'a bunch of old women' and that she was going out of her mind.

She didn't let it stop her having fun for long, though, and soon I was getting reports back from the rest of the crew that she was out partying every night after the show on her own. It seemed there was no stopping her.

Sometimes Sharon's antics could be expensive, too. One memorable occasion was in 1977, just after we'd done the big deal with CBS. I was giving a dinner for some friends at one of those fashionable new restaurants that spring up in New York all the time and then disappear. So I can't remember the name, but I do recall that we had a jolly time, drinking the most expensive champagne, working our way through the choicest items on the menu. At about two in the morning I called for the bill from the maître d' and threw down my credit card. Twenty minutes later, however, he still hadn't returned and I began to wonder what was going on.

Then I spotted him, standing by the cash register, beckoning *me* to come to *him*. I thought, What the fuck is this? I went over and he was very uncomfortable. He said he had someone on the phone from American Express who wanted to speak with me. My temper starting to rise, I grabbed the phone and asked this guy on the other end what he thought he was doing calling me to the phone and embarrassing me in front of my guests.

'I'm sorry, sir,' he said. 'But we just felt it best to check with you personally before approving this latest charge as so much money has already been spent on the card in the last twenty-four hours.'

'What the fuck are you talking about?' I said. 'What money?' He quoted me a figure somewhere in the region of $300,000 and I nearly collapsed! 'I haven't bought anything worth three hundred thousand dollars!' I bellowed. 'No, sir,' he said. 'But it appears your daughter has . . .'

We all had credit cards for the same account: I, my wife, Sharon and David. But they were meant to be used either for family business or other 'getting-around' expenses such as dinner in a restaurant or petrol for the car. Sharon obviously had other ideas, however, and when I got the American

Express man to read me out the list of items she had purchased that day I couldn't believe my ears! She had spent the entire amount on jewellery! There was one item for something like $175,000 from Van Cleef, one for $75,000 from Tiffany's, and one for about $50,000 from Cartier – all bought in the space of a single afternoon.

I hung up the phone, paid the bill and got the hell out of there in a hurry. As soon as I got back to my hotel I called Sharon on the phone. 'What the fuck do you think you are doing?' I yelled at her. She just sighed and said, 'Oh, Daddy, I was so *bored*, I had to do *something*.' I was speechless. She said she'd been feeling 'depressed and so I decided to cheer myself up'. I just sat there staring at the phone in my hand, unable to speak.

I've heard Sharon called everything from 'a chip off the old block' to 'Don in a skirt', as David puts it. And, in terms of her ruthlessly shrewd attitude to business, I suppose I would have to agree with that. She has certainly made a stellar success of her career. But I was born into a house with no electricity and one cold-water tap. We didn't know what the word 'depressed' meant; we were too busy just trying to get by. While I wouldn't have wanted my own children to have gone through that, the fact that she had never been poor made her different from me in lots of ways too.

What really pissed me off was that a couple of months later she gave the $175,000 necklace to Britt Ekland, and then Britt gave it to her nanny! Britt was Sharon's big pal at the time and her kids were always at the house, and so, when I came home to find the place empty one day except for Britt's nanny, I wasn't exactly thrilled, but I wasn't that surprised, either. When I saw this thing she was wearing round her neck, though, I nearly burst a blood vessel.

Paddles was with me and she told me to remain cool and to talk to Sharon about it later, but I was outraged. I followed the nanny into the kitchen and said, 'Excuse me, but can you tell me why you're wearing that necklace?'

'Oh, this?' she said, as if it were a ten-dollar chain from the thrift store. 'Sharon gave it to me.' I said, 'Did she, now? Well, I'm her father and I'm the one who paid for it and I would like it back now, please.'

'Oh, no,' she said, 'you don't understand. Sharon *wanted* me to have it.'

'No, no,' I said, '*you* don't understand. I don't give a fuck what Sharon wanted. It belongs to me and I want it back – now.' With that, I reached over and got her by the throat, not to hurt her, just to hold her still while I took the damn thing off her.

But Sharon was always either losing her jewellery or giving it away. Once, on tour with ELO, in the limo on her way in from the airport, she had a bust-up with the driver, and when she finally got out at the hotel she refused to tip him, just gave him the finger, as if to say, 'Bye, you shit!' The driver took off in a huff but just as the car vanished round the corner she suddenly remembered. 'Jesus, fuck!' she screamed. 'I've left my jewellery in there!' She'd left her leather case with all her most expensive jewellery in it on the back seat.

She spent the next two hours trying to trace the driver but she just couldn't find him. Then it was time to go to the show and so she promptly forgot about it. I'm talking about a collection of jewellery then worth in the region of $750,000 – and this was 25 years ago. Add another zero to that figure to get an idea of what the contents of that bag would be worth now. Sharon just shrugged. 'Don't worry, Daddy,' she simpered. 'It's all insured.' A week later when I asked her how she'd got on with the insurance company, she said something like, 'Oh, yeah! I *must* do that . . .' It meant that little to her.

Considering the formidable woman she grew into, a woman with enormous intelligence, humour and personal style, it took a long time for Sharon to really grow up. It wasn't until she met Ozzy that she finally stopped behaving like a spoiled brat. Having all that responsibility thrust on her suddenly forced her to mature mentally. Until then, however, she was young and impetuous and made many mistakes. For instance, there was the time when she moved into her own place in Beverly Hills for the first time. She invited eight wives of the richest couples from her street for a getting-to-know-you dinner. Afterwards, as they were leaving, her maid stood at the door with parcels and as each one passed she presented them, 'with Madam's compliments', to the women. When they got home and unwrapped them they found a watch in each worth $10,000. Of course, within twenty minutes they were all on the phone to each other talking about it. Who was this extraordinary woman Sharon Osbourne? And how dare she assume they could have their friendship bought so easily. They decided they would all send them back, which they did the next day. That really floored her, I think. But it was a good lesson for her: money can't buy you everything. Or not quite, anyway.

Sharon's choice of boyfriends always left a lot to be desired, too. Sometimes I would think she deliberately chose the worst types she could unearth just to wind me up. And, if it wasn't guys she was in trouble with, it was girls. At least, that was what people thought after they saw the pictures of Sharon French-kissing Britt Ekland that were published at the time in all the tabloids. They were taken at a Jet Records convention party in 1978 by a well-known paparazzo. Sharon and Britt were high on champagne and did it just to give the photographers something to get worked up about. The way the newspapers presented it, though, suggested that they were having a full-blown lesbian relationship.

I went crazy and decided to give the photographer a little wake-up call – literally. I got hold of him on the phone at six o'clock one morning and let him have it. 'You dirty fucking piece of shit,' I said. 'You know I'm gonna have to kill you now.' He began to simper and moan, begging forgiveness, saying it wasn't his fault, he was only doing his job, all the usual bullshit. 'Ah, fuck off,' I said. 'I'm not here to ask for an apology: I'm calling to say you better run and hide, that's all. You know I mean it. I'll see you real *soon*.' Then I hung up. I had to get off the phone before I started laughing. He had received the death rattle, though, and I heard he more or less went into hiding for the next couple of weeks.

Not all Sharon's little adventures ended so amusingly, however. One time on tour in America with Ozzy, Sharon had an almighty row with the hotel manager. This was somewhere down South, where women are supposed to act like ladies and the men openly carry guns. But she got into a spat with the guy at the checkout desk. The reception area was full of people as Sharon started screaming at the man, 'You fucking cocksucker! Fuck you, baby! I'm out of here!' Then she marched over to this big palm tree in the middle of the lobby, pulled up her skirt, squatted down and pissed on it! In the end, they had to call the police to get her to leave.

Sharon had first met Ozzy when I took over the management of Black Sabbath in 1974. We were still living in London then and he was still living in the Midlands with his first wife Thelma, so, although Tony Iommi was a frequent visitor, you saw Ozzy only when the whole band were coming in for a meeting.

It was while Ozzy was living in the house in 1979 that Sharon first became interested in him. I also feel partly responsible because I more or less threw them together when I made Sharon Ozzy's tour manager on his first comeback tour. I was going to put David in that job but his daughter Charlotte had just been born prematurely and he needed to be with his family. So I put Sharon on the job, working as Ozzy's day-to-day handler, and that was how it all started between them.

This was in 1981, when Ozzy was still married to Thelma. It all came to a head in November that year, when Ozzy toured the UK. By then his romance with Sharon was no longer a secret and, when Thelma got to hear about it, all hell broke loose. Ozzy panicked and he and Sharon decided to break it up, in public at least. From now on, we told everybody, they would be working together, not sleeping together. That worked for about three weeks and then, on the eve of the tour, Ozzy couldn't stand it any longer and flipped out and did a runner.

Great, I thought, I've got an artist who's as hot as a pistol – and he's decided to do a bunk. It was time to intervene. I sent the boys to look for Ozzy. It didn't take them long to find him

– he'd gone running back to Thelma. He was in a terrible state when they found him. He'd been on the most almighty binge – booze, coke, dope, you name it, he had it coming out of his ears. He'd also shaved off all his hair so that he was now completely bald. Jesus Christ! I thought. Is this guy deliberately trying to ruin me?

I arranged to go up to Birmingham and see him immediately. I knew he was terrified of what I was going to do to him for messing me around like this, but I wasn't interested in retribution: I just wanted to get him back on the road. I got David to call ahead and reassure Ozzy that it would be a very warm, friendly meeting and that we just wanted him to come back to us. I would promise Thelma I would keep Sharon on a leash. In return, she would talk to Ozzy about going back to work.

However, when I got there, all of that went out of the window. We sat down at the table to talk but before I could open my mouth Ozzy leaned over and said, 'Don, it's as simple as this. I love your daughter and I want to marry her!' Meeting over.

But if that sudden news flash had come as a blow to Thelma – whose face turned black with rage and humiliation – it came as something of a shock to me too. A mere fling between Ozzy and Sharon was one thing – I didn't especially like it, I thought it might be bad for business, and so it had proved – but as long as it was purely a temporary thing I could live with it. The very worst that could happen, I thought, was that it would damage his short-term prospects and I might lose him as an artist. It never crossed my mind I might be inheriting a son-in-law! But they both seemed quite serious about it, and, when two people are in love like that, it doesn't really matter what anyone else thinks. All we could do was wish them well and wait to see what happened next.

Once Ozzy had declared his intentions, Sharon moved quickly to seal the deal. Ozzy divorced Thelma in double-quick time – there was a cash settlement, I believe – and the following summer he was free to marry Sharon. The wedding took place on the beautiful Hawaiian island of Maui on 4 July

1982. It was a strange affair in many ways. Ozzy had apparently been on a 48-hour stag party in the lead-up to the wedding and was now so out of it he had to be carried to bed unconscious long before the party was over.

A few weeks before the wedding, I had walked into the dining room one day and found him banging his fists against his chest. I asked what was wrong and he said he was worried about his mother. I asked him why. Was she ill? He just shook his head and went back to beating himself up. I pushed him further. He was acting so strangely that it was making me uncomfortable, and he blurted it out. 'I can't have my mother at the wedding,' he said. 'She'll steal the fucking plates off the table!'

I thought he was joking and started to laugh. 'What the fuck are you talking about?'

He said, 'No, you don't understand. I'm serious! She'll steal everything!'

Bollocks! I thought, and walked away. I didn't believe for one moment any mother would do something like that at her own son's wedding and decided it must be something else that had happened that he wasn't telling me. I wondered whether, perhaps, Sharon had tried to block Ozzy's mother's coming.

I decided to call ELO's drummer, Bev Bevan. Bev had been close to Ozzy and his family as a kid and I thought he might be able to throw some light on the situation. 'He's not kidding, Don,' he said. 'Ozzy's mother was notorious for pulling stunts like that in the band's early days.' He said that, whenever the record company had a party for the band, Ozzy's family would always be there, stealing the cutlery and anything else they could get their hands on. He said it was such a regular occurrence that the caterers used to keep count of all the knives and forks that went missing and present the bill to the band at the end. What a family! But then they were poor and I could relate to that. Scavenging is what the poor do to survive. I went to Ozzy and told him not to worry. 'Let them take all the fucking cutlery they want,' I said. 'Just make sure they're there.'

In many respects, Sharon and Ozzy were perfectly suited – Sharon was very like Ozzy in that she had a wonderful sense of humour and they could both also be totally unpredictable. In other respects, however, he was no match for her. Where he wouldn't hurt a fly she had her vindictive side. I remember once, when she was pissed off with Paddles over something, she sent a postcard to her in England telling her about a weekend trip Sharon and I were taking to Las Vegas. She ended by writing, 'I'm taking THE CUNT as well' – meaning Ozzy. She wrote it in capital letters so the postman would see it when he delivered it and Paddles would be embarrassed.

Sharon clearly loved Ozzy, though. The things she had to put up with from him, the sacrifices she had to make – she *must* have done. In her wild-child days, Sharon had been a bit of a boozer, too. But after spending time with Ozzy she realised it was never going to work if at least one of them didn't sober up – and she wasn't crazy enough to think that might be Ozzy. So she quit herself, just like that, then spent the next ten years putting Ozzy in and out of rehab. All to no avail – or at least not for long.

I remember once when they were staying at the house in LA, I was awoken in the night by a strange sound coming from somewhere. I jumped out of bed, grabbed the big shillelagh stick I kept by the bed, and tiptoed to the door. I opened it a crack and peered out onto the landing. I couldn't see anything but I could definitely *hear* something now. I stepped out, closed the door silently behind me and stood there in the dark with this big club in my hand, waiting for whoever or whatever it was. It sounded like somebody dragging a dead body down the hall. It was coming nearer and nearer. When I sensed it was close enough, I raised the club, switched on the light, and was just about to strike when I saw it was Sharon!

She was struggling down the hall with a double-bed mattress on her back. 'What the fuck are you doing?' I cried. She didn't even look at me.

'Piss!' she screamed. 'That's all I get night and day – piss, piss, piss!'

Ozzy was drinking himself into such a stupor that he was pissing the bed every night. But then Ozzy would sometimes piss himself when he was supposed to be wide awake. He was pouring so much booze down his throat he no longer had any control over when it came out of the other end. Even when Sharon gave him a whack round the head, which she would do quite often, it didn't make any difference.

By the time Sharon married Ozzy, she was also managing him. I gave her his management contract as a wedding present. Why? Because as usual I could already see where this was going. I woke up one morning and realised it wasn't just Ozzy's hand in marriage Sharon was after – she had her sights set on controlling his career, too. I thought, What's the point in trying to stop her? If he's going to marry her she's going to take him anyway. So I went and got the contract from the safe and put it in an envelope and wrote her name on it. Then I gave it to her and said, 'This is my wedding present to you both. I hope it brings you great success and happiness.'

You might have thought that would be the end of it – a happy ending for all. Far from it, though. Instead, it turned out to be just the beginning. One bad move led to another and the whole thing turned into a catastrophe. Sharon and I did not speak to each other – with a few, fairly horrific, exceptions – for over twenty years.

In the early years after the bust-up, it was suggested in a number of newspaper and magazine articles that the reasons for our spectacular fallout were largely financial. That old thing again – but this time it was Ozzy and my own daughter I was supposed to have ripped off. What crap. In fact, it was the opposite. Sharon was trying to do me. When I had given her Ozzy's management contract, I had done so in the not unreasonable expectation that he would remain as a recording artist on Jet. But that wasn't enough for Sharon and the first thing she did as his manager was inform me, through her lawyers, that she was taking Ozzy from Jet and signing him directly to Epic, a much larger CBS imprint.

OK, I had given her the management contract of a major, platinum-selling star for nothing. If she wanted then to break his *recording* contract with me too, that was an entirely different story. She would have to pay. Or, rather, CBS would have to pay. That was only right and proper. I'd taken Ozzy out of the gutter and made him a bigger star than ever before. I hadn't put a foot wrong. But that meant nothing to Sharon, and eventually I was forced to sue them both after Sharon had persuaded CBS to put a freeze on Jet's share of the profits from Ozzy's record sales after alleging we hadn't paid Ozzy his share of the royalties.

More bullshit. In fact, Ozzy had been into the office just a few months before to receive all his royalty statements – plus a six-figure cheque. I'd made sure he signed for them personally. It was the first time I'd ever done that – I knew something was coming and had decided to keep a detailed record of everything. Ultimately, the whole thing was a deliberate tactic by Sharon to get at me. By then she had it in for me, and she wasn't gonna quit, so everything she could do to mess me up or blacken my name, she did.

I took her to court and she was eventually forced to settle. The figure we finally agreed on – somewhere in the region of $1 million – was a modest one compared with what I could have earned if I had kept his contracts. But my policy in such situations – where the artist wants out – has always been to take the money and run. I didn't put the boot in and go for a much larger figure, as my lawyers had urged me to do. She was still my daughter, after all. I just wanted to get a severance fee that was respectable and wave goodbye. I figured, what's the difference whether he's worth one million or twenty million? This is just too much aggro to bear. Take the money and go.

So that was what I did. It was a case of getting rid of everything before the war started. Because once it did I knew that would be it and all bets would be off. And that is exactly what happened, of course.

10

I was still trying to sort out the mess with Ozzy when I found myself splashed across the newspapers back home in Britain again after a so-called 'investigative reporter' named Roger Cook did a radio programme about me for the BBC, in which he resurrected my tabloid image as 'the Al Capone of rock', albeit from the opposite point of view to the original *News of the World* story. While the newspaper had made me seem like Robin Hood, Cook's programme painted a crude portrait of me as a crook and a gangster, somebody who stole from his own artists and bent the charts to suit his needs. He had dug up the usual suspects to help blacken the picture and, though none of them had anything new to say, I didn't see the funny side for a long time.

Indeed, Cook was extremely fortunate I didn't live in England any more when the programme was aired in 1980, otherwise I would have been standing in his office waiting for him to arrive one morning. I did make several attempts to get him on the phone, but he avoided me for weeks. When I did finally get through to him I told him exactly what I thought of him and his nasty little programme. What I hadn't realised, however, was that he was taping the call.

'You worthless piece of shit,' I said. 'You've been avoiding me. You talk big on the radio but you're nothing but a fucking coward.'

'Oh, no,' he said, 'I'm not afraid of you.'

'Great,' I said. 'That's what I was hoping you would say. Because I think you and I should meet and have this out man to man. What do you say? We could have a little wager on the outcome. What shall we say? Fifty thousand? A hundred? More, if you like, I don't mind. We'll make it as high as you want; we'll fix it now through your lawyer. What do you say?'

'Oh,' he said, 'and how many heavies are you gonna have there with you?'

'Let me tell you something,' I said. 'I don't need any help sorting out the likes of you. I could beat you with one hand stuck up my arse.' When an edited version of the conversation was later broadcast in a follow-up piece on the radio all the papers turned it into a big story and it became a famous line throughout the UK: 'I could beat you with one hand stuck up my arse.' Everybody found it hysterical. Hundreds of letters were sent to the papers, they told me, two-thirds of which were from people saying they would be only too pleased to pick up Roger Cook and throw him out of the window for me. There were even a few from women. One I recall said, 'I like Don but does he think he's Humphrey Bogart?'

So I didn't come out of it too badly, really. Despite the sly way he edited the programme, I had publicly proved him to be a coward and, if the show had any effect on my career at all, it was to reinforce the idea that I was untouchable. It just became a huge joke and after that the BBC warned him off because by then they had double-checked on me. The BBC had their own security watching the activities of various people, and they were told by them that I wasn't kidding around, that I wasn't like the people Roger Cook was used to picking on and that they should take any threat from me very seriously indeed.

Nevertheless, I wanted him dealt with. I began simply by suing both Cook and the BBC, separately and together. I hired Marvin Mitchelson, who later became known as a famous divorce lawyer when he established the legal concept of 'palimony'. Marvin started firing off writs left, right and centre, and suddenly the BBC became jumpy. They must have feared there was nothing in the Roger Cook programme that would stand up in court, so they hired a retired policeman named Roy Ransome to dig up as much dirt on me as possible. I was tipped off and David and I set him up with a couple of stooges. We had them wired up when they went to meet Ransome, and we ended up with recordings of him offering them money to spill the beans. We actually had this guy on tape telling them how I had buried people in Regent's Park, people I'd apparently shot dead with my own gun, and all kinds of other stories, none of which were true. So that screwed it up for them. I then began a legal action against Ransome for slander and, as soon as it came out that we'd stitched their man up, the BBC approached us quietly to drop the case and settle out of court. They knew they were onto a loser.

Whatever brief satisfaction that news brought me, however, was tempered by the fact that the whole thing had also made a star out of Roger Cook. Consequently, they gave him his own TV show. So now I wanted to kill him. But I wanted him to be available to me. I didn't want to actually get on a plane and go looking for him. It wasn't like the old Carnaby Street days when I'd have enjoyed hunting him down. He simply wasn't a big enough rat for me to waste any more time trying to smash him. By then, I didn't just live in a different country: I lived in a different world.

But if I had walked into a restaurant any time over the next ten years, say, and Roger Cook had happened to be there, I'd have gone for him immediately, no question. I would have got hold of him and I wouldn't have let go until he died in my hands.

If the Roger Cook programme had been the only setback I suffered in the eighties, however, I wouldn't have had much to complain about. Instead, it became the least of my worries as, over the course of the next decade, I saw first my life and then my business change beyond recognition.

The most tragic occurrence for me personally was the complete breakdown of my relationship with Sharon. Although the split was superficially over Ozzy, deep down it was nothing to do with business. It was purely personal, the sort of thing that happens to families all over the world, but in our case the whole thing was played out in public. The fact is, the rift began in earnest when Sharon discovered I was having an affair with a woman in Los Angeles that I had fallen seriously in love with. Her name was Meredith Goodwin and Sharon hated her before she'd even set eyes on her.

David saw things differently and decided to stick by me, no matter what. But even he had his reservations about this unexpected new development in my life. If you talk to him now, he'll probably tell you that, in effect, I gave up my family and my business for Meredith, that I became completely obsessed with her – and I suppose I did. For a long time, I confess, I couldn't keep my mind on anything else. But it wasn't as simple as that. I had met Meredith during a visit to England in 1981. I went to look at some property and she was with the people who owned the place. They say opposites attract and there was something in that, I suspect, in my initial attraction to Meredith. I liked it very much that she knew nothing whatsoever about my business, my world. Her own life was so different, and it seemed that she was coming from a much purer place.

Because Meredith was some years younger than I was, Sharon claimed it was merely my money she was in love with. But Meredith was hardly a groupie or a gold digger. She already had her own very successful career in America as an academic, and her father had been one of the top engineers at NASA during the space programme in the sixties. When Meredith met me she didn't know anything about rock 'n' roll – and didn't *want* to know anything. All this nastiness with Sharon deeply upset her. Frankly, she had never met such people before.

It was tragic. Up until then, Sharon and I had been very close and, at root, I think her hostility to Meredith stemmed from resentment that her own place in my affections might be usurped. She simply couldn't bear the thought that she might no longer be number one in my life. That's how it seemed to me, anyway. And the way it came out was her thinking she had the right to criticise me because I had another woman; to pass judgment on me. I didn't react well to that, of course, and one bad move led to another, turning it into a catastrophe for the whole family.

It was a great shame. Paddles certainly didn't see it the way Sharon did. Our love would always be unbreakable but our relationship had reached a very advanced level of understanding. Being a good ten years older than I was, Paddles was now in her mid-sixties and she accepted that Meredith gave me something in my life that she was no longer able to – youthful companionship and all the excitement that goes with it. I didn't abandon or neglect my wife, though. I was still spending a great deal of my time with Paddles in England, where I had bought her Kimberley House, a wonderful place on its own land in Dorking, Surrey, one of the most beautiful counties in England, and just a short drive from London. Because of that, she always had friends and family staying there with her. David and his family also lived there for a time.

As far as I was concerned then, the new situation with Meredith was entirely manageable. I really couldn't see why Sharon was making such a fuss. If her mother had been suicidal with grief, then I might have understood. But she wasn't. In fact, I think Paddles secretly enjoyed the freedom the new arrangements gave her. When you've been through as much as we had during our 35 years together, a little space between you can be a good thing. Sharon simply refused to acknowledge that fact, though, and over the next twenty years she took it upon herself to try to do me down at every available opportunity. It was 'I'll fix him,' that type of thing. I tried not to retaliate, tried to stay calm and hope that she would eventually come to her senses and see that things were actually all right as they were. But it was a good job I didn't hold my breath while I waited, or I would have been long gone by now.

It was all the wrong approach to settling anything, but that became only part of it. Every time I turned round it seemed that she'd done something else. First there was the business of freezing the royalties I was owed for Ozzy by CBS; then she interfered in the sale of the Howard Hughes house, forcing me to sell the place for a much lower price than I should have just to get the deal done quickly and get her out of my hair. And she stopped speaking to her mother, too. That hurt me more than anything to do with money ever could – which is why she did it of course.

I was sad to see the old house go, I have to admit. But the fallout from my affair with Meredith and subsequent rift with Sharon meant that nobody wanted to live there any more. I'd been there for over five incredible years; I'd certainly had a lot of fun out of the place. But now it was time to move on. I had a new life now with Meredith and so, in 1983, I put it back on the market, and Meredith and I bought a new place for us together over in Century City.

Of course, it took a while to find a buyer rich enough to afford the old place. Steven Spielberg came to see it and fell in love with it immediately. I told him he could have it for not much more than the $10 million I'd laid out on it. He went away to think about it but I knew he'd be back. His wife just loved the place, you could see. And the connection with a legendary filmmaker and inventor like Hughes was just too tempting for Spielberg. But then he bumped into a friend in the business who told him I'd certainly never paid that much for it. Spielberg pulled out of the deal. Apart from the fact that nobody ever sells a house for *less* than they paid for it, I thought it was a crummy thing for this guy to do. Not only did he end up shafting me out of a sale, but he also shafted his so-called buddy Spielberg out of his dream home.

The house was eventually sold in 1983 and everybody tried to get on with their lives again. Business, for me, was still booming with or without Ozzy. I had also become the manager of another big chart act in America called Air Supply.

Air Supply were one of those successful but largely faceless rock acts that dominated mainstream radio in the US in the early eighties, along with fellow travellers such as REO Speedwagon, Journey and Toto. With a wonderful blend of top musicianship and catchy generic rock tunes, Air Supply were easy on the ear and very popular – but not the sort of group who were written about much in the music press. Because of that they never made it in Britain or Europe, but in America they were gold dust for about five years.

I had the band signed with Clive Davis at Arista Records in New York. At the time they were his number-one group. It all began to turn sour between us, though, when the band were making what should have been their biggest album yet, a Greatest Hits collection including a new track: 'Making Love Out of Nothin' at All'. Written and produced by Jim Steinman of Meat Loaf and *Bat Out of Hell* fame, 'Making Love . . .' would become Air Supply's biggest hit of all when it was recorded as a single that year. David and I had come up with the concept of having a *new* hit on there; it was the perfect vehicle to really sell the compilation.

Clive wanted to dictate how the record should sound to Bob Ezrin, the producer. I'd listened to Ezrin's mix and was happy with it; it sounded great. But Clive wasn't satisfied and had the album remixed.

Clive has had a lot of success over the years, but in my opinion he'd ruined the new album of one of my best-selling groups. When I found out, I was close to murdering him. I stormed into his office and told him what I thought of him in front of his whole staff.

It was also around this time that Black Sabbath – or what was left of them – came back to me. It began when I bumped into Tony Iommi at the airport one day in 1983. It was in Detroit, where I'd been at an Air Supply show the night before. We went for coffee and got talking. He told me the Dio situation had fallen apart after just two albums. Bill had been first to jump ship; he didn't even make it through the first tour with Dio. This was not because of remorse for Ozzy, though, as he likes to say now, but because by then he was a hopeless alcoholic. That left just Tony and Terry. Well, at least it was the creative half of the original four, so there was still hope for them yet, I thought.

By then they had seen what an incredible job I'd done on

Ozzy. They couldn't believe it. They were so certain his career would be over without Sabbath. Now they wanted me to do the same for them. 'Will you take us back, Don?' Tony asked me. Well, what could I say? There was so much history between us by then it seemed pointless being stubborn about it. Besides, I admit I rather fancied pitting my wits against Sharon in the Sabbath-versus-Ozzy battle that would now inevitably ensue.

For once, however, I underestimated the size of the task before me. Ozzy was about to release his first solo album that year under Sharon's management (*Bark at the Moon*) and the proof of how effective her operations would be without me to lend weight to them had yet to be established. Ozzy had also lost his talented guitarist and songwriter Randy Rhoads in a plane crash. In many ways, then, his next album would be a make-or-break one for him and it seemed to me that, if Sabbath were ever to regain the ground they had lost with Ozzy's fans in the Dio years, it was right then.

Determined to give it my best shot, I set about reassembling the band from the ground up, and I still think I pulled off one of my greatest moves when I acquired the services for them of the singer Ian Gillan and the drummer Bev Bevan. Gillan had fronted Deep Purple in the early seventies when they enjoyed their greatest success with hits like 'Smoke on the Water' and 'Black Night'. Despite having launched his own successful solo band in Britain after he had left Purple in 1974, Gillan had not done anything in America for years, and so, profile-wise, I thought he'd be perfect. He was known and respected enough in America to be taken seriously, but he had been out of the spotlight there long enough to now be considered in a new guise – as the singer in Black Sabbath. Bev, of course, was the drummer in ELO and before that the Move, and he was therefore someone I had known and worked with for years. Being from Birmingham, too, Tony and Terry had also known him a long time and, with ELO then in hiatus, again I thought he would be the perfect fit for the revamped Sabbath line-up.

It certainly seemed that we had a winner on our hands when the album they recorded together with this line-up, *Born Again*, was released in the summer of 1983. The arrival of Gillan in the band had put them back in the headlines again and the album was generally well received throughout America. By the time the US tour was ready to roll I thought we were on the verge of cracking it. And so we might have if Ian Gillan had been able to cut it on stage. But for some inexplicable reason he couldn't manage it. Here was an ultra-experienced old pro, and he stiffed out! It was nuts. He should have been great. Vocally, he was, in my opinion, the only one out there who could match what both Ozzy *and* Dio had done with the band previously. Unfortunately, we had brought him in maybe five years too late. His voice was still in good shape but it was as if his brain had gone.

He had a terrible habit of forgetting the lyrics. He would go off on weird vocal scats – 'doobie-woobie-jabba-wabba' – to disguise the fact that he didn't know what the hell he was supposed to be singing. That might have worked in the more bluesy style of Deep Purple, but in Black Sabbath, where the lyrics were a big thing, it was a complete disaster. Terry, who wrote most of them, nearly died the first night on tour when he looked over and saw Ian on his knees leafing through big sheets of paper with the lyrics written on them. Sabbath had thick dry ice pumping out across the stage throughout the show and so he couldn't see the words if he was standing up. He ended up doing most of that tour on his knees. We might as well have had Ronnie Dio back up there!

The band capped it all off, though, by insisting on having stage props built around the idea of recreating Stonehenge – the very stage set, in fact, that inspired the famous scene from the spoof rock movie, *This Is Spinal Tap*, which came out the following year. In the movie, when the band's new Stonehenge stage set is unveiled, the stones are so small as to be ridiculous. In real life, however, Sabbath had the opposite problem: they'd made the damn things so big they didn't fit the stage! They did ninety concerts on their US tour and they managed to get the

Stonehenge gear up at just one of them. It cost them a couple of hundred grand, and it was a fiasco.

When they saw my face they all ran. I had told them not to do it. 'For fuck's sake, why bother?' I'd said. 'In America they don't even know what Stonehenge is!'

'Yeah, man, you're probably right.'

Then as soon as my back was turned they got the tour manager to find someone in England to build it for them. However, nobody thought to ask for actual measurements, and so the builders just made all the stones life-size. When word got out that they couldn't put their planned stage show on because they'd made the thing too big, it made a laughing stock of them.

That was the icing on the cake as far as that line-up of Sabbath was concerned. Despite successes like their headline appearance before 50,000 people at that year's Reading Festival in England, as soon as the tour was over Tony and Terry came to me and said they wanted Gillan gone again. That was fine by me. My only concern was that they might start talking to me again about the midget Dio! But by then even he had gone on to greater success as a solo artist with his own band, Dio. It didn't last, but by the mid-eighties Dio was now bigger than Sabbath. Ozzy, meanwhile, was still bigger than both of them put together. By 1985 even Terry had thrown in the towel and, although I did one final album that year (*Seventh Star*) with Tony and a bunch of session men posing as Black Sabbath, that was it for me and I bailed out of the Sabbath story for the third and final time not long afterwards. One thing about me: I've never been afraid to pull the plug. And by then it was apparent to me that without Ozzy the rest of the band might as well pack in.

In truth, by the mid-eighties I suppose I was simply getting bored with the whole business. With the ELO empire long since established there seemed little left to do. It soon became apparent that Jeff Lynne was of the same opinion. When he put the band on what was supposed to be a temporary hiatus I already knew in my heart that it was probably the end – that Jeff wouldn't be back. And so it proved. Although the band never officially broke up and we did release a couple more ELO albums, the days of the big money-spinning tours were over. I suppose we'd made our money – and then some. Now it was time simply to move on.

In which direction, though? Being with Meredith had shown me there was more to life than just show business. But I still had a yen to be involved in things. It was in this frame of mind that I first became involved with the Republican Party in America. It started innocuously enough when I asked my lawyers about getting green cards for me and the family plus some of the staff from Jet in England whom I now wanted with me permanently in LA. They advised me to enlist the services of a lobbyist who was willing to act on my behalf, which I did. He recommended I make a sizable donation to the Republican Party, so I did that too. You're not supposed to say how much you gave exactly, or on which occasion, but let's just say it was a large enough cheque to get me noticed – and the next thing I knew I had fifteen green cards in my hand!

A few months later I got a letter from the guy who was the head cook and bottle washer, as they say, at a top Republican club. Working on behalf of Ronald Reagan, he made similar approaches to everyone who had made a substantial contribution to the Republican coffers over the past year. As a result, I and fifty other guys were invited to spend a weekend at the White House. Reagan was starting new money-raising campaigns, but they were for 'special causes' and he wanted to approach only people who had given a certain amount already – and I was one of them.

Before you can spend the weekend at the White House, though, you've got to see the FBI. I went to see them and weeks later they were still investigating me. But they eventually cleared me and I went with Meredith. It was fabulous. We were treated like visiting royalty from a foreign country. Back then, my next-door neighbour had been Cary Grant, whom I had come to know quite well over the years. It turned out Cary was at the White House too that weekend. He'd been one of Reagan's closest friends back in his Hollywood days and so, as we were waiting in line to be greeted by the president and his wife, Cary came up and said, 'Oh, don't stand here, come with me. I'll introduce you to Ronnie.' And he took Meredith and me up to meet Reagan. He said, 'Mr President, I want you to meet these friends of mine. They live next door in the house that I wanted but couldn't afford!' It was a lie, for Cary was one of the richest men in Hollywood, but what an intro!

And that was how I became involved in helping raise money for the Republican Party. All in all I must have invested more than $2 million personally over the years, on top of which I also helped the president get money for all his other friends who needed it. I'm not allowed to reveal names or what the money was for. But let's just say there was a certain etiquette involved. The king of America is not going to come out and say, 'I want half a million from you, a million from you . . .' He can't do that. Instead, he sends in his people to talk to you. You'd get a friendly little tug on the sleeve: 'Here, we wanna show you this, we wanna show you that' – and while they are showing you these things they're mentioning figures in the most delightful way. 'Oh, so-and-so was here last year and he gave the president two million dollars for this much-cherished project . . .' And that's how you knew what they wanted – the ballpark figure, anyway.

So I put in a fair old stake of my own and started to think about the opportunities it might bring me. At that point I felt I could do anything, I really did. The success of ELO and Jet Records was one thing, but being plugged into the main players in the Republican Party, the ruling government of America throughout the eighties, was a whole other ball game. There were all sorts of things I could have got into: finance houses, banks. These are the steps you take that turn you from a millionaire into a billionaire, involving the sorts of guys you very rarely read about in the press but who are there pulling the strings behind the scenes. I should have grabbed at that but I was stupid, I never followed it through. I was so cocksure that

I didn't think it was necessary for me to schmooze up to anything or anybody.

I once got a letter from Reagan thanking me personally for all my efforts at raising money for him. It ended by saying, 'We are proud to know there are Americans like you in this world.' I thought that was a strange thing to say. I might have had a green card, but I wasn't an American. So I showed the letter to Cary and asked him what he thought of it. He said, 'What it means is that, if you want to get even more involved, the door is now open for you. If I were you, I'd take them up on the offer – now. You don't usually get asked these things twice.' Cary was right, but I passed. It was a great opportunity, and could have put me in a phenomenal position, but it had come just a little too late for me. By then, there were other, more pressing, issues for me to deal with.

The mail never stopped coming from Reagan though. For fun, he would send me official government badges. When I went to Las Vegas once, I lost the key to my suite, so I went down to the VIP department to get a replacement. When they asked me for ID I realised I didn't have my wallet on me – it was in my suite. But I did have a small gold pin Reagan had recently sent me, with official words on it to the effect that I was a party to the party of the president, or some such. Anyway, I pinned it on, scowled at him and said, 'That's my identification!' And the security guy was so stunned he actually stepped back and saluted me.

He got me a new key and I managed to keep a straight face as he followed me to the elevator. As he held the door open for me he leaned forward and whispered, 'Excuse me, sir. But do you look out for the president?' I just looked at him very sternly and tapped the side of my nose. 'Of course, sir,' he whispered as he backed away, almost bowing. 'Of course, your secret identity is safe with me.'

They say that every empire must one day crumble and fall. And so it was with me in the late eighties. For undoubtedly the low point of my career – and the event that symbolised the beginning of the end of my own towering business empire – was my arrest in 1985 and subsequent trial in 1986 on charges of kidnapping, blackmail, torture and assault. The victim was one Harshad Batyu Patel, an English-born Asian who had begun working for me as an accountant in my new Century City offices when I moved Jet's main headquarters over to LA. When I felt he had not been straight with me, I went crazy.

The singer Harry Nilsson, who'd turned into a bit of a wheeler-dealer, was talking to me one night and he happened to say how sorry he was that the radio station we had both invested in had gone belly-up. I asked him what he was talking about – what radio station? He said, 'Oh, I know you had nothing to do with it personally, it was all done through your accountant.' That was my tip-off. The very next day I started looking into things, checking the books in the office, and that was it!

This was in LA. David was on tour with Air Supply at the time and so I acted alone. I just got a few of the boys together to grab Patel and bring him to my house for interrogation. I bashed him up a bit on a point of principle: I wanted him to know who it was he was dealing with. He denied everything and that just made me even madder. I took an antique shotgun I had on the wall and started hitting him with it. *Smack!* I gave him a whack right across the nose with the butt of the gun. 'That's what you're gonna get every time you say that to me!' I roared at him. After that, he started to be co-operative.

In the end I gave him the phone and told him to call his bank and tell them he wanted to withdraw a large sum of money from his account – my money I felt. But he insisted he didn't have any more money. I laughed in his face, then whacked him in the balls. He fell to the floor screaming. Then I stuck both barrels up against his ear and said, 'Pick up the fucking phone.' He dragged himself to his feet and got straight on the phone to his bank manager. He got me a banker's draft for $100,000.

At that point, though, I still didn't know exactly what Patel had been up to, so when I'd finished with him I told him he had 24 hours to come back to me with the rest of my money, and threw him out onto the street. Big mistake. Sure enough, 24 hours later he'd failed to appear, so I went looking for him again. It turned out he had hopped on the first available flight back to England.

I might have left it there but over the next few weeks I had a complete audit done of the accounts in his control and was now painfully aware of the real story. So now I not only wanted what I felt I was owed, but I was looking for revenge. That was when I decided to follow him to London.

You might ask why I didn't just go to the law about it. He held money that my lawyers couldn't present to the IRS (the Internal Revenue Service) – money from what are known as 'double-breasted' deals we had done. It was simply from business deals that wouldn't have been worth the paper they were written on if I'd submitted all the details to the IRS. We went through millions in such a short space of time that there was no way of keeping track of it without a full-time accounts guy looking after it – which was where Patel came in. I did sue him and we eventually got a judgment against him in the US courts.

In the meantime, I had five Mafia guys with me when I arrived back in London looking for him. The men they sent over were the best: Bobby Bomps and the crew, including one character called Legs (so called because he had the biggest legs in the world, each thigh so gargantuan that it was almost grotesque). If there was a locked door to be opened in a hurry, Legs was the guy you called for. Legs would come and knock it down with one almighty kick.

That was what they did to Patel: got Legs to smash his door down. He almost fainted when Legs then picked him up like a baby and carried him out to the car. They brought him to me at my office in London where this time I really went to work on him. 'You dirty bastard!' I said, 'I want all my money back! Now you're going to pay!' I wanted to make sure he never had a child. So I got my tools out and battered his prick. I could have battered his head but I didn't. I just wanted my fucking money back.

Once again, David wasn't there that day. He was actually at the tax office with my accountant. When he returned that day to find Patel under lock and key he went mad. He told me I'd gone too far. It was his birthday, and we were all supposed to be going out for a big celebration dinner. But when he saw the state Patel was in he told me and everybody else to go on ahead without him, that he would join us later. Then when we were gone he went and spoke to Patel. He told him to pay us back what he could as soon as he could, then get lost and never come back. Then he unlocked the door and let him go. Second big mistake. This time he went straight to the cops. And that was when they issued warrants for the arrest in England of both me and David, whom they threw a 'conspiracy to kidnap and blackmail' charge at. My own charges were more serious, but it was David's arrest that hurt me more. He hadn't done anything. Quite the opposite: as usual, he had just tried to keep the peace. But they tried to nail us both.

I was arrested on four charges. Top of the list was 'kidnapping' – very tasty, that. If you've got a bad lawyer you can go down for a long time just on that alone. But then there was also blackmail, torture and assault. As if that were not bad enough, my QC (queen's counsel) told me that the judge, Justice Smedley, had been his enemy inside the court for over 35 years. Outside it, though, they were the best of friends and he said that Smedley hated everything I stood for. He said he thought at best I had a fifty–fifty shot, and that if things went badly I could go down for ten years. Maybe longer.

David and I were both tried separately at London's most famous criminal court, the Old Bailey. Without thinking, David had hired his usual music business lawyer to defend him. He may have been brilliant at record contracts but he didn't know much about kidnapping or blackmail. He advised me not to be there when David's trial came up. He said that if we were seen in court together the press would make a circus out of it and we were both sure to go down. So I stayed in LA – a decision I would come to regret when David's trial started to go badly wrong.

They tore David to pieces. It looked like a stitch-up from start to finish. The guy from the tax office who could have verified that David was with him on the day in question was suddenly struck down by a mystery illness, which prevented him from coming to court. As the trial went on, David's defence seemed to be going deeper and deeper into the mire. In the end, David was given two years with a year suspended. He served seven months.

I was devastated, as were the whole family. My going to jail would have been bad enough. But it wasn't me; it was my beloved son, the one who had actually tried to stop me going after Patel. It added insult to injury and while David now says that going to jail was actually one of the best things that ever happened to him – he became physically fit and, ironically, learned some lessons in life he would never have had otherwise – as far as I was concerned, it was the worst thing that had ever happened to me and my family.

The trial had other unfortunate repercussions. I was just about to settle out of court with the BBC over the Roger Cook programme when the Patel court case blew up in all the papers. Suddenly the BBC decided they didn't mind if I wanted to take them to court. They knew that the bad publicity from the Patel trial would mean I would never get a fair hearing against the good old Beeb. So that was that.

To rub salt into the wound, the BBC seemed to be hand in glove with the police. The Patel thing could have been resolved with a slap on the wrist but they seemed to have it in for me and David personally, and to be trying very hard to screw us.

It took a long time for my own case to come to trial. David was already out of nick by the time I arrived at the Old Bailey. I had had a long time to think about things and to prepare. I had learned things from David's trial, from making sure I had the right lawyer to knowing how to play the jury. I felt I had a good case for the defence. Meanwhile, the police simply refused to accept that I had any reason to feel aggrieved by Patel. They just wanted to nail me for something, anything.

They never even looked into any of the accusations I made about Patel. It was as if, because it had happened in America, it had nothing to do with them.

There was no support, so I had to go and get it myself – sometimes from the most unexpected quarters. For example, when the Los Angeles Police Department (LAPD) began requesting information about Patel from Scotland Yard in London in connection with the case I had brought against him in LA, they either couldn't get anything out of them or what they did get turned out to be total rubbish. It was obvious the London cops just didn't want to know and the LA cops were so appalled that one of them actually offered to come all the way to London and stand up for me in court, both as a character witness and to tell the jury what Patel had done to me in America. It was fantastic. This straight-shooter LA cop stood up in the witness box and took the oath in full uniform. The jury almost applauded.

I had also hired one of the most experienced criminal lawyers in London, the one who looked after the Kray twins – Ralph Hyams. Ralph not only knew every trick in the book, but had *written* the book. I also got myself a top QC in Gilbert Grey. Gilbert was amazing. He looked like a movie star. In fact, he should have been a movie star because he was a top performer. I knew he was a genius from the moment we met. He began by telling me exactly how he wanted me to act in court both when I was in the witness box and – just as important, he said – when I was out of it. I had to remember that the jury's eyes would be on me all of the time and that every little thing I did would be read by them like a book. Then he asked me what knowledge of the case I had, and that was when I surprised him. I had already worked hard on it for over a year. I knew that if I failed at the Old Bailey I was finished for life, so I'd studied like a maniac. I interrogated people. I went to see different court cases, made notes and tried to guess the verdicts, just to see if I was on the right track with my own case.

When I showed Gilbert my notes and extensive research, he said, 'Congratulations, you've done a wonderful job.' Because I had already highlighted all the obstacles and possible dangers, he was free to work that material into something he felt he could use. I'll never forget our first day in court. Gilbert opened up with one of the most vicious attacks I've ever heard – he just pulverised Patel. He turned to him and said, 'You stole this man's money, his fortune, because you wanted money, any man's money. And, even though this man took you from the gutter of Birmingham and put you into a high-paying job in America, you chose to steal from him.'

The jury sat there nodding their heads, taking it all in. Then Grey tore into him, portraying Patel as utterly low down and despicable. It was so wonderful to hear this guy tear into him. Every day the place was packed out, and you couldn't get a seat.

The only thing that worried me was what effect the judge's summing up would have on the verdict. Sure enough, just as Gilbert had predicted, Smedley seemed to go out of his way to give me a good working over for the jury. In the end, I think he made me sound like Adolf Hitler! His criticisms backfired, though – when the jury came back in after their deliberations, they returned a 'not guilty' verdict on all four charges! David and I were jumping up and down with glee. The judge's mouth just dropped.

With one of the jurors absent through illness, it had taken the remaining six men and five women less than an hour to reach their verdict. Afterwards, several of them actually waited outside for me on the steps of the Old Bailey. The men wanted to shake my hand and the women wanted to kiss me. They all said they knew I was innocent from day one and that the police should never have brought the case. It was bizarre. Mind you, by then, I swear, all the women on the jury had fallen in love with me. I had been getting surreptitious little smiles and nods and winks throughout the trial. Some of them were actually crying when I walked out of court a free man.

Although it was a great day, in many ways, it was also a terribly sad one. If I had been proven not guilty of all charges, then what had David gone to prison for? When the trial was over, as we were walking from the court, I went over and collared the detective who'd been in charge of both my and David's prosecution cases. I stuck my face right into his and said, 'I know you had it in for me and my boy. Well, let me tell you something: this isn't over yet by a long way. Now it's your turn to suffer.'

We were standing right there in the middle of the Old Bailey and I was half expecting to be rearrested there and then. But all he did was just deny everything. 'No, Mr Arden,' he said, 'it was nothing personal at all. The case just came to my desk.' I told him to shut up. 'Listen to me and listen good,' I said. 'If you ever come near me or any of my family again you'll have me to answer to – and this time you won't have to wait for a fucking trial. You won't fucking live that long, do you understand?' I waited for him to do something, say something. But he just stood there looking at me, his face turning grey.

After the Patel trial, I went away for a long holiday. I don't think I even spoke to anybody on the phone for about eight weeks. In the year and a half I had been working on my case I don't think I slept properly even once. I would keep going until I virtually collapsed from physical and mental exhaustion. Now I just wanted to go somewhere and blank it all out. I'd had enough excitement for a while.

So I disappeared with Meredith to an island in the South Seas. There were only about fifty people on the whole island and the peace and solitude did me the world of good. But even after I returned home to LA it took us all a very long time to regroup. Both David and I were not really ourselves again for a few years after that. It took me a long time even to get back behind a desk. I had to think things over.

I was sixty years old in 1986 – retirement age for most top executives. I had been in show business for over 45 years, working pretty much nonstop, night and day, building everything towards what now looked like a peak. Along the way, I had had some fun – oh, yes. I'd lived in the biggest houses, had always travelled first class, and had always eaten in the best restaurants. In that respect, I had lived my life large. I'd had holidays, but I had not actually had what you would call a proper break since I was fourteen and had won the talent competition that took me into my first show. I intended to have one now and for the next few years I lived a different sort of life from any I'd known previously, and spent quality time with Meredith, either at home in LA, or travelling all over the world – London, New York, Paris, anywhere that took our fancy. It allowed me to reconsider what I wanted from life.

Did I take my eye off the ball, though? Yes, I suppose I did. Often I would leave David to run the LA office while I went off on another trip with Meredith. David became torn between the two sides – Sharon's and mine. I knew it wasn't right or fair but I didn't know what else to do. I had already begun selling off various parts of the business. By the late eighties ELO were virtually over, as Jeff Lynne went off to work with superstars such as Bob Dylan and the ex-Beatles. I had also ditched Sabbath and then Air Supply and one or two other projects. After so many years spent working, fighting, clawing my way to the top, the truth is I simply couldn't be bothered with it any more. There had to be more to life. Being with Meredith made me see that there was.

The one situation that proved impossible to resolve, however, was my relationship with Sharon, which had now deteriorated into all-out war. I always used to refer to my long separation from my daughter as 'the war' because that was exactly what it was. Not just in the beginning, either, when things were at their worst, but right through the entire twenty years. She never let up. If she could stick one to me, she would, and it did have an effect on some of my business deals back then. People suddenly wouldn't want to know because Sharon had put the word in.

At first I was hurt. After all I had done for her I couldn't believe she could act so hatefully towards me, her own father. But the longer it went on, the more the hurt turned simply to anger and for a while, I'm afraid to say, I got into tit-for-tat retaliation. For example, there was the time I tried to stop the original Sabbath line-up from re-forming for the day at Live Aid in Philadelphia in

1985. Because they needed Ozzy for that, Sharon had taken charge of the deal – and that rubbed me up the wrong way, as I still technically managed the band. So I took out a legal action against them. I actually had the band served with papers as they were being interviewed on TV the day before the show. It didn't actually stop them appearing but it did tie Sharon up in lots of phone calls for several hours and manage to piss her off mightily – which was exactly what it was supposed to.

There was no surrender between us for over twenty years. We couldn't even manage to become professional rivals: we had to become bitter personal enemies. It just screwed with everything. There was the time former Sex Pistols manager Malcolm McLaren approached me about making a film of my life. It was in 1995. He'd already raised the funds for a movie of Peter Grant's life story, but, once the film production company financing the deal had actually seen it all written down, they weren't convinced there was enough good material there for a whole movie. Malcolm knew there would be no such problems with me and so, in an effort to keep the deal alive, he had suggested a movie based on *my* life story instead. The film company gave it the green light and so I agreed to meet with them. The rest of the family were never mentioned. Three months later they'd finally got the contracts done and they arranged a lunch so that we could all meet and sign.

As soon as we sat down, though, a guy from the film company – Goldenberg – said, 'I've got some great news for you, by the way, Don.'

'Oh yes?' I said. 'What's that?'

'I have finally got Sharon to agree to work with us on this, too.'

I looked at him. 'Who?' I said, genuinely bewildered. When you haven't spoken to someone properly for years you don't always think of them first when their names are mentioned. 'I beg your pardon?' I said. 'Sharon who?'

He laughed: 'What do you mean "Sharon who"? Sharon your daughter!'

'What!' I cried. 'You've been talking to my daughter behind

my back? You're fucking insane!' I went nuts, had a big blow-up and walked out on them. 'You might be a nice fella,' I said, 'but don't ever call me again!'

I left him sitting there with Malcolm, who was busy trying to hide under the table. But that's always been the thing with Malcolm: he wanted the explosion, he wanted the volcano. He asked too much because he thought he was smart enough to pull it off. He wasn't.

Amidst all the hurt, however, I have to admit there were some funny situations with Sharon, too – not that they seemed particularly hilarious at the time. There were things you don't expect from a grown woman, like going into the Polo Lounge at the Beverly Hills Hotel and throwing a hot bowl of soup over someone – which was what Sharon once did to Meredith. It was an embarrassment to me that my own daughter would do something like that to her. But you couldn't convince Sharon that this wasn't the right way for a lady to behave in public.

Then there was the time Sharon tried to run me down in her car. It was in LA, in about 1992. Meredith and I had just been to the cinema in Century City, around the corner from where we lived. We were on our way home, just crossing the street, when suddenly out of nowhere a car came zooming towards us. We managed to jump out of the way just in time! Then the car screeched to a halt and started reversing at full speed back towards us. We both ran for our lives and it missed us again.

It was Sharon, of course. Ozzy actually rang me later and told me about it. He had been in the car, too, hiding behind the seats saying, 'Beam me up, Scotty!' They had been to see the same movie and had spotted us as they were driving home. The fact that I was with Meredith, too, acted on Sharon like a red rag to a bull and she just stamped her foot on the accelerator and went for it. We were lucky we weren't both killed or maimed.

Despite my feud with Sharon, I had never had a cross word with Ozzy, and so we actually stayed in touch throughout those years, as a result of which he came off much worse than I did on occasions. Sharon was always accusing me of plotting to steal Ozzy back from her – and it's true. I would have done if I could, just to spite her. But there was no way she was going to let that happen. There was the time Ozzy called me on the phone out of the blue one day and asked me to go over and see him. 'I'd love to,' I said. 'But I don't think Sharon would like that.' He cackled and said, 'It doesn't matter what she likes, she ain't here.'

Sharon had just left for the airport, he explained, to catch a flight to London. So I drove over to the Beverly Hills Hotel, where he was staying, and he started to tell me all his woes concerning Sharon. He wanted to get rid of her as his manager and come back to me. I had to laugh. God, she'd have hit the roof if she could have seen us there right then, hearing what Ozzy had to say about her. I remember calling David from Ozzy's suite and saying, 'You'll never guess where I am right now.' Then I passed the phone to Ozzy, who said, 'Hey, Dave, I want your father to manage me again – what do you think?' David didn't know what to think. He was more worried what Sharon would think when she found out.

I couldn't stick around too long that day, as I had other business to attend to. But he persisted about me managing him again, and so I said, 'Let's have dinner tomorrow night and we'll talk then.' But when I left he got the stupid idea into his head to call Sharon and tell her what he'd done. They'd had another big row before she left and now he wanted to get his own back on her.

He thought she'd be in the air by then and just wanted to get a message to her – something that would stop her from sleeping on the long flight. But when he called the airline they told him the flight had been delayed and that he could speak with her on the phone in the VIP lounge. They found her for him and gave her the phone and she said: 'Yes, what do you fucking want?' He replied, 'I just thought I'd let you know what my dinner plans are for tomorrow night.'

'OK,' she said. 'Let's have it.'

He laughed and said, 'I'm having dinner with your father!' He told me later that at that point she let out an almighty howl, like a wolverine shot down by hunters.

Then she let him have it. 'You're dead!' she screamed at him. 'Can you hear me? You're fucking dead!'

Ozzy told me he didn't know whether to laugh or cry, so in a panic he hung up on her. Of course, that only made Sharon even crazier. She got hold of the airline people and said, 'Now look, I don't care how late this fucking plane is, I've got some important life-or-death phone calls to make!'

Next thing, she's on the phone again to Ozzy. 'I'm not fucking standing for this, you cocksucker!' she screamed at him. 'I'll fucking fix you!' Then she hung up on him. But she wasn't done yet. She'd had a brainwave and got on the phone to a well-known celebrity drink-and-drug rehab joint in Hollywood. She told them her husband, the famous Ozzy Osbourne, was in a suite at the Beverly Hills Hotel surrounded by drug dealers and that she needed someone to go over there and rescue him from the grave danger he was in.

Sure enough, at six o'clock the following morning, Ozzy's suite was raided by these professional do-gooders hired by Sharon. Poor old Ozzy didn't know what the hell had hit him! One minute he was asleep in bed, the next he was in a car being taken to hospital for 'special treatment'. No sooner had they thrown him in his padded cell than Sharon called him again. 'Now if you don't behave yourself,' she said, 'you're going to be in there for a very long time.' Ozzy said she kept him in there until she returned to LA a few weeks later. All to stop him from seeing me!

That's why I say it was like a war between us, because it became very nasty like that at times. As recently as the mid-nineties she was still out to get me in any way she could. Sometimes it could be excruciatingly embarrassing what she would do. For many years now, for instance, it has been my custom to have Sunday lunch at Nat 'N' Al's, a famous Jewish deli in Beverly Hills. It's the sort of classy, forties-style Hollywood place that the same faces have been going to for years, the kind of joint where everybody knows everybody. Sunday afternoons have always been great times for me there. The place is always packed but they always hold back the same table for me, where I like to have lunch and pass the time with some of my old cronies, mainly these old wise guys from my days with the Paganos – just a bunch of good old souls, like me, semiretired now.

Anyway, it was outside Nat 'N' Al's one Sunday afternoon just a few years ago that Sharon made her last serious assault on me in public. We had just finished another long and enjoyable lunch there and were standing outside saying our goodbyes when we suddenly heard tyres screeching to a halt. We looked and saw a car doing a fast U-turn in the street. Then it came hurtling towards us at full speed. God knows what these old Mob guys thought was happening but I was surprised one of them didn't pull out a piece and take aim.

I could see it was Sharon behind the wheel as soon as the car came skidding to a halt on the pavement about five feet from where we were standing. I thought, Oh fuck, no, not here! Then Sharon leaned out of the window and started laying into me. 'You fucking asshole! You dirty cocksucker! I hope you die soon and rot in hell!' On and on she went with all this type of stuff. I didn't know where to look. Finally, she'd said her piece and the car did another wild U-turn and screeched off down the road.

Ozzy and all the kids were in the car too. He phoned me a few days later and told me that, because Sharon had always told the kids her own father was dead, when they all wanted to know who the hell it was she had just gone off at, she told them it was Tony Curtis! I had to laugh. She frightened the hell out of me but I had to laugh.

'Who the fuck was that?' asked one of the old boys as the car sped off down the street in a dust cloud.

'My daughter,' I said. 'She's always like that when she sees me.'

He looked at me and shook his head sadly. 'Those woids,' he said in his old Bronx drawl, 'those woids she said – where did she loin dem?'

I smiled. There was no answer to that. Or was there? I went home that night and thought about it . . .

Whatever my personal travails with my daughter, at least she never stole from me.

I made a final attempt to keep ELO alive in 1992 when I came up with the idea for ELO II. We couldn't get Jeff Lynne interested – he didn't even want the others to do it – so to distract attention from the fact that the group were missing their principal member, I invited the hundred-piece Moscow Symphony Orchestra to do the shows with them. The end result was absolutely marvellous – one of the best shows I ever produced. But it lasted only for the five shows we did in Britain. They were all arenas, all sold out, but a combination of a lack of new material and the fact that we simply couldn't afford to keep an entire orchestra on the road for any longer than that meant the whole thing fizzled out again pretty quickly. But it was great while it lasted.

As a result of that, though, I finally wound up Jet Records the following year. The back catalogue was still there of course, still earning big money. But I sold everything concerning Jet and ELO in 1993, including my publishing interests. I was 67 years old and had simply decided that it was time to close down the store. Or at least hand it over to somebody in exchange for a nice fat cheque.

And that is what duly happened. Once again, the guy in the frame to do the deal was Walter Yetnikoff at CBS (or CBS/Sony, as they were now known, following Yetnikoff's recent precedent-setting deal with the Japanese technology giants). After much haggling, we eventually agreed on a figure of $40 million.

The saddest event of recent years had nothing to do with money or business. It was the death of my beloved wife Paddles, from lung cancer, a week before Christmas in 1999. She had been ill for some time and I saw her death as a blessed release for her. For years I had begged her not to smoke. But smoking was something most people of our generation did. I was always the odd man out in those days because I didn't. It was such a part of our world, though, that I don't think Paddles even wanted to stop. And though it was the saddest thing that had ever happened to me, saying goodbye to her like that, I like to think she at least died happy, knowing her life had been a full and exciting one, full of love and family and adventure.

What made her passing an even more tragic occasion was that she died with Sharon still refusing to see her. Sharon, regretfully, couldn't even bring herself to go to the funeral. Why? I don't think even Sharon could tell you that now. I suppose all my enemies had assured her that she was right in what she was doing and nobody could alter that. But I think if you really pressed her, even Sharon would admit that it was probably a mistake. I'm sure she feels badly about it now. But once Sharon declared war, she really did mean to-the-death it seemed. She had long ago decided she wasn't going to speak to either me *or* her mother again and that was that. How she blamed Paddles for what had happened, fuck knows, but there you go. Sharon just couldn't forgive either of us, I suppose. The last time they had seen each other had been almost fifteen years before. Sharon had arranged to go on holiday to South Africa with her mother and Ozzy later that month, and, as they kissed and waved her goodbye, they said, 'We'll see you in two weeks, darling' – and that was that. Paddles saw neither of them again.

How that made Paddles feel as the years went by I don't know. She never talked about it much. My wife put up with it all because she had faith in me. In spite of the fact that I had a girlfriend in Hollywood, we never ever had any feelings for anybody else like those we had for each other. It's hard to explain but true. We simply loved each other in an entirely different way. I still miss her, God rest her soul.

Ironically, what finally ended the war between my daughter and me was the very thing that indirectly led to the recent war in Iraq: the astonishing attack on the Twin Towers, in New York, on 11 September 2001. Sharon and Ozzy had actually been staying in New York on the day it happened. They saw the whole thing unfold from their hotel windows. It must have been ghastly for them. It certainly frightened the wits out of Sharon. But she later told me that it was in the wake of all that that she first started to think kindly about the old man again. And that was when she decided it was time to put a stop to the terrible goings on between us and call a truce.

It was just a few weeks after the World Trade Center attack that she called David to ask him to let me know she would like to see me again. She wanted to bury the hatchet – not in my head this time, but in the spirit of love and understanding. I must say I was amazed – and not a little suspicious – when David phoned and told me. Now, though, I'm very glad that she did.

David arranged for us to have tea together at a hotel in Los Angeles one day towards the end of 2001. I went along not knowing what I would find there. I half expected some sort of scam, or showdown. But when I got there I realised she was quite nervous, too, and that she didn't really know what to expect from this meeting, either. And that was when I realised she was being genuine and I started to relax.

David poured the tea – I think he was more anxious than both of us put together – but we started chatting and within a few minutes we were laughing our heads off, recalling the various horrid things we had done to each other over the years. Since then we've become the most tremendous friends again. Just like that. She even accepted Meredith. It's amazing how it's all just blended in and everybody laughs when they tell these stories now. That's the wonderful thing about Sharon and me: at the time we were plotting to ruin each other, and now we sit there and hug each other and laugh about it until we cry.

It was good to be able to see Ozzy again, too, without having to hide behind doors to do so. These days he and Sharon phone me every other day. I've also become a frequent visitor to their home in LA – as you might have seen in the second series of *The Osbournes*. I was even a guest on one of Ozzy's *Ozzfest* shows in the summer of 2002. God, what a scene! Looking out from the side of the stage I realised I couldn't tell any more who were the bigger freaks, the artists or the people in the audience. Judging by the crowd at *Ozzfest*, I'd say it was neck-and-neck.

The other thing that's changed about Sharon, of course, is that she's now become a huge star in her own right with *The Osbournes*. Ever since it started broadcasting on MTV in the spring of 2002, I have not stopped being told how funny it is. Well, it's certainly a remarkable show that will go down in history, of that I have no doubt. But I rarely laugh when I watch it. To me, *The Osbournes* is less a comedy show and more like a documentary, or a home movie. If anything, it makes me want to cry more than it makes me want to laugh. I must finally be getting old!

It's impossible to describe how proud I am, though, of the fact that one of my children has made it as an entertainment star in her own right. I took it as a great compliment, from one artist to another, as it were, when she invited me onto the show for the second series, recorded over the latter half of 2002. Months later, watching myself arriving at their house, being invited in to meet their children, Jack and Kelly, for the first time, I found it all faintly embarrassing. But it was also strangely touching – from watching myself acting the goat to cheer Sharon up, to walking her down the aisle on New Year's Eve, as she and Ozzy prepared to retake their wedding vows, to Ozzy putting my eardrops in for me as I lay on the couch one day. What a strange and remarkable television show that is. But look at the main characters: you couldn't make them up. It must be something in the blood, because, let's face it, Sharon makes a fabulous star: beautiful, funny, immensely strong. As I write this, she is just about to begin presenting her own daytime TV chat show in America and I'm already convinced it's going to be the biggest success since Oprah Winfrey.

It seemed especially unfair, therefore, that she was diagnosed with cancer of the colon in the summer of 2002. Being a born fighter like her old man, Sharon would, I knew, beat her illness into submission and come back stronger and wiser than ever. But for a while it was touch and go. The news knocked us all off our feet for weeks. In fact, it was Sharon who kept the rest of us going. But she had the best doctors and we all rallied round to do what we could, and now, as I write this several months later, the prognosis could not be more positive. The doctors have told her that, if she takes good care of herself, she could live to be a hundred. It seems the world will have to suffer both my daughter and me for a while longer yet.

Looking back at my life now, as I write these final words, I realise that, in spite of my various setbacks over the years, I have been luckier than most. Of course, luck is what you make of it and it's not as if I have been a lottery winner: I had to work hard all my life to get where I am today, and I'm proud of that fact. But don't expect me to faint whenever I hear an old song on the radio by the Small Faces or ELO or whoever. I wasn't there to persuade snotty-nosed musicians to love me: I was there to make us all rich. If people did as they were told, I nearly always managed to do it.

To a certain extent, my whole life was a big act. So many moves I made – from threatening to chuck Robert Stigwood over the balcony to holding Patel prisoner – were done deliberately to cause as much of a stink as possible. I saw myself as the Jewish Marlon Brando starring in a movie called *My Life*. I was proud of the fact that I would do things other guys didn't have the guts to do. My reputation was built on the fact that I always had the chutzpah to go in first – whether it was getting into rock 'n' roll in the early days or seeing off Mafia hoodlums at an ELO show in the seventies. And, when your reputation is running along in front of you, the battle has often been won before you've even stepped through the door. It was something that I studied, something that became part of my life. I can still remember practising alone in a room with the door locked – what I was going to do, what I was going to say, rehearsing the role until it fitted like a glove.

No, I have never killed anybody – yet. But there is a knack to creating fear and terror, and my scene has always been creating it in such a way that the people I scare are going to have to keep looking over their shoulders for the rest of their lives.

There are people still out there today who are terrified of what I might still do to them – and the last time they heard anything from me was thirty years ago.

And that's the reason, too, I think, why my story has become such an intriguing one for this generation. When Channel 4 in the UK made a TV documentary about me in the late nineties called *Mr Rock 'n' Roll*, it proved to be such a hit that they repeated it twice more, getting bigger and bigger ratings each time. They later came back to me when they discovered I was writing this book and asked to make a feature-length film of my life. (We were all set to proceed when Channel Four Films dissolved in 2002 and the idea was necessarily shelved.)

The fact is, I am 77 years old and I have never given less of a fuck in my life. Money is no longer an issue with me. I know I'm going to eat breakfast every day. And I still go to the same tailor's – the same guy who used to fit Frank Sinatra. I started out in the ghetto and finished up a very powerful man in this business, and I'm still powerful. But I know my time is short, and so I have decided to go out with a bang. I have a hit list. And no one whose name is on it will be able to rest until I've gone. None of you are free to go just yet. Wait and see.

David says I should leave all these things in the past. But with me it doesn't matter: my time's limited now, so I might as well do what I want to do before I kick the bucket. I'm just looking to write myself a big ending.

Why? Because I'm Don Arden. And that's the way it is with me. The way it always has been.